Interpreting the Sindhi World

Essays on Society and History

Interpreting the Sindhi World

Essays on Society and History

Edited by

Michel Boivin and Matthew A. Cook

OXFORD
UNIVERSITY PRESS

OXFORD
UNIVERSITY PRESS

Great Clarendon Street, Oxford OX2 6DP

Oxford University Press is a department of the University of Oxford.
It furthers the University's objective of excellence in research, scholarship,
and education by publishing worldwide in

Oxford New York

Auckland Cape Town Dar es Salaam Hong Kong Karachi
Kuala Lumpur Madrid Melbourne Mexico City Nairobi
New Delhi Shanghai Taipei Toronto

With offices in

Argentina Austria Brazil Chile Czech Republic France Greece
Guatemala Hungary Italy Japan Poland Portugal Singapore
South Korea Switzerland Turkey Ukraine Vietnam

First published 2010

ISBN 978-0-19-547719-1

Typeset in Adobe Garamond Pro
Printed in Pakistan by
Pixel Graphix, Karachi.
Published by
Ameena Saiyid, Oxford University Press
No. 38, Sector 15, Korangi Industrial Area, P.O. Box 8214,
Karachi-74900, Pakistan.

Contents

Note on Spellings

The editors and authors have given attention to retaining historically accurate grammar and spellings. Stylistic inconsistencies, such as multiple spellings of Sindh, reflect original source materials and have deliberately not been 'updated'.

Introduction

Notes on the Study of Sindhi History and Identity

Michel Boivin and Matthew A. Cook

It is not popularly known that the word Sindh derives from Sanskrit. The word *sindhu* means river or ocean in Sanskrit. The Rig Veda uses the term to describe a large flowing body of water in western South Asia. Sindhi nationalist Ghulam Murtaza Shah (a.k.a., G.M. Syed), in his 1943 welcome address to the thirty-first session of the All India Muslim League, states that the nation of Pakistan is, historically, nothing else than Sindh. While Syed considers Sindh a metaphor for Pakistan's polity, the word has a much wider socio-political etymology: Hindustan and India both derive from it.[1]

Despite its status as a wide-ranging namesake, Sindh is historically and socially under studied. In comparison to other South Asian regions, there is little scholarship on Sindh. This dearth of scholarship is ironic given how 'unlocalized' Sindhi cultural practices are over history. These practices are not restricted to the contemporary Pakistani province of Sindh. A cursory overview of Sindhi-speakers leads to many locations. In the Las Bela district of Balochistan, people speak a Sindhi dialect.[2] Sindh's sphere of influence during the medieval period includes Multan in Pakistani Punjab. This region, linguistically known as the 'Siraiki Belt', speaks a form of Sindhi. Communities living across the border in India also communicate in Sindhi. People speak a Sindhi dialect in the Kutch and Saurashtra regions of Gujarat. Others speak the Dhatki version of Sindhi in south-western Rajasthan.[3] Various communities of overseas Sindhis (both Hindus and Muslims) speak their mother tongue, not only in Asian countries but in Africa, Europe, and the Americas.

Many histories locate Sindh's socio-historical roots in Mohenjo Daro.[4] Sir John Marshall published the first major study on this ancient city, entitled *Mohenjo Daro and the Indus Civilization*, in 1931.[5] He utilizes the region's material culture to argue that urban life in Sindh stretches back to the third millennium BCE. Marshall convincingly maintains that

Mohenjo Daro, along with Mesopotamia and China, is one of the oldest civilizations in the world. Despite its antiquity, much remains unknown about Mohenjo Daro's exact socio-historical connections with Sindh. The failure to decipher the ancient Indus Valley writing system helps maintain historical speculation about Sindh's connections to Mohenjo Daro. Some of this speculation even suggests that Sindh's socio-historical roots are Dravidian and/or Semitic.[6]

Despite an ambiguous connection to Mohenjo Daro, Sindh remains a historically important region of South Asia. The region is a geographic gateway to South Asia and historically the target of invasions into the area. Whether under the influence of Greco-Macedonians (like Alexander the Great), the Kushans, the Hephtalites, or the Mauryas, Sindh has historically been part of larger polities. Being part of large and diverse polities impacted the cultural character of Sindh. A region of many cultural practices, both Hinduism and Buddhism were Sindh's principle religions prior to the arrival of Islam in the eighth century.[7] Material remains from eastern Sindh even attest to the popularity of Jainism.[8]

This diversity of cultural practice makes establishing a unique Sindhi identity chronologically complex. Language and literature are often good comparative elements for establishing such a chronology. However, in the case of the Sindhi language, tracing history through these elements is difficult. For example, the use of Sindhi cannot be attested to prior to the tenth century.[9] Scholars from South Asia frequently use the literary genres of legend and folklore to identify the 'aboriginal' roots of Sindhi identity.[10] They point toward 'marginal' communities such as the Mohana, Bhil, or Koli as Sindh's original inhabitants.[11] In support of this assertion, scholars employ a tautology that identifies these communities as 'primitives' whose current marginal status results from being Sindh's oldest inhabitants. Nonetheless, linguistic data clearly illustrates that communities like the Mohana, Bhil, and Koli are non-Sindhi speakers who migrated to the Indus Valley region in the nineteenth century.[12]

The eighth century arrival of Islam did not stunt the diversity of people's cultural practices in Sindh. Islam's arrival marks a period of continued socio-cultural negotiation. Islamic values were not imposed on Sindh—rather non-converts could continue their traditions by paying a special tax. This multi-cultural situation lasted for many centuries: the majority of Sindhis did not become Muslim until the fifteenth century (i.e., seven hundred years after the Arab conquest). One reason for this gradual cultural transition was that local dynasties (e.g., the Somras and the Samas) replaced Sindh's Arab rulers between the eleventh and fourteenth centuries. During this period, it is difficult to speak of people converting to Islam in the way that the languages of western Christianity imply. Collective groups of families, clans, and tribes merely paid homage to 'saintly' figures who, more often than not, were Muslims. The worship of a Muslim saint in Sindh, either Ismaili or Sufi, did not demand a conversion to Islam (this is still the case in much of present-day Sindh). Preachers during this period also often incorporated pre-Muslim rituals (interpreted from an Islamic perspective) to convince people to subscribe to their teachings.[13]

By the sixteenth century, Sindh was firmly under the influence of the Mughal Empire. Nonetheless, it was a somewhat 'peripheral' imperial location. The choice of Sindh for Emperor Humayun's flight of exile in 1541 highlights the region's distance from the Mughal Imperial metropole. Humayun took refuge at Umarkot, in eastern Sindh, where his successor, Akbar, was born in 1542. The oldest known examples of Sindhi poetry also date from this period.[14] Given Sindh's status as a cultural 'shatter zone' at the edge of Mughal authority, this Islamic-style poetry is not particularly orthodox.[15] At the historical crossroads of Persian and Mughal influences, it points toward a fusion of multiple traditions. With various influences, this poetry reflects a multi-faceted Islamic identity that, despite later challenges, continued to socio-culturally dominate the Indus River region until Partition in 1947.[16]

Like much of the subcontinent, the eighteenth century in Sindh was a time of transition. In 1731, the Mughals recognized Mian Nur Muhammad Kalhora as Sindh's governor. He and his relatives subsequently broke with the Mughals and established their own state. The Kalhora state fell when the Talpur clan from Balochistan took control of Sindh in 1783.[17] During this same period, migrations from the Punjab and Rajasthan expanded Sindh's population of local traders (cf. Cook's chapter). These traders used their toehold in Sindh to build trade networks that extended to Central Asia and other parts of the world.[18] Many of these new migrants brought with them cultural practices associated with Sikhism (i.e., Nanakpanth). However, the practices of Sufism remained popular. This 'easy' mix of faiths during the eighteenth century produced both cultural opponents and advocates. It led to a conservative reaction spearheaded by the Naqshbandis, who desired to 'purify' Sufism from 'non-Islamic' practises like dance and music.[19] It also produced a cultural environment in which Sufi poets like Shah Abdul Latif who, in *Shah jo Risalo*, praised Hindu *jogis* as the best ascetics and most authentic followers of Ali.[20]

In the course of the nineteenth century, Sindh increasingly came under the influence of Great Britain.[21] Major General Sir Charles Napier conquered Sindh in 1843. In 1847, the British placed the region directly under the Bombay Presidency's control.[22] While the cultural impact of colonialism on Sindh was great (e.g., the British standardized the Sindhi writing system), the region (like under the Mughals) remained on the periphery of the imperial imagination. Nonetheless, being on the colonial, and subsequently nationalist, 'fringe' helped Sindh maintain a historical cultural fusion when other regions of South Asia—under the tensions of both colonialism and nationalism—experienced greater communalism.[23]

While communal division was not a major socio-political factor in Sindh until the twentieth century, the period after 1843 did witness an increased socio-political gulf between the urban and rural milieus. In Karachi and in other larger cities (e.g., Hyderabad and Shikarpur), endogamous merchant communities wielded great influence. Regardless of community, these urbanized Hindu, Parsi, and Muslim traders increasingly reflected a social commitment to education and social upliftment as a 'sacred' duty.[24] As in other regions of South Asia, the establishment of women's rights and the promotion of individual freedoms increasingly informed public debate in urban Sindh (particularly through neo-humanist organizations like the Freemasons and the Theosophical Society).[25]

Sindh's rural milieu, in contrast to its urban spaces, remained essentially 'feudal'.[26] Reflecting Sindh's fused cultural identity and lack of communalism, feudal landlords were both Hindus and Muslims.[27] Also in concert with the region's fused identity, peasants' allegiances were often to religious figures who followed local forms of Sufism.[28] In rural areas, the twentieth century rise in communal-oriented nationalist organizations (e.g., the Muslim League) led to increased social cohesion within historically open Sufi sects. Books and pamphlets published from this period attest to increasing communal and sectarian divisions in Sindh, which some authors compare to Nanakshahi and Akali Sikh differences regarding the control and administration of sacred sites.[29]

With the growth of Karachi as a port city and the development of large-scale irrigation projects, merchants and marginal populations from neighbouring regions increasingly flocked to Sindh during the later colonial period. Despite greater cultural diversity, this period witnessed increased cultural fission. The Hindu and Muslim components of Sindh's cultural landscape increasingly disaggregated following the First World War. While it is difficult to identify an exact point of schism, a public break did historically occur prior to Partition. For example, the Manzilgah Affair of 1939, in which seventy people lost their lives, was clearly a communal killing that divided Hindus and Muslims.[30] While communal violence in Sindh was less than in other parts of South Asia, it is worth noting that circumstances devolved to such a state that most Hindus migrated to India after 1947.

After Partition, Sindhis increasingly identified along different geo-cultural axes: Sindhis in Pakistan, in India, and in the diaspora increasingly lived distinct lives. Within the diaspora community, there were also pre- and post-Partition distinctions.[31] Nonetheless, most members of the Sindhi diaspora participated—as highly educated and qualified professionals—within an increasingly global and interconnected community. In recent years, the diaspora Sindhis were at the forefront of utilizing new communications technologies for socio-cultural purposes. They used technologies, like the Internet, to promote their own sense of 'Sindhiness', which some feel may dissolve given the community's 'deterritorialized' condition. The past decade therefore has witnessed an explosion of Sindhi managed websites on society, culture, and history as the community attempts to harness modern technologies to re-invent a virtual motherland—a place where Sindhis (both Hindu and Muslim) can work together to freely exchange ideas about their cultural world and their history.

RESOURCES FOR THE STUDY OF SINDH'S HISTORY AND CULTURE

Prior to Partition, Sindh had no PhD programs that focused on the Indus River region. Pre-Partition students had to take their examinations in Bombay. Many early dissertations on Sindh were therefore written at the University of Bombay.[32] After Partition, the government of Pakistan formed the University of Sindh in Karachi (then the national capital). In 1951, the University of Karachi replaced the University of Sindh (which the government shifted to Hyderabad). Eleven years later, the University of Sindh established an institute, the Sindhi Academy, with the goal of, (1) establishing a research library of multi-language resources about Sindh, and (2) publishing PhD dissertations from all over Pakistan. In addition to dissertations about Sindh, the Sindhi Academy published research about the region from a variety of languages (e.g., Persian, Arabic, English, and regional Pakistani languages).

The Sindhi Academy's main aim was to help scholars obtain primary and secondary sources on the Indus River region. The driving force behind the academy was M. Raziuddin Siddiqi, Vice-Chancellor of the University of Sindh. To administer the academy, Siddiqi hired scholars who studied Sindh: Nabi Bakhsh Khan Baloch, Muhammad Hanif Siddiqui, Pir Hussamuddin Rashdi and Ghulam Ali Allana. In 1964, the academy's advisory board expanded the institute's research away from language and changed its name to the Institute of Sindhology. The advisory board outlined three goals for the newly renamed institute: use Indology and Egyptology as a model to shape the study of Sindh, encourage the historical study of the Indus Valley, and contextualize Sindh's contribution to world history and civilization.

Initially established in a small room at the University of Sindh (Old Hyderabad Campus), the Institute of Sindhology's beginnings were modest. Nonetheless, the university allocated increased funding. Construction of a new three-storey building to house the institute began in late 1972. It shifted from the old Hyderabad campus to the new Jamshoro campus in 1978. A fusion of Islamic and Buddhist architecture, this new building (decorated in magnificent Hala tile-work) not only housed the Sindhology Institute's research library and administration, but (under its main dome) an anthropological research centre/museum, an art gallery, a film and photograph collection, and audio-visual materials. Prior to Silver Jubilee Celebrations in 1987 the university built extensions to the main building and, in an attempt to popularise the study of Sindh, included a bookstore and gift shop.

On the Indian side of the border, Sindhis lived in scattered locations after Partition. While many relocated to Mumbai and Gujarat, others settled in Kandla on the Gulf of Kutch (the Maharao of Kutch, in response to a request by Gandhi, allocated land to Sindhi refugees). Following Partition, the reestablishment of the community's material base was a priority. Little was done during this time to promote the study of Sindh's peoples, languages, or history. However, this 'apathy' changed when the community was on firmer material ground. In 1989, a group of Indian Sindhis gathered in Pune to create an institute for the promotion of Sindh. Later that year, they began building the Indian Institute of Sindhology at Adipur (near Kandla). In addition to sponsoring research and lectures on Sindh, the institute houses a Sindhi medium school. The institute plans to expand its activities in the future by becoming a full-fledged university campus (a.k.a., Bharati Sindhu Vidyapeeth) affiliated with the Shamji Krushna Verma Kutch University of Bhuj.

Beyond the Indian Institute of Sindhology (Adipur) and the Institute of Sindhology (Jamshoro) what other locations are there for the historical and cultural study of Sindh? Unfortunately, a dearth of up-to-date bibliographic catalogues hinders answers to this question—Muhammad Husain Panhwar's *Source Material on Sindh* from 1977 remains the main bibliography on Sindh. As a result, there are a variety of sources and locations that remain under explored and catalogued.[33] For example, the Sindh Archives, the National Museum, and Government Department of Archaeology in Karachi all house bodies of information about Sindh and its past. There are also scattered smaller collections (both private and public) in Pakistani cities like Hyderabad, Sukkur, and Khairpur.[34] Islamabad's National Archives also contains important research information.[35] Since nineteenth century British relations with Sindh were largely conducted via the Bombay Presidency, there are many documents concerning Sindh at the Maharashtra State Archives in Mumbai.[36] These documents are particularly helpful for understanding Sindh as part of the Bombay Presidency (i.e., 1847 to 1937).

Outside of South Asia, the most extensive collection on Sindh is the British Library's Oriental and India Office Collection. The Oriental and India Office Collection contains not only manuscripts and printed materials, but maps and photographs. While the collection indexes many printed government documents and manuscripts, numerous materials remain under catalogued.[37] Despite such archival 'loose ends' for the colonial period, Martin Moir's 'Archival Materials for the History of Sind Prior to British Annexation' is an excellent description of the British Library's pre-1843 materials regarding Sindh.[38] Also in London, the Institute of Ismaili Studies, the British War Museum and the Public Records Office (along with the School of Oriental and African Studies and Edinburgh University libraries) are frequently overlooked for the study of Sindh and its colonial history.[39] Primary source materials about Sindh are also found in the United States—the Library of Congress contains numerous books in Sindhi, as well as copies of materials that are difficult to access in London.

An important (and recent) resource for the study of Sindh is the Internet.[40] A virtual explosion in Internet forums by Sindhis wishing to discuss their heritage and past drives this resource.[41] In North America, many community associations are quick to utilize this new communication technology to build collective cohesion among overseas Sindhis from different regions, religious, and class backgrounds.[42] While the internet greatly expands these associations' ability to reach community members, many community groups pre-date the internet age. Regardless of when people establish these associations, their aims are relatively consistent: (1) preserve and transmit the heritages of Sindh, (2) dispatch Sindh-related news and information to those within and outside the community, and (3) bring international attention to difficulties experienced by the people of Sindh in Pakistan.

Among Internet sites that promote Sindh, there are two categories: overtly political and socio-historical. The latter are nodes that aspire to spread news and assist diaspora Sindhis. The first promotes *sindhiyat*, a political ideology based on Sindhi nationalism. Unfortunately, websites of both types are often short-lived. Nonetheless, some are long-term. For example, the Worldwide Sindh Network hosts a detailed website: it consists of multiple sections that direct users to information about arts (i.e., the fine arts and crafts of Sindh), culture and history, as well as business, employment, entertainment, media, and tourism.

While a large variety of virtual and non-virtual research locations exist, this diversity of sources does not necessarily challenge the disciplinary nature of much university-level research on Sindh. Since studies on Sindh often split along disciplinary lines, this volume aims to cross the divisions of interest that separate scholars working on Sindh and with Sindhis. Within a single forum, it seeks to unite scholarship from multiple research locations to map a 'snap shot' of contemporary scholarship about Sindh and its people. By combining an interdisciplinary and multi-local approach, *Interpreting the Sindhi World* not only investigates the diversity of Sindh's 'voices,' but raises questions about how these voices are historically and socio-culturally defined.

CONTRIBUTING TO THE DESCRIPTION OF SINDH AND SINDHIS

Interpreting the Sindhi World surveys contemporary Sindhi Studies through the oculus of society and history.[43] Its contributors practice a variety of disciplines in an equally diverse set of locations. Some live in Pakistan, while others reside in Europe, North America, or India. Yet others are diasporic Sindhis. The contributors' disciplinary range covers socio-cultural anthropology, history, literature, politics, and linguistics.

The collection opens with an essay by Lata Parwani. She begins the discussion on Sindhi culture by teasing apart histories of Udero Lal, a charismatic and mythic figure for both Hindus and Muslims. Parwani argues that Udero Lal is a metaphor that reflects the cultural integration of Sindhi society. Farhana Ibrahim and Rita Kothari's chapters also focus on the theme of cultural integration. However, they focus on Sindhis living in the Indian state of Gujarat. Ibrahim addresses the reception of post-Partition Sindhis in Kutch. The Kutch region is often noted by Sindhologists since, despite being in India, its mother tongue is a variation of Sindhi. Ibrahim examines how, despite linguistic kinship, the people of Kutch treat migrants from Sindh as 'outsiders'. She invokes the idea of *Asmita*, a local form of *Hindutva*, to explain this cultural disassociation. Kothari focuses on Sindhis in Gujarat who live outside of Kutch. She identifies Gujarat as the largest Sindhi cultural zone within India. She, like Ibrahim, investigates negative stereotyping of Sindhis and explains them within the larger cultural context of Gujarat and its politics.

Steven Ramey discusses religious practices and cultural identity in a South Asian location that is distant both from Sindh and Gujarat. He focuses on Lucknow to explore how new socio-cultural contexts shape innovative religious practices among Sindhis. Ramey analyzes how saint-movements impact cultural choices, as well as the different options available in Lucknow to Sindhis for developing their religious heritage. Maya Khemlani David takes us even further from the Indus River region by focusing on Sindhis in Malaysia. She examines how Malaysian Sindhis linguistically code switch within their community to communicate across age and gender lines.

Michel Boivin's contribution focuses this collection of essays back on Sindh by historically analyzing the tradition of Pithoro Pir. He deciphers how an upper caste, the Rajputs, succeeded in establishing their authority over an outcaste community, the Menghwars, in the Sufi saint tradition of Pithoro Pir. He questions how such a process can still be relevant in Pakistani Sindh.

Matthew Cook's chapter also analyzes Sindh's past. In contrast to other contributors, he addresses the themes of culture and migration by focusing on Sindh's pre-British past. Cook examines the case of the Lohanas of Sindh, a community historically transformed by the cultural dynamics of migration since the eighteenth century. He argues that the Sindhis who fled Pakistan after Partition are largely part of a community which has always been mobile, and that state disintegration and formation have always played a major role in this mobility.

Contributors to this collection also analyze Sindh's colonial period and events after Partition. Paulo Lemos Horta traces how Richard Burton's mid-nineteenth century experience of Sindh's religious fusion impacts his conception of folklore, syncretism, and empire. Unlike other histories of

Burton, Horta stresses how Sindh's cultural life makes its way into this author's writings on literature, faith, and imperialism. Vazira Zamindar's contribution turns to a crucial moment in the history of Sindhis: the exodus from Karachi in 1947. She critiques positions that consider exodus as a natural post-Partition phenomena by examining its complex reasons in light of re-making the subcontinent into a two state national order. Oskar Verkaaik concludes the volume by focusing on Sindhi nationalist discourse during the post-Partition period. He describes transformations in Sindhi nationalism and how they relate to the writings of regional saintly and political figures.

Conventional area studies approaches of South Asia bend regions and their people upon themselves to analyze society and history.[44] In contrast, this collection of essays treats Sindh and its people not as isolated entities, but as comparative entries in a wider socio-historical web. Such an approach does not treat history and society as particularly localized.[45] In the comparative process, it celebrates rather than erases diverse cultural faces from Sindh's human tapestry. Through cross-disciplinary studies from across the world, this collection challenges claims that the Sindhi world is anything but complex. By exploring its socio-historical complexity, this volume not only looks to illuminate details about Sindh and its past, but provide insights into its people and the multi-faceted worlds they inhabit.

NOTES

1. John Stratton Hawley, 'Naming Hinduism', *Wilson Quarterly* 15.1 (Summer 1991): 20–34.
2. More than 60 per cent of Las Bela's population speak the Lassi dialect.
3. Laurent Maheux, 'Moumal-Mahendra: Contextes et Variations d'un Cycle Légendaire du Thar' (PhD Dissertation in Literature at the National Institute for Oriental Languages and Civilizations [Paris], 2004).
4. For example, see: Sohail Lari, *History of Sind* (Karachi: Oxford University Press, 1994).
5. Sir John Marshall, *Mohenjo-Daro and the Indus Civilization* (Delhi: Asian Educational Services, 2004 [1931]).
6. Ghulam Ali Allana, *Papers on Sindhi Language and Linguistics* (Jamshoro: Institute of Sindhology, 1998).
7. Derryl MacLean, *Religion and Society in Arab Sind* (Leiden: E.J. Brill, 1989).
8. Murlidhar Dawani, *Hindu Architecture in Sind: Preservation, Conservation and Restoration of Gori Temple* (Karachi: Department of Architecture, Dawood College of Engineering and Technology, 1986).
9. Motilal Jotwani, *A Dictionary of Sindhi Literature* (New Delhi: Sampark Prakashan, 1996), 152.

10. Ghulam Ali Allana, *Sindhi Culture: A Preliminary Study* (Karachi: Indus Publications, 1986), 94.
11. Sohail Amirali Bawani, 'Beyond Hindu and Muslim: Rethinking Iconographic Models and Symbolic Expressions from Sindh (A Case of the Tradition of Rama Pir)', *Nukta Art* 1/2 (2007): 64–71.
12. E.H. Aitken, *Gazetteer of the Province of Sind* (Karachi: Mercantile Steam Press, 1907), 182.
13. Michel Boivin, 'La Danse Dans Les Cultes Musulmans Du Domaine Sindhi', *Revue d'Histoire du Soufisme* 4 (2005): 179–187.
14. Annemarie Schimmel, *Sindhi Literature* (Wiesbaden: Otto Harrassowitz, 1974), 11.
15. Bernard Cohn, *An Anthropologist Among the Historians and Other Essays* (Delhi: Oxford University Press, 1987), 109.
16. Jethmal Gulraj Parsram, *Sind and Its Sufis: Life, Poetry and Philosophy of Sufis in Sind* (Adipur: Indian Institute of Sindhology, 2000 [1929]).
17. Lari, 144.
18. Claude Markovits, *The Global World of Indian Merchants, 1750–1947: Traders of Sindh from Bukhara to Panama* (Cambridge: Cambridge University Press, 2000).
19. Schimmel, 18.
20. Shah Abdul Latif, *Shah jo risalo alias Ganje Latif*, Volume II (Revised), trans. Muhammad Yacoob Agha (Hyderabad: Shah Abdul Latif Bhitshah Cultural Centre Committee, 1985), 752.
21. Robert Huttenback, *British Relations with Sind, 1799–1843* (Karachi: Oxford University Press, 2007). For an alternate perspective on this process, see: Matthew A. Cook, ed., *Observing Sindh: Selected Reports* (Karachi: Oxford University Press, 2008), vii–xiv.
22. For the analysis of the period between conquest and Sindh's formal integration into the Bombay Presidency, see: Matthew A. Cook, 'After Annexation: Colonialism and Sindh During the 1840s' (PhD dissertation in anthropology at Columbia University, 2007).
23. Sandria Freitag, *Collective Action and Community: Public Arenas and the Emergence of Communalism in North India* (Berkeley: University of California Press, 1989).
24. Alexander F. Baillie, *Kurrachee: Past, Present and Future* (Karachi: Oxford University Press, 1997).
25. Aitken, 167. The Theosophical Society established itself in Karachi during 1895 and is still active today.
26. David Cheesman, *Rural Power and Indebtness in Colonial Sindh* (Surrey, U.K.: Curzon Press, 1997).
27. Aitken, 409.
28. Sara Ansari, *Sufi Saints and State Power: The Pirs of Sind, 1843–1947* (Cambridge: Cambridge University Press, 1992).
29. Dayaram Hemraj Tajwani, *Hindu Dharam Rakpal Shri Nanak Deva* (Karachi: Unknown Publisher, 1915).
30. Keith Allen Jones, *Politics in Sindh, 1907–1940: Muslim Identity and the Demand for Pakistan* (Karachi: Oxford University Press, 2002).
31. Michel Boivin, 'The Dynamics of Identity Reassertion in the Sindhi Diaspora', in A. Ranbirsingh and T. Chakrabati, eds., *Theorizing and Critiquing Indian Diaspora* (New Delhi: Creative Books, 2004), 136–165.
32. One important example is: S.J. Narsain, 'The Amil Community of Hyderabad, Sind' (PhD dissertation in Sociology at the University of Bombay, 1932).
33. Martin Moir, 'The Sind Government Archives in Karachi', *Sind Quarterly* 16.3: 32–37.

34. Afzal Ahmed Sheikh, *Critical Study of Sind Provincial Museum Library* (Hyderabad: Provincial Museum, 1981).
35. Martin Moir, 'Prospects for the Development of Archives in Pakistan', *Sindhological Studies* 16.1–2: 8–16.
36. For additional details on the scope of the Maharastra State Archives Collection, refer to chapter one in Matthew A. Cook, 'After Annexation: Colonialism and Sindh During the 1840s' (PhD dissertation in anthropology at Columbia University, 2007).
37. J. Blumhardt, *Catalogue of the Hindi, Panjabi, Sindhi and Pushtu Printed Books in the Library of the British Museum* (London: British Museum, 1893); J. Blumhardt, *Catalogue of the Marathi, Gujarati, Bengali, Assamese, Orya, Pushtu and Sindhi Manuscripts in the Library of the British Museum* (London: British Museum, 1893).
38. Martin Moir, 'The India Office Library Records: Archival Materials for the History of Sind Prior to British Annexation', in Hamida Khuhro, ed., *Sind Through the Centuries* (Karachi: Oxford University Press, 1981), 290–301.
39. The Institute of Ismaili Studies shelters a particularly important collection of manuscripts in Sindhi. The institute collected these manuscripts from the Khoja community (followers of the Aga Khan).
40. Boivin, 136–165.
41. http://www.worldsindhicongress.org
42. An estimated twenty associations of Sindhis are active in the United State in locations as diverse as Chicago, Michigan, New York, Florida, Houston, Long Island, North and South Carolina, New Jersey, San Francisco, South California, New England, Washington, and Georgia.
43. A similar, but Franco-centric account, is: Michel Boivin, ed., *Sindh Through History and Representations: French Contributions to Sindhi Studies* (Karachi: Oxford University Press, 2008).
44. Thomas Metcalf, *Forging the Raj: Essays on British India in the Heyday of Empire* (Delhi: Oxford University Press, 2005), 283.
45. This approach distinguishes *Interpreting the Sindhi World* from other collections of essays on Sindh (e.g., Fahmida Hussain, ed., *Sindh: Past, Present and Future* [Karachi: Institute of Sindhology, 2006], and Pratapaditya Pal, ed., *Sindh Past Glory, Present Nostalgia* (Mumbai: Marg Publications, 2008).

CHAPTER 1

Myths of Jhuley Lal: Deconstructing a Sindhi Cultural Icon[1]

LATA PARWANI

He who invokes Jhuley Lal
Will find his desires fulfilled
Followers of Lal, call out
Jhuley Lal!

Jhuley Lal is popularly regarded as the patron saint of Sindhi Hindus. For millions of followers worldwide, this charismatic figure represents the essence of *Sindhiyat* or 'Sindhiness'. Intrinsically linked with this personification of Sindhi culture is the notion of Jhuley Lal as a symbol of what is typically described as a Sindhi Sufi identity. In speaking to Sindhis today, one would be led to believe that the figure of Jhuley Lal belongs to the immemorial past and has always played this essential role in informing and shaping Sindhi imaginaries. A closer examination shows that this has not been the case historically. This representation of *Sindhiyat* is a conscious construct, an 'invented tradition',[2] and the numerous colonial era accounts of myths associated with a Sindhi river god have been integral to this process of invention. In this context, these myths are 'a coding device in which important information is conveyed…a discursive act through which actors evoke the sentiments out of which society is actively constructed'.[3]

A closer reading of the Jhuley Lal myths affords a deeper understanding of Sindhi society and a study of their re-formulations is integral to understanding contemporary representations of *Sindhiyat*. Building on the notion of constructed traditions and expanding on the definition of myths as a coding device and a discursive act, this chapter traces the evolution of these myths, from their origins in the fishing villages of Sindh to their present day global span. Contextualizing these accounts historically, this chapter analyzes various concerns—Orientalist, cultural, nationalistic, ethnic, and diasporic—that have influenced and perpetuated multiple interpretations of these myths. Finally, there is a consideration of Jhuley Lal as a symbol of Sindhi culture and a representative of Sindhi identity.

DOCUMENTING THE SINDHI RIVER GOD

Sindh was one of the last areas to be added to Britain's Indian Empire. The region first assumed geo-political importance for the British in the early nineteenth century as the gateway to Afghanistan, which had come to be seen as a crucial buffer against Russian expansion. After their military debacle in Afghanistan, British officials in India sought to secure the border and recover their military prestige by conquering Sindh in February 1843. The introduction of colonial rule to the region marked the beginning of a new chapter in Sindhi history, as for the first time in centuries, the region was brought under non-Muslim rule. With its subsequent 1847 annexation to the Bombay Presidency, Sindh's geographical, cultural, and political seclusion from the rest of India came to an abrupt end. Its distance from imperial centres of power had allowed the region to develop a distinct socio-cultural legacy—one that was embodied in a fluid Sindhi identity, which articulated an accommodation of Hindu, Muslim, and Sikh religious influences.

With the establishment of a permanent colonial presence, there was a spate of British officers and travellers writing about Sindh. These colonial observers meticulously recorded the ethnic, caste, linguistic, and other distinctions that constituted the social mosaic of Sindhi society. Their accounts commented on the 'openness' of Sindhi culture and on the absence of a 'proper' caste system among Sindhi Hindus.[4] Observing the 'cultural media',[5] they sought to understand the widespread Sindhi participation in the worship of saints belonging to the 'other' community and their enthusiastic involvement in each other's religious festivals. Confounded in the endeavour to slot Sindhis into tidy 'Hindu' and 'Muslim' categories, popular religious practices were typically described as a concoction of various faiths. According to Richard Burton:

> Hindoo religion is not to be found in a state of purity in Sindh....Hinduism here is mixed up with the heterogeneous elements of Islam, and the faith of Nanak Shah. A Hindoo will often become the Murid (follower) of a Mussulman, and in some cases the contrary takes place...all great Pirs revered by the Moslems have classical Hindoo names....From the Sikhs, the Sindh

> Hindoo has learned to simplify his faith: to believe in one God whom he calls Khuda, Thakur and Bhagwan....The male and female [deities] are considered by them as intercessors with the Deity, and hold the same position as the Paighambar or Prophets of the Moslems....The Pirs and holy men are revered as sub-intercessors, whose superogatory piety enables them to aid their fellow creatures in a spiritual way.[6]

Writing in 1907, E.H. Aitken concurred: 'There is very little religion in Sind that would be recognized as Hinduism in India...the prevailing religion of [Hindus] is a blend of the two faiths in varying proportions'.[7] In 1940, H.T. Sorley similarly commented: 'The complex religious history of [Sindh has produced] a great accretion of superstitious practice in the belief of multitude, and a common basis of understanding by Muslim and Hindu alike'.[8]

As part of the effort to know and construct a Sindhi 'other', stories of a religiously syncretic riverine cult garnered special attention from colonial ethnographers. Even while declaring Sindhi Hindu religious practices to be 'so intermingled...that we can scarcely discern the line of demarcation',[9] they presented 'Hindu' and 'Muslim' understandings of these myths. Documented at great length, the legends of Udero Lal, Amar Lal, Zinda Pir, Shaikh Tahir, and Khwajah Khizr featured prominently in accounts of Sindh and a hitherto localized deity became emblematic of Sindhi religious eclecticism.[10]

THE RIVER GOD AS A HINDU INCARNATION

In these versions, the river god is variously known as Udero Lal, Jhuley Lal, Amar Lal, Darya Shah, and Zinda Pir. The most popular narrative is set in the mid-tenth century, when Mirkh Shah was ruling over Thatta with his tyrannical vizier Yusuf Ahio.[11] Mirkh Shah believed that Islam should be the only religion practiced in his realm and ordered all Hindus to convert. This greatly distressed Hindu elders, who negotiated for a reprieve. Mirkh Shah agreed to a brief respite, on the expiration of which they would have to concede to his demand. At this difficult juncture, the Hindus turned to Varuna (the river god) and prayed and fasted at the banks of the Indus. Finally, Varuna emerged and promised that a divine saviour would be born at Nasarpur to Ratan and Devki, an old childless couple.

The baby was named Udero Lal at birth. The baby's cradle swung by itself; hence, he was also called Jhuley Lal. On being informed of this development, Mirkh Shah sent his vizier, Ahio, to confirm the news. Ahio went to Nasarpur where he saw the baby in a cradle; within moments, the baby transformed into a youth, a black-bearded man and an old white-haired man. The astonished vizier asked Udero Lal to accompany him, but the river god asked the vizier to proceed ahead of him. On reaching Thatta, Ahio was shocked to see Udero Lal emerging from the river, dressed as a warrior, and followed by a well-equipped army. A frightened Ahio asked Udero Lal to come alone since the king did not intend to engage in a battle with the Hindus. Udero Lal relented and went to visit the king. Ahio reported the miracles to Mirkh Shah and introduced Udero Lal as a god of the Hindus. Mirkh Shah asked him to convince the Hindus to convert to Islam. Udero Lal engaged in an extended theological debate with the king and using Quranic references explained that all were creations of the same god hence equal. Mirkh Shah was almost convinced, but Ahio advised him to stand firm. Swayed by the vizier, Mirkh Shah ordered Udero Lal imprisoned. However, Udero Lal evaded capture by transforming himself into wind and water. An enraged Mirkh Shah decided to proceed with his plans of forced conversions. Angered, Udero Lal commanded fire to destroy Thatta. Scared by the prospects of economic loss and destruction, Mirkh Shah conceded defeat and sought forgiveness. Udero Lal relented and Mirkh Shah instituted freedom of worship in Sindh.

After some time, Udero Lal asked his cousin Pugar Thakur to found a new cult called the *Daryapanthi* faith. Thakur consented and became Udero Lal's first disciple. Udero Lal travelled to Juhejo where he saw a barren plot of land with a dry well, owned by a Muslim named Shaikh Mamman. Udero Lal expressed interest in buying the land to establish a temple there. Mamman went off to consult with his wife. Meanwhile, Udero Lal struck his spear in the ground, a verdant tree sprung up and the dry well was miraculously filled. On his return, the stunned owner offered his land *gratis*. Pleased, Udero Lal again struck his spear on the ground and brought forth gems, which he presented to Mamman. The astonished landowner fell to his knees and became a devotee. Soon after, Udero Lal and his horse jumped into the well and disappeared. According to some versions, Udero Lal disappeared into the earth while other accounts mention him returning to the Indus. After the deity's disappearance, guided by a dream, Mirkh Shah ordered a shrine to be built which would embody Udero Lal's teachings and accommodate religious practices of both communities. An eternal flame was also lit at the spot to memorialize the deity. In the 1920 *Gazetteer,* J.W. Smyth reports that upwards of fifty thousand people attend the annual fair held at this shrine.[12]

Another widely circulated account situates Udero Lal in the mid to late seventeenth century. Here, Mirkh Shah is presented as a Muslim *kazi* with a similar agenda: to force conversion of Hindus.[13] When Udero Lal was five years of age, he went with other children to sell boiled grain in adjacent villages. Every day he would stop by the river to pray and cast his basket of rice as an offering to the river god. His basket was always returned filled with 'money, honey, and other delicacies'.[14] In time, his parents became suspicious. One day his father followed him to the river and saw two men emerge from the water and take the boy with them. The distraught father was comforted when his son returned with the usual gift-laden basket. Meanwhile the *kazi's* vehemence towards non-Muslims increased. Frightened Hindus pleaded to the river god and were informed that Udero Lal was their divine protector. When this news reached the *kazi*, he decided to persecute non-Muslims, beginning with their saviour. The *kazi* met with the boy and forced him to convert to Islam. The youth countered with his superior knowledge of Islamic teachings and Quranic injunctions regarding forcible conversions. This debate moved from the courthouse to the banks of the Indus. Here, the boy invited the *kazi* to continue his arguments on the water, throwing down the gauntlet that if the *kazi* had faith in his religion then he would not drown. The *kazi* agreed but soon started sinking; frightened he called out for assistance. Udero Lal promised to help but only if the *kazi* stopped proselytizing and promised freedom of worship. The chastised *kazi* repented and was spared.

THE RIVER GOD AS A MUSLIM SAINT

In these versions, Jhuley Lal is variously described as Shaikh Tahir, Khwajah Khizr, Zinda Pir, and Darya Pir. The earliest mention of this saint (who is worshipped by members of both communities) is provided by a local historian, Mir Shir Ali Qani:

> Juhejo is well known for the shrine of Shaikh Tahir who is known as Udero Lal by the Hindus. Intoxicated with the wine of Divinity he spent the early part of his life roaming in the desert. One day when he was holding some seeds in his hands to eat them, a camel, running away from its owner, appeared at the doorstep of his humble abode. Observing the camel with his inner spiritual eye he saw God residing in the camel. He addressed God and said: 'Oh Lord, since you have blessed me by appearing in front of me in this form, deign to

> share my food with me'. The camel would not stop to take this offering, but the Shaikh persisted in following it, until he attained a high spiritual station. After his death his sanctuary has become a pilgrimage centre for the masses. Every year there is an unusual fair here, Hindu women gather from all over Sindh and can be seen dancing through the streets of the village.[15]

A later account, citing nineteenth century sources, provides more details. According to Din Muhammad Vafai's *Tazkirah-i Mashahir-i Sindh*, Shaikh Tahir was a Muslim convert from Hinduism and a devotee of Shaikh Bahauddin Zakaria Multani.[16] Vafai further adds that Shaikh Tahir's Hindu name was Udero Lal, son of Ratan Shah. Accounts by colonial officers like Burton, Aitken, and Hughes also mention that the Hindu river god Udero Lal is known to his Muslim followers as Shaikh Tahir.[17]

This duality is inscribed structurally as well: the fort-like shrine complex at the village of Udero Lal (in Sindh, Pakistan) includes a domed tomb and small temple for the eternal flame. Describing it as built in the 'usual style of Mussalman tombs', Smyth notes that, while it is known as the shrine of Shaikh Tahir, an inscription on the building credits a Hindu, Bedarang son of Shamdas Thakur, as having supervised the construction of the tomb in CE 1634. Revenues from the annual fair are split between Hindu caretakers, who look after the eternal flame, and Muslim shrine attendants.[18]

A different set of myths is associated with a small island shrine near Rohri, in Sindh. Abbot writes that one night a shepherd, Baji, saw a bright flame burning in the distance on the water. Thinking there were lost travellers, he sent his wife after the light to help the travellers. However, the closer she got the further the light moved away from her. On hearing her account, her husband took her inability to get the light as a sign of fear and went after it himself. Nonetheless, the light proved as elusive as before. This filled him with awe and he erected a shrine and became a devotee. Soon after that the Indus changed its course. Abandoning the walls of Alor, it encircled the shrine built by Baji. In the colonial period, this was known as the island of Khwajah Khizr.[19]

Another version credits a merchant, Shah Husain, as the builder of the shrine. In the 1876 *Gazetteer of the Province of Sind*, A.W. Hughes writes that a Delhi merchant named Shah Husain reportedly built the shrine of Khwajah Khizr in CE 925.[20] One day Husain was travelling with his daughter in a boat on the Indus to Makkah. On his arrival at Aror (also Alor), Dalurai—the debauched Hindu king of that city—asked to marry the merchant's daughter. The merchant refused, saying a Muslim could not marry a Hindu. The king was not swayed and plotted to kidnap the girl. The distraught girl prayed to Khwajah Khizr. The saint responded and directed her father to loosen the boat. As soon as this was done, the Indus changed its course and the boat was carried away to safety (while the city of Aror was completely flooded). In gratitude, the merchant built a shrine dedicated to the saint in Bakkhar. In his 1892 study of the Indus, H.G. Raverty notes that in Sindh, Khizr (believed to have drunk the waters of life and become immortal) is known as Zinda Pir and that 'Muhammadans of Hind are in the habit of offering him oblations of lamps and flowers'.[21] Raverty further observes that the Hindus worship Khizr as a river god under the name of Jinda Pir.

A related legend states that annually the palla fish, a species indigenous to the Indus, ascends the river as far as Bakkhar. At Bakkhar, the fish circumambulate the shrine and turn back, and thus never present their tails to the hallowed abode. J. Abbot reports that it is popularly believed that the palla are performing a pilgrimage to the shrine.[22]

READING THE RIVER GOD MYTHS

This corpus is remarkable for a variety of reasons. Besides the fact that they highlight Sindhi religious eclecticism, these myths are like a palimpsest of Sindhi history and culture. They amplify the dominant role of the Indus in determining the socio-economic fortunes of Sindhis, a people who derive their name from an indigenized form of the river's name—the Sindhu. Since antiquity, Sindhis have worked as farmers, fishermen, or tradesmen. In the eighteenth and nineteenth centuries, river routes connected merchants in Shikarpur, Sukkur, and Hyderabad with commercial markets in the Persian Gulf, Middle East, and Central Asia. Many Sindhi idioms highlight this maritime aspect of Sindhi culture as well. For instance, *Shala Bero Budeii!* (may your boat sink!) is a popular curse, *Bera Bana Laeen* (may you bring boats ashore safely) an oft-repeated entreaty, and *Shala Beri Tarayee* (may your boat stay afloat) a frequently expressed good luck wish.

These myths also successfully tap into ancient practices of river worship in Sindh. U.T. Thakur notes that the Indus cult was the principal religion of the early inhabitants of the region.[23] G.E.L. Carter points to a fragment of pottery with a fish painted on it found at the site of a fourth century Buddhist Stupa near the banks of an old riverbed.[24] Sindhi literature is replete with allusions and oblations to the river. Shah Abdul Latif Bhittai, the premier Sindhi poet, highlights the central role of the Indus in the daily lives of Sindhis. Dedicating *Sur Samundi* as an ode to the Indus,

Bhittai's verses speak of peasant women making offerings of ghee and rice, as well as lighting oil lamps along riverbanks while praying to the Indus to bring their seafaring men safely back home.[25]

It is suggested here that for early Sindhis this intimate relationship with the Indus facilitated what A.R. Radcliffe-Brown calls the 'personification of a natural phenomenon'.[26] Udero Lal is presented as an incarnation of the river and his vehicle is the palla, a fish indigenous to the Indus. Its peculiar movements render it an appropriate companion for the incarnate deity. Throughout the story, the connection to the river is continually strengthened. Varuna emerges from the river. The swinging cradle is reminiscent of the undulating waves of the Indus. The vizier sees Udero Lal emerging from the river. The debate between the *kazi* and the boy concludes when the Indus decides the validity of the *kazi's* claims. When the youth makes daily offerings to the river, his devotion is rewarded with a basket filled with 'money, honey, and other delicacies',[27] all symbols of prosperity. This then is the promise the river holds out—as long as followers remain devoted—it will protect them. The identification with the Indus is complete.

In the Khizr myths, the annual pilgrimage of the palla presents a local reading of a natural phenomenon. It is understandable that a locale where the palla circumambulated would be considered sacred, the same spot which bore the annual brunt of the Indus floods. Abbot points to parables about saints like Pir Badar, Zinda Ghazi, and Ghazi Miyan, who are similarly associated with dominion over waters and control over storms. Abbott further suggests that it is very likely that, 'such saints are the transformation of old animistic spirits, perpetuating an ancient Nature worship of daimonia [*sic*] and tutelary spirits'.[28] Subsequent transmutation of this cult into a Hindu deity Udero Lal/Zinda Pir and a Muslim saint Shaikh Tahir/Khwajah Khizr affords a deeper understanding of incoming religious influences on modes of Sindhi worship. Given its geographical position, at the confluence of the Indic and Iranian–Arab worlds, Sindh has historically been a meeting place of distinct cultures and varied religious traditions. Pottery fragments at various archaeological sites hint at the influence exerted by the river during that period. While Buddhism and Jainism eventually died out, Hinduism and Islam continued to flourish and left discernable imprints on this cult.

In reading these myths, there is detectable evidence of accretions, intermingling, and aggregation of rituals. The Udero Lal story begins with invocations of the teachings of *Bhagwad Gita* and bears remarkable similarities to the Krishna story. However, while the vocabulary is

Hinduized, the rituals are those associated with the older cult of water worship. Similarly, the language of the Khizr/Zinda Pir legends reflects a thinly applied veneer of Islamic explanations to indigenous understandings of the change in the flow of the Indus. The Sindhis recast the Quranic figure of Khizr and moulded it to fit that of the river god. Khizr's association with water made him an obvious candidate for indigenization by a culture that had worshiped the river since pre-historic times. John Renard defines this as a process by which, 'the receiving culture makes acceptable to itself stories from other cultures'.[29] Thus, an originally Islamic hero is seen to gradually take on the features of a local character and participate in a process in which evolving local, social and political structures cloak themselves in the authority, antiquity, and universal claims of Islam.

Concurrently at work is the concept of 'Islamization', which Renard explains as a process by which non-Islamic heroic figures take on a distinctly Islamic religious cast.[30] As the Vafai text suggests, a tentative explanation for this could be that Shaikh Tahir is an Islamicized version of the Udero Lal legend. When the local populace converted to Islam, these figures, too, were gradually 'converted'. By virtue of being Islamicized, Shaikh Tahir participated in a 'legitimation of Islam', by conferring on it the kind of credibility that an incoming religion needs to take hold in a foreign culture. Islamization provided a means for the recently converted Sindhis to recast their modes of worship in an Islamic hue. As described by Qani, Shaikh Tahir's spiritual capacity to see beyond the externalities and see God in every living thing (even a camel) points to the essence of the saint's appeal: *Wahdat-ul-Wujud* (i.e., the Unity of Being) or looking beyond the narrow confines of religion. This rationalization of religious differences made it easier for recently converted Sindhis to carry on with pre-Islamic practices of worship cloaked in an Islamic understanding. Thus, the temple dedicated to the river god, Udero Lal was designated as the shrine of Shaikh Tahir.[31]

Co-existence of multiple versions of essentially the same myth points to the integration of society and offers an insight into the 'social organization' of Sindhi society. Robert Redfield uses this term to 'account for the choices and resolutions of difficulties and conflicts' that occur in a given context.[32] Commenting on continued circulation of these myths, Carter writes:

> Think of the Hindus as worshipping the river and of the Mahomedans with a veneer of Arabic learning, carrying on to the full all their old customs and folklore. The early years...gave the Sindhi much to think about and one result

> was the realization by both, the Hindus and the Mahomedans, that both could worship at the same shrine and pray for help, for both worshipped the living God....It seems indeed that the later invasions...must have hammered into the understanding of the Sindhis, that Hindu or Mussalman, they were of the same stock, supported by the same river and bound together by common interests.[33]

Reading these myths, therefore, is akin to reading a social charter legitimating the social structure of Sindhi society. These myths describe a formative moment, in which enduring tensions threatened to divide the two religious groups and where emphasis is placed on accommodating, not erasing, religious differences. Beginning with communitarian conflict, the story concludes with a negotiated resolution that alludes to a pragmatic conciliation. It thus offers a valuable insight into the intricately imbricated socio-economic relationship that had evolved over time between the two communities.[34] When the British arrived in Sindh, relations between Sindhis were such that conflict and hostility mingled easily with congenial amity, making for a layered social complexity that defied easy categorizations. Moreover, the much-vaunted shared culture was not always able to override differences, particularly over economic matters.[35] In the early twentieth century, even as colonial observers continued to reify Sindhi religious culture, the shared icon was embroiled in a legal battle. Dispute over the rights to collect revenues arose between Hindu and Muslim attendants of the shrine, leading to a civil case petitioning colonial courts to adjudicate whether Udero Lal was Hindu or Muslim.[36]

Given the central importance accorded to the river god in colonial accounts, it is noteworthy that while there is evidence of river worship in the region, the figure of Jhuley Lal/Udero Lal/Tahir Shaikh/Zinda Pir is remarkably absent from pre-modern sources, Sindhi or otherwise. Carter reports that this cult of river worship was prevalent in areas of Lower and Central Sindh.[37] In his recent study, Mark-Anthony Falzon notes that this appears to have been a localized cult. Urbanized Sindhis and those living away from riverine areas report unfamiliarity with these myths before their migration to India. For those who worshiped the deity, the river god was one of the many they revered.[38]

Nonetheless, Orientalist observers were attracted to these myths because they offered a way of approaching and understanding the socio-cultural interaction between Sindhis. Through publication of widely circulated travelogues, gazetteers, and hagiographies, the fables/legends of the River God were invested with authority and credibility that elevated them to the status of myths, thereby making these available as a means with which new social forms could be constructed.[39]

POST-COLONIAL REPRESENTATIONS: INVENTING *SINDHIYAT*

In 1947, as the subcontinent was cleaved to create the nation-states of Pakistan and India, the Muslim majority region of Sindh became a constituent province in newly independent Pakistan. While Punjab saw the worst of the bloodshed and brutality (compelling entire communities to migrate), Sindh did not face similar levels of violence nor did it witness comparable population transfers. Nevertheless, with increasing communal rhetoric, equivocation of political leaders, and a steady influx of refugees, the pragmatic communitarian accommodation that had been characteristic of Sindh was severely jeopardized. Increasingly disenfranchised and fearful for their lives, particularly after the riots of January 1948, the majority of Hindus fled their homes and left Sindh. By August 1948, over a million had migrated from Sindh.[40] From there, many moved to South-East Asia, Africa, Europe, Australia, and North America.

In India, Bombay received the first wave of Sindhi immigrants. From there, they were shuttled to refugee camps in Ulhasnagar, Ajmer, Marwar, and Ahmedabad. Lack of housing and unfamiliar territory made it very difficult for Sindhis to establish themselves. Added to this was the attitude of the local population, who viewed them with varying degrees of sympathy, apprehension, and antagonism. The government offered some degree of help, but for the bulk of Sindhis, who had left behind thriving businesses, life in overcrowded refugee camps was extremely difficult. Nanik Motwane, a Sindhi refugee, wrote: 'With tardy rations and insufficient clothes, no one can say that the condition of the refugees is as satisfactory as it should be. Most of them are found to be sleeping on the ground huddled together'.[41] *The Bombay Chronicle* reported: 'The exodus of a large number of non-Muslims from Sind created a special problem for the whole country and for the refugees themselves...there is no place the Sind refugees could call their own'.[42] Describing the Sindhi plight, Popati Hiranandani wrote: 'Here, being a stateless Sindhi...you are just like a tiny wave in an ocean, nay, a particle of salt and they use you for the flavour of their dishes'. Sindhi religious practices were perceived as not being 'Hindu' enough and ridiculed as 'Islamic'. Faced with such 'subtle forms of discrimination and often pronounced hostility', Sindhis were often likened to tribes of wandering Jews in search of a homeland.[43]

During the 1950s, as Sindhis settled in, efforts were made to recreate the cultural climate they had left behind in Sindh. Integrally tied to this endeavour was the attempt to promote the language. Initially, Sindhi was not recognized as an Indian national language by the 1950 Constitution of India. After much debate it was included as one of the national languages in 1966.[44] Concurrently, efforts were also made to preserve and promote Sindhi culture. This was accomplished with renewed attention towards an icon popularly associated with Sindhis, Jhuley Lal. Professor Ram Panjwani (a Sindhi educator, writer, and singer who migrated to India after Partition) is generally credited with the revival of Jhuley Lal.[45] Baldev Gajra, a contemporary of Panjwani, notes that Panjwani's efforts were inspired by the institution of Ganesh Puja, founded by Lokmanya Bal Gangadhar Tilak to bring the Maratha community on one platform.[46] Gobind Malhi added: '[Panjwani] has rallied [Sindhis]...around the community deity—Jhulelal—and has given them a slogan which has unified them: *Jeko chavando Jhulelal, Tenhja thinda bera par* (he who will utter the name Jhulelal will find salvation)'.[47] Panjwani himself said that, 'Faith has established Jhule Lal as Asht Dev of Sindhis—Community God of Sindhis...[he] inspires us to believe in unity and brotherhood of mankind. He raises us above the differences and distinctions of caste, colour and creed'.[48]

In order to spread his message, Panjwani travelled in India and around the world wherever the Sindhis had settled. Drawing on the treasure trove of myths circulated in the colonial period, he reached out to Sindhis and reminded them of Sindh and Sindhi songs, their shared heritage, and, above all, the figure of Jhuley Lal who had previously rescued oppressed Sindhis and whom he urged them to invoke again as Sindhis began to build new lives for themselves. Temples dedicated to this deity were built in cities wherever there was a sizeable Sindhi population, thus adding Jhuley Lal to the pantheon of Sindhi gods. Idols and pictures of Jhuley Lal were soon to be found in Sindhi households. In this iconography, he is generally seen seated cross-legged on a lotus placed on the back of the palla, floating on the Indus with an indistinct waterfront shrine in the background. He is depicted as an ascetic with a flowing white beard, a sectarian mark on his forehead, holding a generic holy text. Occasionally he is shown as a warrior astride a steed, sword in one hand and flag in the other, highlighting his martial nature. A third rendition portrays him standing on the palla holding a staff, portraying him as a leader of this community. In rare representations, he is shown as sitting on a crocodile.

Using popular media to increase awareness, Panjwani produced and starred in a Sindhi film *Jhooley Lal*. He also recorded a number of devotional songs, in praise of Jhuley Lal, sung by popular singer Bhagwanti Navani. Given below is a sample:

My boat is in mid-stream
I entreat before Zinda Pir
Oh! Lal Udero! You of the eternal lights
Many supplicants come to your threshold
Your blessings are for rich and poor alike
I entreat....[49]

Invoking vivid images of women praying and lighting lamps on the banks of the Indus, these songs were immensely popular as they fostered a sense of community by stirring memories of a shared loss and evoking nostalgia for a lost homeland and a rich cultural heritage.

Panjwani had astutely recognized the potential of myths for use as crucial elements of cultural (re)production. Using discursive force, defined by Bruce Lincoln as 'the chief means whereby social borders, hierarchies, institutional formations, and habituated patterns of behaviour are both maintained and modified',[50] these myths were simplified and revived. Various epithets assigned to the river god were subsumed under one name: Jhuley Lal. While earlier accounts generally end with Jhuley Lal disappearing into the river, in post-colonial hagiographies this charismatic figure is reported to have visited other Hindu pilgrimage centres in Sindh, thus connecting disparate religious sites.[51] In colonial Sindh, this local deity had been primarily worshipped by Daryapanthis, but in post-Partition India Jhuley Lal was transformed into *the* Sindhi Hindu God and elevated above social and caste distinctions. In this process of construction, there is an almost complete erasure of the Islamic aspects of the river god tales. Relevant facts, like his being revered as a Muslim saint in Sindh or that the shrine at Udero Lal bore close resemblance to a Sufi *dargah* (unlike the temples built in India), were downplayed. However, even as Jhuley Lal was valorized as the saffron flag-wielding saviour of Hindus (*à* la Shivaji Maharaj for the Marathas and Guru Gobind Singh for Sikhs),[52] a concomitant emphasis was also placed on Sindhi Sufism described as a 'fusion of the stern monotheism of the Persian mind and the deep philosophical thoughts of the Vedanta'.[53] Panjwani elaborated: 'A Sindhi is a Sufi, above all considerations of caste and creed. He does not discriminate...[Sindhi] poets and saints have given us glimpses of the light that has lit up the soul of Sind. It matters not at all whether these saints were Hindus or Muslims, for saints have no religion, or, rather they are the essence of all religions'.[54] Such internally inconsistent articulations are indicative of Sindhis' ambivalent relationship with Muslims/Islam and were a vital element in the development of a burgeoning Indian Sindhi Hindu identity.

Evoking a sentimental response, these myths acted as a means of standardization that helped Sindhis recognize that they broadly shared a 'mindset'. These myths also aided in the construction of social borders. By recollecting specific moments from the past, their oppression, and subsequent triumphal deliverance (as well as their distinct cultural legacy), Panjwani helped Sindhis recall their heritage. Deploying the past to shape the present, invocation of the river god was a simultaneous evocation of a co-related Sindhi community. In this act of memory, the Sindhis re-defined themselves as a singular social group. In the colonial era, these myths had been a means of understanding the pragmatic accommodation of religious differences. However, in the post-1947 context they underlined cultural distinction. 'Every community', Panjwani explained, 'has its own patron deity [and] Udero Lal is the patron god of Sindhis…[he] is their presiding deity'.[55] This discourse, therefore, was a key element in the 'creation of closures and in the constitution of collectivities…vital to the establishment of coherence…and generally in making cosmos out of chaos'.[56]

In order for these myths to capture popular imagination, other necessary components were required as well: ritual and symbol. 'Myth', according to George Schopflin, 'is the narrative, whereas ritual is the acting out, the articulation of the myth; symbols are the building blocks of myths and the acceptance or veneration of symbols is a significant aspect of ritual'.[57] As a part of this ongoing construction, the ritual of *bahrano* was popularized. In this ritual, rice, ghee, flowers, fruits, and kneaded wheat flour are placed decoratively on a *thal* (a flat metal dish) and 'offered' to the image of Jhuley Lal. This is accompanied by *chhej*, a traditional dance in which the dancers' undulating movements are reminiscent of the waves of the Indus. The *bahrano* culminates in the form of a procession leading to the water's edge. On reaching the water's edge, amidst enthusiastic cries of 'Jhuley Lal! Jhuley Lal', offerings are immersed in the water. The ritual of *bahrano* and the associated festival of Cheti Chand, marking the beginning of the Sindhi New Year, are standard features of Sindhi worship. In pre-Partition Sindh, Cheti Chand was a localized festival but, thanks to Panjwani's inspired efforts, it is now also known as Jhuley Lal Jayanti. On this occasion Sindhis organize festive processions, complete with music and dancing. Elaborate idols of the river god and decorated floats highlight different aspects of Sindhi culture.[58] Public celebrations or ritual performances such as these are an authoritative mode of symbolic discourse and powerful instruments for evoking sentiments of affinity out of which society is constituted, maintained, and expressed. For Sindhis, this public staging of collective activity became the moment for anchoring *Sindhiyat.*

Importantly, these myths and rituals succeeded because participation did not presuppose the internalization of belief. The manner in which these myths were re-articulated meant that they were stripped of their original context and were no longer associated with the older practices of river worship. Rather they were now primarily used to articulate culture. As Panjwani asserted:

> [Udero Lal] laid stress on unity...[and] to promote this unity, the Sindhis celebrate...Cheti Chand and refer to it as 'Sindhiat' day....On this auspicious day, fairs are organized all over the country, where people get together. They sing and dance...they sing panjras...songs that express their love of, and praise for, Udero Lal. But more [importantly] at these get-togethers, efforts are made to popularise Sindhi art, literature and folklore.[59]

Even as *Sindhiyat* was being constructed, cultural entrepreneurs were mindful that this public expression of affinity with a region now in Pakistan could be construed as transgressing the boundaries of Indian nationalism. Thus, Panjwani clarified: 'Let no one fear or imagine that Sindhiat, or the Sindhi way of life would dominate [other ways] of life. You might as well fear that the river will swallow the ocean. The river, after all merges in the sea becomes one with it...this is equally true of the Sindhi culture of India'.[60] Accordingly, these myths and the associated *Sindhiyat* allowed members to construct their identities as Sindhis while simultaneously participating as members of a larger community. This pragmatic approach helped Sindhis adapt to their environments, no matter where they lived. As K.R. Malkani notes: '[Sindhis] like to be always "sugar-in-milk" with the locals....It is at once natural and desirable'.[61] Such vocabulary provided a sustained way of imbuing collective expressions of a relational community with a more ideological and broad based definition of the collectivity.

With myth and ritual firmly in place, the figure of Jhuley Lal was the obvious symbol for articulating the nebulous *Sindhiyat.* Today, a mere reference to Jhuley Lal is sufficient to convey the relevant information, without recalling associated myths or returning to ritual. This network of symbols, rituals, and myth is a part of the web of communication shared by the community and is more significant than language itself.[62] Jhuley Lal is a profound symbol of *Sindhiyat* and Sindhi identity. There are numerous websites dedicated to the legend of Jhuley Lal. In the recent Bollywood blockbuster, *Koi Mil Gaya*, one of the characters is immediately identifiable as a Sindhi because of his exasperated exclamations of 'Jhuley Lal! Jhuley Lal!'

RE-IMAGINING JHULEY LAL

Panjwani and his associates were so successful in their endeavours to restore a sense of belonging to Sindhi refugees that in less than fifty years they were able to (re)invent what it meant to be Sindhi in a post-colonial world. Integral to this invention of tradition were the river god myths. 'Though Sindh is not on the map of Independent India', said Panjwani, 'Sindh is wherever Sindhis live [and] Udero Lal continues to be a bond of unity between Sindhis all over and everywhere'.[63] The crucial element in this success seems to have been the use of emotionally and symbolically charged, yet deliberately ambiguous, signs of what constituted *Sindhiyat. Sindhiyat* invokes strong sentiments of kinship, strong enough to create what Benedict Anderson calls a de-territorialized 'imagined' community.[64] It is imagined, according to Falzon, in that in the imaginaries of Sindhis that they are all connected via kinship and a nostalgic bond to the homeland.[65] Hence, even as individual Sindhis remain largely unaware of most of their fellow community members, each is intuitively aware of the ties of *Sindhiyat* that bind him/her to the others. *Sindhiyat* is intensified with the help of symbolic rituals that help strengthen these imagined ties with what Victor Turner calls the building up of 'communitas'.[66] By actively participating in symbolic activities, the individual member is inextricably linked to all others who act likewise. At this moment of communitas individual Sindhis become part of a larger Sindhi network, both in India and abroad.

Sindhiyat thus created is being harnessed to bring about political awareness of a Sindhi presence in the national arena. Cheti Chand festivities present an appropriate occasion for marking a public presence. Concerted efforts by community leaders have resulted in Cheti Chand being included in the roster of Indian official holidays. Among the diaspora, participation in ongoing cyber-efforts to protect and foster *Sindhiyat* can be seen as an addition to the constellation of symbolic rituals that affirm identity. In January 2005, Sanjeev Bhatnagar, a Delhi advocate, petitioned the Indian Supreme Court asking for the deletion of the word 'Sindh' in the Indian national anthem. This anthem, written in 1911 by Rabindranath Tagore, highlights different regions of undivided India, Sindh included. The crux of Bhatnagar's complaint was that Sindh's presence in the Indian anthem was a geographical anachronism and should, therefore, be deleted. Generating spontaneous communitas, this political issue served to bring cosmopolitan Sindhis together as no other event had in recent times—here was an issue that directly threatened and attacked their heritage. There was a tremendous outcry from Sindhis all around the world. The *Times of India* highlighted Sindhi resentment on this issue:

> Once again, salt has been rubbed into an old wound. A dispossessed people, torn from their homeland 57 years ago, now find themselves at the receiving end of another emotional assault...the literalism of the stance has piqued Sindhis who retort that Sindh is much more than a geo-political entity—it is a people, a culture and a civilization, and deserves at least the dignity of a name....Sindh is not a piece of territory—it has its own civilization...Sindhis may be stateless but they are still live representatives of this civilization. And as far as the anthem is concerned, Sindhis glow with pride when they hear the word 'Sindh' in the national anthem. Do you want to take that away too?[67]

In addition to print articles, cyber-Sindhi groups started e-petitions to register their outrage. Numerous Sindhi websites helped create a global awareness of the issue, seen as a direct attack on Sindhi identity. Here, the role of the print and electronic media cannot be over emphasized. After consulting with the Centre in New Delhi, the Supreme Court ruled against the deletion. It noted that 'Sindh' referred to more than a region; it referred to a civilization.[68] Mobilizing their shared imaginary, the Sindhis had successfully rallied together as a community and staked their claim to be counted politically.

In September 2005, Renuka Chowdhuri, Minister for Tourism, called for renaming parts of the Indus, known regionally as Sindhu, which flowed through Ladakh in India. She contended that the river was known as the Sindhu River 'only in Pakistan' and should, therefore, be given the local Buddhist name Singhe River. Accordingly, the offending word was removed from the Sindhu Darshan programme by renaming it Singhe Darshan. This was seen as yet another assault on Sindhi heritage. Spearheaded by Sindhis in the US, another online protest was launched. Not mincing words, the e-statement sternly stated:

> [Sindhis realize that] people often made no effort to understand the sacrifices made by Sindhi Hindus. [They] fought for India's freedom right along side

> others. In the end it was the Sindhi[s] who were forced to make the ultimate sacrifice vis-à-vis flee the land of their forefathers or be the victims of massacre or religious conversion....Sindhis feel that all these endeavours are aimed at dispossessing Sindhis of their memory, roots and heritage. [Sindhis are distressed by] the Minister...who refers to Sindhu as the river known only in Pakistan. [T]his shows [her] ignorance and lack of appreciation not only of the very roots and heritage of India but of Vedic literature as well...the songs of Rig Veda, composed from 4600 BCE, echo and resound as they chant with ecstasy and delight in reverence and devotion of Sindhu River....[69]

Seen here is an endeavour to reaffirm Sindhis as belonging within the broader context of the Indian state, shifting them from the margins and placing them right at the centre of the nationalist discourse. There is an explicit demand to be included, not as marginalized refugees, but as legitimate citizens. This self-confident assertion is paralleled by efforts to re-work the past. The invocation of the Rig Veda points to a need in the present to (re)assert identity in terms of a primordial Hindu past by establishing Sindhi Hindus as rightful inheritors of ancient Vedic heritage and thus, the earliest citizens of *Bharat Varsha*. This move is tied to the recent trends of saffronization. The rise of Hindutva, its promotion of 'pure Hinduism' and efforts to highlight the 'Hindu' heritage of India, all play an important part in this development.[70] At this juncture, political exigency dictates that Sindhis articulate new ways of belonging. The vision of a Sufi *Sindhiyat*, as outlined by Panjwani, is no longer deemed sufficient to meet contemporary needs.

Change in Sindhi self-perception is discernable in representations of Jhuley Lal as well. Sindhi cultural entrepreneurs are now actively deconstructing earlier visions to reconstruct *Sindhiyat* by modifying details in the narration of an established myth, 'thereby changing the nature of the sentiments (and the society) it evokes'.[71] In this discourse, eclecticism of Sindhi religion/culture is no longer highlighted. Rather, the past is re-constructed in terms of simplistic Hindu/Muslim binaries. A perusal of recently published versions of the Jhuley Lal myths reveals that, though the basic plot remains the same, the narratives are vividly embellished. Themes such as Muslim tyranny, the attempted genocide of Hindus, and Hindus as victims of forced conversions are emphasized, garbed as history and added to the shared memory of the community. A sampling of the opening paragraphs of recent mass-market hagiographies illustrates this point. In an English language monograph, the story begins with:

> The early Muslim rule in Sindh has had a chequered history, for off and on over the centuries of invasions also many times they were overpowered by the

> Hindu kings but they persisted in their attacks...whatever be the other attributes of the different Muslim rulers, whatsoever the period of their supremacy, in one respect they were all alike, they uniformly sought to spread Islam, converting Hindus at the point of sword or various threats....Thatta a township in southern Sindh had fallen to a Muslim chieftain Makrabkhan, a tyrant, who killed the invader king and himself took over the reins, changing his name to Mirkshah. [He] was a fanatic and a tyrant and many-a-Muslim fanatic sycophant surrounded him and instigated him against the Hindu population. In tune with the Muslim belief, he also believed that only with the spread of Islam will he be awarded *jannat* where he will be received by heavenly *hoors* (beauties) and thus acquire eternal bliss after death.[72]

According to a Sindhi booklet:

> Mirkh Shah had ruled for ten years when he decided to convert all Hindus of Sindh to increase the influence of Islam. History is witness to the fact that Muslims have spread Islam by might, money, force, and persecution...Mirkh Shah ordered all Hindus be brought within the fold of Islam. Instead of their own religious texts, they were to be compelled to read the Quran, and were to either be forcibly converted or be beheaded by the sword. After this proclamation, Mirkh Shah would partake his meals only after one and half *seers* of Hindu *janeyos* were collected and weighed in front of him daily. Young girls were also victimized; some were forced to marry Muslims and others kept as slaves.[73]

Another Sindhi hagiography historicizes the narrative:

> In seventh century AD...India was ruled by [Muslim] Caliphs. They ruled over much of India, most of which had been conquered by force. Whenever they conquered a new region, the Caliphs would install a handpicked Nawab to ensure proper governance and enable further expansion....Mirkh Shah Nawab was the ruler of Thatta city, in the province of Sindh. In order to appease the Caliph...he ordered his non-Muslim subjects to convert to Islam and to ensure this he increased atrocities to such an extent that it became unbearable. Violence was perpetuated on young and old, adults were killed, and mothers and sisters molested, such that it became difficult to save the [Hindu] faith. Raja Dahir Sen of Sindh also became a prisoner after being defeated.[74]

Along with inflammatory language, 'Hindu' elements of Jhuley Lal's identity are made more explicit. In a commemorative volume celebrating the golden jubilee of a Jhuley Lal temple in Delhi, readers are informed that, 'Amarlal sucked stepmother's milk. This can be compared with Lord Krishna doing similarly of Mata Yashoda....When the child grows older, he is taken to a Vedic scholar and acquires worldly as well as spiritual knowledge and receives the Guru-Mantra of Alakh Niranjan…from Guru Gorakhnath'.[75]

These modifications are visible in iconography also. A poster from Ahmedabad depicts the river god as Vishnu, complete with all the accoutrements associated with that deity. Though Jhuley Lal is portrayed as standing on a palla, the waterfront scenery and the shrine in the background are markedly absent. A mural in Mumbai depicts the deity similarly. There is also an increase in the production of images showing Jhuley Lal as a warrior, reflective of the increasingly militant religious rhetoric. Jhuley Lal, once emblematic of the idealized social integration of Sindhi society, today represents the move towards a self-conscious Sindhi Hindu/Indian identity.

JHULEY LAL IN SINDH

Given the popular view of Jhuley Lal as the patron saint of Sindhis, those familiar with these myths are generally surprised to find that the deity does not play a similarly central role in shaping Sindhi imaginaries in Pakistan as it does in India.[76] Worship of the river god continues to remain a localized practice. Unlike in India, there are very few temples dedicated to Jhuley Lal. The main shrine, located at Udero Lal, near Hyderabad (Sindh), was reportedly built around the seventeenth century. The shrine complex is built like a fort; gates open into a spacious courtyard with rooms lining its entire perimeter. The most important building within this complex is the edifice that holds a Muslim style tomb (designated as Udero Lal/Tahir Shaikh's *mazar*) and a small temple. The temple consists of a small room containing relics and images associated with Udero Lal. Included among these are some pictures of the deity, a cradle and an oil lamp that burns continuously. The temple, though clearly dedicated to a Hindu deity, does not contain any idols or holy books. Festivals at this shrine are attended by members of both communities. Importantly, attendees do not see themselves as followers of the same deity. For Sindhi Hindus this site is associated with the Hindu incarnation Udero Lal, whereas for Sindhi Muslims, this is the burial place of the Sufi saint Tahir Shaikh. Other religious sites, Sadhbela, Manora, and Rohri, associated with Jhuley Lal by Sindhi Hindus in India and abroad, remain disparate and unconnected with the shrine of Udero Lal/Tahir Shaikh. Concomitantly, the river god is also described and visualized as a Muslim saint. A poster entitled 'The King of Waters: Hazrat Khwajah Khizr-ul Islam' transmutes one of the most popular images associated with Jhuley

Lal, the deity floating on the Indus, into that of a Muslim saint reading the Quran. Addition of iconography depicting Madinah and Makkah makes the Islamic connection explicit.[77]

After Partition, along with the steady influx of refugees, Sindhis were faced with a rapidly changing political scenario. Karachi became the capital of Pakistan. Its designation as a 'federal capital area', followed by the later implementation of the One Unit Scheme, meant that even though they had not lost their homeland, Sindhi Muslims, too, faced a marginalization similar to that faced by their Hindu compatriots in India. Political sidelining was accompanied by denigration of Sindhi language and culture evident at the highest levels of governance. For instance, Liaquat Ali Khan remarked, 'What is Sindhi culture, except driving donkeys and camels?'[78]

In fashioning a response to their changing socio-political circumstances, Sindhi Muslims, too, looked to the past, where they sought and found novel ways to agitate for change in the nature of existing social formations. Whereas Sindhi Hindu narratives were employed to locate, legitimate, and later consolidate Sindhi status within the discourse of Indian nationalism, for Sindhi Muslims the river god myths bolstered the ethno-nationalist challenge to the hegemonic discourse of Pakistani nationalism. A growing sense of Sindhi deprivation led to the 1967 launch of the *Jeay Sindh* movement spearheaded by G.M. Syed, who demanded autonomy from the 'Urdu imperialists who have pillaged the land of Sindh'.[79] In 1972, disillusioned with official efforts to mitigate Sindhi grievances, Syed called for the creation of a *Sindhu Desh*. Calling the creation of Pakistan 'a mistake' and sharply critical of the state-sponsored ideology of religious nationalism, Syed's counter-narrative argued that Sindh 'has for a long time been an independent and sovereign state'.[80] Noting that the region's distinct identity lay in its tradition of Sufism, Syed explained:

> An amalgam of different religions and philosophies took place here...Buddhism was born in India, but it flourished here. When Islam appeared in Sindh, Buddhism was still extant. Islam added a positive element to the teachings of Buddha. Philosophies of Vedanta and the Unity of God (Wahdat-ul-Wajud) first interacted on each other in this land. [This] influenced the thinking of the Hindus, reducing their interest in idolatry...religious or sectarian prejudices, caste differences and the impulse for violence are absent in this land as perhaps nowhere else.[81]

In his manifesto, *Sindhudesh: A Study in its Separate Identity through the Ages,* Syed drew the picture of an idyllic Sindhi milieu by glossing over the bitter acrimony of pre-Partition politics and the subsequent Sindhi Hindu exodus:

> [In Sindh] Hindus used to go the shrines of Muslims and asked for their guidance...took education from Muslim saints and teachers...Muslim fakirs and Sufis [visited Hindu] temples and religious places. [Muslims] used to listen the teachings of Hindu Dervishes...several Muslims gave Hindu saints their own Muslim names, as Jind Pir Rohri was Khawaja Khizir, Udero Lal was called Shaikh Tahir...all this means that by adopting mixed traditional customs and rituals, the people of Sindh showed religious broad-mindedness and sense of toleration.[82]

For Syed, these illustrations of Sindhi Sufism, which he equated with secularism, constituted the essence of *Sindhiyat.* In this regard, the Jhuley Lal myths, highlighting the saint's dual nomenclature, were particularly attractive. A related website entitled 'SindhuDesh.com—The Sindh Nation's Story' features a number of articles about the legend of 'Jhulelal—The Sindhi God'.[83]

CONCLUDING REMARKS

Today, Sindhis are easily identifiable by their greetings, rituals, festivals, and slogans. Jhuley Lal is regarded as an immutable part of Sindhi tradition and culture, a powerful symbol of Sindhi identity. Sindhis, both Hindu and Muslim, speak warmly of the *Sindhiyat* ties that have historically defined their culture and society. Nonetheless, *Sindhiyat* is not a primordial entity, static and unchanging. Even as Sindhi Hindu and Muslim discourses converge to define identity in terms of *Sindhiyat* by locating and interrogating this notion as a historical entity, there are conspicuous divergences. Invoked in response to radically different socio-political concerns, Sindhiness was, and continues to be, a series of imbricated identities that have emerged in interaction with and, at times, overshadowed other forms of belonging, be they local, cultural, religious, ethnic, or national. In this context, Jhuley Lal myths are the locus of a 'management of meanings' by which historically contingent understandings are generated and maintained, transmitted and received, applied, exhibited, and remembered.[84]

Historically, it is seen that the notion of Jhuley Lal as a representation of *Sindhiyat* is not the original product of Sindhi imaginaries, rather it draws quite heavily on pre-existing colonial discourse. Extensive documentation of the river god in Orientalist accounts imparts an apparent historic legitimacy to these myths. It renders them suitable for adaptation in the post-colonial period. Responding in very different ways to the ideological demands of state-sponsored nationalism, Sindhi communities on both sides of the border have appropriated and selectively modified these myths. Struggling to adapt in a new environment, Sindhi Hindus were able to lose their immediate past and creatively reconcile their present with an appropriate vision of a distant past. Sindhi Muslims, on the other hand, sought an idyllic future based on lessons learned from a 'secular Sufi' past. However, contrary to (re)constructions that took place in the post-independence era, a close reading has shown that rather than painting either a rosy or an antagonistic picture of relations between religious communities, these myths highlight the nuanced manner in which complex socio-economic relations made for pragmatic communitarian accommodations in pre-colonial and colonial Sindh.

Today, Jhuley Lal and his myths wield the most influence among Sindhi Hindus. The reason being that this invention of tradition grew out of a crisis in their lives at a time when being Sindhi was akin to a social stigma. Jhuley Lal myths were integral to concerted efforts that led to the creation of *Sindhiyat*. The intrinsic value of these myths (and the secret of their success) lies in their construction of coherence. With time, as Sindhis have settled in India, their lives have changed. Though the original concerns for invoking these myths no longer remain relevant, they continue to shape and inform Sindhi imaginaries. Even as culture is viewed as stable and possibly static, these myths are continually being reproduced and are thus perpetually re-created in the present. The original group of marginalized refugee mythmakers has been replaced by a new generation of more confident cultural entrepreneurs. Change is also evidenced in the discourse of recently published hagiographies of Jhuley Lal. It reveals a pernicious trend: a move toward the articulation of a rigidly defined 'Hindu' identity. The polemic portrayals, provocative vocabulary, and extensive reworking of the past shows that even while Sindh continues to be popularly designated as 'the cradle of Sufism, which [has] distilled the essence of many religions [and the Sindhi Sufi outlook] is synonymous with India's secularism', there are noticeable slippages in this rhetoric.[85]

NOTES

1. This essay is a preliminary attempt at approaching some of the questions that I examine in a larger project on Sindhi identity. I am grateful to Michel Boivin for his thorough

reading of this essay. I would also like to thank Matthew A. Cook and Derryl Maclean for their comments on an earlier draft.

2. Eric Hobsbawm and Terence Ranger eds., *The Invention of Tradition* (Cambridge: Cambridge University Press, 1983), 1.
3. In this essay, the term 'myths' is applied to narratives that are distinguished not by their content, but by the truth-claims forwarded by their narrators and the manner in which these are subsequently received. Myths therefore possess credibility and authority, and are to be differentiated from fables (stories accepted as pure fiction), legends (that make some truth-claims, but lack credibility), and history (that which makes truth-claims, has credibility, but lacks authority to evoke an emotional response). For more on this classification see, Bruce Lincoln, *Discourse and the Construction of Society: Comparative Studies of Myth, Ritual and Classification* (New York: Oxford University Press, 1989), 24–25.
4. This ought to be understood within the context of the colonial obsession with systems of religious and sectarian classification. For discussions of the colonial endeavour in India, see: Ronald Inden, 'Orientalist Constructions of India', *Modern Asian Studies* 20.3 (1988); Bernard S. Cohn, *Colonialism and Its Forms of Knowledge: The British in India* (Princeton: Princeton University Press, 1986); Nicholas B. Dirks, *Castes of Mind: Colonialism and the Making of Modern India* (Princeton: Princeton University Press, 2001).
5. A term used by Milton Singer to describe the songs, dances, dramas, festivals, ceremonies, recitations, and prayers with offerings that are used to express culture (Robert Redfield, *Peasant Society and Culture: An Anthropological Approach to Civilization* [Chicago: University of Chicago Press, 1956], 98.)
6. Richard F. Burton, *Sindh and the Races that Inhabit the Valley of the Indus* (Karachi: Oxford University Press, 1973 [1851]), 324–325.
7. E.H. Aitken, *Gazetteer of the Province of Sind* (Karachi: Mercantile Steam Press, 1907), 164.
8. H.T. Sorley, *Shah Abdul Latif of Bhit: A Study of Literary, Social and Economic Conditions in Eighteenth Century Sind* (London: Oxford University Press, 1940), 166.
9. Burton, 310.
10. Here I do not mean to imply that the British were the first ones to make note of this deity, there might have been earlier accounts, but I have only been able to locate one brief mention by Mir Shir Ali Qani in his 1768 gazetteer-like account of Sindh. The British documentation of these myths was followed by the publication of numerous Sindhi Hindu accounts of Udero Lal; these accounts, however, tend not to mention the dual nomenclature of the river god and generally focus on Udero Lal solely as a Hindu deity. For a selection see: Vasanmal Kishanchand, *Uderola'lu Sahabu: Baitan Men* (Hyderabad, Sindh: Vasanmal Kishanchand, 1916); Harisingh, *Daryashah jun Gadu Panju Madahun* (Sakhar Na'in: Harisingh, 1913); Hiranandu Gulrajmalu Thakur, *Janam Sakhi: Sri Amar Uderolalu ji* (Karachi: Harcandani Thakur Kevalramu 'ain Thakur Kundamalu Citirmalani, 1923). The extent to which these later publications were informed by colonial insistence on viewing Indian society through a religious lens is an important concern.
11. This story is culled from J. Abbott, *Sind: A Re-Interpretation of the Unhappy Valley* (Karachi: Indus Publications, 1977 [1924]), 101–102 and G.E.L. Carter, 'Religion in Sind', *The Indian Antiquary* 47 (1918): 197–208.
12. J.W. Smyth, *Gazetteer of the Province of Sind: Volume II, Hyderabad District* (Bombay: Government Orient Press, 1920), 56.

13. This was the time of Aurangzeb's reign and the story plays on the stereotype of Aurangzeb as a fanatical and proselytizing Muslim ruler (see Burton, 329–332).
14. Ibid., 331.
15. Mir Ali Shir Qani, *Tuhfat al-Kiram* (Hyderabad: Sindhi Adabi Board, 1957 [1768]), 389–390.
16. Din Muhammad Vafai, *Tazkirah-i Mashahir-i Sindh, Vol. II* (Jamshoro, Hyderabad: Sindhi Adabi Board, 1985), 333–335.
17. Burton, 333 and Aitken, 165–166.
18. Smyth, 56–57.
19. Abbot, 98.
20. A.W. Hughes, *Gazetteer of the Province of Sind* (Karachi: Indus Publications, 1996 [1876]), 680–681.
21. H.G. Raverty, *The Mihran of Sind and its Tributaries* (Lahore: Sang-e-Meel Publications, 1979), 345.
22. Abbot, 98.
23. U.T. Thakur, *Sindhi Culture* (Bombay: University of Bombay, 1959), 19–21.
24. Carter, 206.
25. For an extended discussion of the legends associated with worship of the Indus, see: Carter (1918).
26. A.R. Radcliffe-Brown, *The Andaman Islanders* (Glencoe, IL: The Free Press, 1948), 377.
27. Burton, 331.
28. Abbot, 99.
29. John Renard, *Islam and the Heroic Image: Themes in Literature and the Visual Arts* (Columbia, S.C.: University of South Carolina Press, 1993), 16.
30. Ibid., 15.
31. Thakur discusses this issue at length, pointing to the Muslim practice of burying their dead in Hindu temples and re-designating them as *dargahs* or shrines (18).
32. Redfield, 102.
33. Carter, 207.
34. For an extended discussion of the socio-economic relations in colonial Sindh, see: Claude Markovits, *The Global World of Indian Merchants 1750–1947: Traders of Sind from Bukhara to Panama* (Cambridge: New York: Cambridge University Press, 2000), 32–56.
35. David Cheesman, *Landlord Power and Rural Indebtedness in Colonial Sind, 1865–1901* (Surrey: Curzon Press, 1997) and Hamida Khuhro, *Muhammad Ayub Khuhro: A Life of Courage in Politics* (Karachi: Ferozesons Limited, 1998).
36. Smyth, 56.
37. Carter, 205.
38. Mark-Anthony Falzon, *Cosmopolitan Connections: The Sindhi Diaspora, 1860–2000* (Leiden: Brill, 2004), 60.
39. Lincoln suggests this as being one of the many ways in which myths can be used to construct new unfamiliar social forms (25).
40. Given that this migration did not take place at one time and from one exit point, the estimated number of migrants remains contested. Various sources cite figures ranging from one to two million migrants.
41. Nanik Motwane cited in Subhadra Anand, *National Integration of the Sindhis* (New Delhi: Vikas Publishing House, 1996), 85.
42. Ibid., 79.

43. Popati Hiranandani, *Sindhis: The Scattered Treasure* (New Delhi: Malah Publications, 1980), x and 39–40.
44. The decision to include Sindhi as a national language was taken on 4 November 1966. This was implemented as the Twenty-First Amendment to the Indian Constitution on 10 April 1967 (see http://indiacode.nic.in/coiweb/amend/amend21.htm).
45. There are numerous websites detailing Panjwani's ceaseless efforts to promote the Sindhi language and culture (see http://www.sindhishaan.com/ourroots/ram_panjwani.htm; http://www.jhulelal.com/sindhiarticles/ziyaa.htm, http://www.sydneysindhi.com/chetichand.html). In 1981, Panjwani was awarded a Padmashri—the highest Indian civilian award—for services rendered on behalf of the Sindhi community.
46. Baldev T. Gajra, 'Ram Panjwani: The Man and His Mission', in Moti A. Gidwani ed., *Professor Ram Panjwani: 70th Birthday Commemoration Volume* (Dubai: Felicitation Committee, 1981), 5.
47. Gobind Malhi, 'The Man with the Healing Touch', in Moti A. Gidwani, ed., *Prof. Ram Panjwani: 70th Birthday Commemoration Volume* (Dubai: Felicitation Committee, 1981), 28.
48. Cited from http://homepages.nyu.edu/~md77/jhulelal/completestory.htm
49. A loose translation of the Sindhi original.
50. Lincoln, 3.
51. Ram Panjwani writes: 'After subjugating Mirkh, [he] set out on a tour of Sind, shrines were built to him wherever he went, at Sroghat and Shahi Bazar in Hyderabad, at Larkana, in Jhijhan, at Bukkhur, Nasarpur, Manora, Mangha Pir, Lar, Sehwan, Shikarpur, Sukkur and Thatta' (see Ram Panjwani, *Sindhi ain Sindhiyat* [Bombay: Sita Sindhu Bhavan, 1987], 4). Also see: Naraindas S. Thakur, *Jai Jhoole Lal: Life Story*; Lekhraj 'Hans', *Rakho Rakhanhar: Shri Amar Udero Lal* (Ajmer: Kohinoor Printers, 1979).
52. Panjwani, 3.
53. Hiranandani, 42.
54. Panjwani, 7.
55. Ibid., 3 and 10.
56. George Schopflin, 'The Function of Myth and a Taxonomy of Myths', in Geoffrey Hosking and George Schopflin, eds., *Myths and Nationhood* (New York: Routledge, 1997), 20.
57. Ibid., 20.
58. For festivities in Kanpur, see: 'Cheti Chand Festivity Takes City By Storm', *The Times of India*, 11 April 2000. For New Delhi, see: 'Prosperous against All Odds', *The Hindustan Times*, 19 August 2005. For celebrations in Saurashtra, Kutch and Ahmedabad see: 'Sindhi New Year "Chetichand" Celebrated', *Indo-Asian News Service*, 30 March 2006.
59. Panjwani, 4–5.
60. Ibid., 7–8.
61. K.R. Malkani, *The Sindh Story* (New Delhi: Sindhi Academy, 1984), 175.
62. Schopflin, 20.
63. http://www.sindhudesh.com/sindhudesh/thesindhi_jhulelal_4.html
64. Benedict Anderson, *Imagined Communities: Reflections on the Origin and Spread of Nationalism* (London and New York: Verso, 1991), 5–7.
65. Falzon, 70.
66. Turner defines communitas as an intense community spirit, a feeling of social equality, solidarity, and togetherness. This feeling is typically experienced during liminality, best described as a betwixt and between stage and continues into the aggregation phase of

the ritual process. The feelings of communitas created in this process are used to support structure, which is rooted in the past and extends into the future, through language, law, and custom (Victor Turner, *The Ritual Process: Structure and Anti-Structure* [New York: Aldine Publishing Company, 1969], 94–97 and 113).

67. 'The Land's Lost, Let the Anthem Alone', *Times of India,* 9 January 2005 (Mumbai Edition).
68. 'Poetry and Patriotism', *The Hindu,* 10 January 2005 (Online Edition).
69. http://www.sindhulogy.org/news-details.php?id=6; http://www.sindhulogy.org/news-details.php?id=7
70. In her work on the Sindhi Hindus of Gujarat, Rita Kothari has analyzed the gradual move away from a porous Sindhi identity to a more hardened Hindu identity (Rita Kothari, *The Burden of Refuge: Sindhi Hindus of Gujarat* [New Delhi: Orient Longman Pvt. Ltd, 2007]). Steven Ramey, too, has studied the increasing emphasis on a publicly Hindu identity (Steven Ramey, 'Defying Borders: Contemporary Sindhi Hindu Constructions of Practices and Identifications' [PhD Dissertation in Religious Studies at The University of North Carolina at Chapel Hill, 2004]). Falzon and Markovits have commented similarly on this trend as well.
71. Lincoln, 25.
72. Mira Govind Advani, *A Saga of Trials and Triumphs of Sindhis: 1947–1997* (Bombay: Gopushi Publishers, 1997), 26–28.
73. Paroo Chawla, ed., *Jhoolan ja Geet 'ain Panjra* (Mumbai: Vashi H. Lilaramani, 2000), 5.
74. *Artiyun (Puj Jhulelal ji Jivani, Chaliho Sahib, Bahrano Sahib, Bhajan, Paintis Akhri, Aurana, Palau 'ain Gayatri Mantar Samet),* (Ahmedabad: Suresh Bookseller & General Store, 2001), 29–30.
75. *Golden Jubilee Year of Lal Sain's Behrana in Lajpat Nagar* (Delhi: Managing Committee, 2005).
76. This is, admittedly, a simplified look at very complex issues. However, a detailed analysis of the interplay of politics and religion in Sindh is beyond the scope of this essay. Here, I limit myself to a discussion of Jhuley Lal myths in Sindh, a brief comparison of the trajectory, circulation, and the extent to which, if any, these myths inform Sindhi identity in Pakistan.
77. For the poster see: Jürgen Wasim Frembgen, *The Friends of God—Sufi Saints in Islam: Popular Poster Art from Pakistan* (Karachi: Oxford University Press, 2006), 15.
78. Liaquat Ali Khan made this remark in a meeting with a delegation led by the Sindh Muslim League President Syed Ali Akbar Shah (Suranjan Das, *Kashmir and Sindh: Nation-Building, Ethnicity and Regional Politics in South Asia* (London: Anthem Press, 2001), 114.
79. G.M. Syed, *The Case of Sindh: G.M. Syed's Deposition in Court* (Karachi: Naeen Sindhi Academy, 1995), chapter 7.
80. Ibid.
81. Ibid., chapter 5.
82. G.M. Syed, *Sindhudesh: A Study in its Separate Identity Through Ages* (Karachi: G.M. Syed Academy, 1991), chapter 5.
83. http://www.sindhudesh.com/sindhudesh/thesindhi_jhulelal_1.html
84. Schopflin, 28.
85. Ram Jethmalani in 'The Land's Lost, Let the Anthem Alone', *Times of India,* 9 January 2005 (Mumbai Edition).

CHAPTER 2

Mobility, Territory, and Authenticity: Sindhi Hindus in Kutch, Gujarat[1]

Farhana Ibrahim

INTRODUCTION

In 2002–2003 I was living in Bhuj, capital of Kutch District in the Indian state of Gujarat, just beginning my dissertation fieldwork. During this time, I found few overt traces of Sindh, a province that lies about 85 miles away from the town centre across an international border, in Pakistan. Over the course of my fieldwork, I had become interested in purchasing some recorded *kafis*, a poetic genre from Sindh popular among the Muslim pastoralists of northern Kutch. A *kafi* is a form of metered verse, usually in four-line sequence, set to classical *ragas* or sung to folk tunes and having rich narrative content. It is a style of folk music that is popular in Sindh. The most famous regional exponent of this genre of poetic narrative was Shah Abdul Latif of Bhit in Sindh, circa CE 1689–1752.[2] I had grown to enjoy these haunting tunes, sung in the wide expanses of the Rann of Kutch. A much favoured way of passing the time of day, as the pastoralists have wandered in groups with their animals through the centuries, these oral narratives are also a rich source of regional history for Kutch and Sindh.

I browsed through all the music shops in Bhuj. None of the wide variety of well-stocked shops had what I was looking for, until I was finally directed to my source. Tucked away behind the main market street of Bhuj—at that time also the city's primary thoroughfare, subsequently much changed in the town planning initiatives undertaken after an earthquake in 2001 nearly decimated large swathes of the city—was a parallel narrow lane of stalls. It is almost hidden from view as it lies behind the constant din and bustle of the central bus station. I had walked by here innumerable times, but had little idea of the veritable treasure-trove of goods that lay obscured from view until I found myself in their midst. Smuggled and second-hand goods thrive here: leather and electronic items, Islamic literature, cassettes of music and religious discourses, cloth, and a myriad other sundries. Here, I finally found what I was looking for. Amid tall stacks of cheap copies of music cassettes from popular Indian films, I found an equally large selection of music from 'across the border'; popular Pakistani singers singing in Urdu and in Sindhi (some of whom were born in Kutch, the shop owners told me with pride). This narrow row of shops, glittering well into the night in the heart of Bhuj and yet somewhat hidden, is a transformed space. Kutch is here no longer insulated from its neighbour across the border; Sindh thrives here, most notably in its folk music. But you will not stumble upon these stalls unbidden; you have to look long and hard, or know the right people, before you can find them.[3]

For all its proximity in space, I found during my research that there was a remarkable lack of reference to Sindh in Kutch. Certainly, political rhetoric in Gujarat made reference to Pakistan regularly. But it was a generalizing rhetorical reference one used to extract political mileage by advocates of right-wing Hindu nationalism, such as the representation of Islam, Pakistan, and by extension Indian Muslims in general, as isomorphic and therefore 'other'.[4] Reference to cultural traits shared by Sindh and Kutch such as language, clothing, and music, tended to be conspicuously absent in such rhetoric.

It is not too difficult to speculate on the reasons for this absence. Modern territorial nation-states are ideologically invested in imagining themselves to be, at the level of nationalist discourse at least, territorially discrete and internally homogenous entities.[5] After the creation of Pakistan as a separate nation-state in 1947 for the Muslim majority areas of British India, Kutch gained a new significance as a strategic border territory; it lay on a newly defined boundary that needed to be naturalized and legitimized politically and socially. In Kutch, and Gujarat more generally, this has been produced through a relatively consistent othering of Pakistan and Muslims within Gujarat.[6] This generates a peculiar ambivalence in the relationship between the adjacent spaces of Kutch and Sindh; they are immediate neighbours and they share close historical and cultural ties but they lie across a problematic boundary.

EXPERIENCING A REGION

In this chapter I attempt to examine this ambivalent relationship between the adjacent territories of Kutch and Sindh in order to be able to reflect critically on how regions are imagined and counter-imagined. In speaking of a region as an analytical concept, I refer not only to its geographical, political, or legal referents but also to the subjective and affective dimension of how regions are experienced and inhabited by their occupants. In an early essay, Bernard Cohn pointed out some of the complexities inherent in the use of the term 'region' or 'regionalism'. He argued that 'regions are far from fixed, enduring things, especially if any historical perspective is taken. They are not absolutes and they are difficult, if not impossible, to define by objective criteria'.[7] He proposed a typology of regions that went beyond a physical sense of space; for Cohn, regions were best understood as historical, linguistic, cultural, or structural. Inherent in each of these types is a subjective element in the making of a region. Following the manner in which I invoke the concept here, how a region is experienced and where its boundaries are placed depends clearly on who is doing the outlining. Thus, as E. Valentine Daniel remarked in his study of the cultural construction of space, the culturally more significant conception of territory is not concerned with boundary lines as much as it is concerned with what lies within.[8] The cultural construction of territory is thus a subjective enterprise; one that engages with varying criteria that contains within it room for disagreement and one that is concerned with notions of compatibility between inhabitants and territory. Of course, this point must be exercised judiciously, for taken to an extreme it may become a politically dangerous argument positing an essentialized relationship between persons and territory based on an imagined shared substance. But I find Daniel's point useful to think about the subjective construction of territoriality. Instead of a fixed and immutable space, the meaning ascribed to place can perceivably morph and change depending on one's perspective. While this is not in itself a problematic assertion, it is also clear that subjectively experienced aspects of territory, space, or region must contend also with their political and legal counterparts. Even though Daniel suggests that it may be more rewarding for anthropologists 'to turn away from the notion of boundaries to that of the centres of regions', the physical and legal aspects of boundaries continue to present real constraints for those who live straddling such divides.[9]

In what follows, I suggest that within such political and legal constraints, a region (i.e., its borders as well as its centre) is experienced rather than encountered *a priori*. Therefore, I attempt an unsettling of the fixity of the concept of region in its political and legal referents, in order to engage the uncertainty and fluidity of the concept when viewed as a subjectively experienced category. On the one hand, Kutch is legally a constituent of the state of Gujarat. In this capacity, officially, it lies squarely within the space of the Indian nation-state, a district in one of its provincial units. Sindh is, from this perspective, an 'outside'. But it is an ambivalent 'outside' as the following anecdote reveals.

In 2004, an Indian scientist filed a Public Interest Litigation (PIL) with the nation's Supreme Court, petitioning for the removal of the word 'Sindh' from the Indian National Anthem. A respected English language daily, *The Hindu*, reported:

> The petitioner...approached the court stating that the recitation of Sindh in the National Anthem was an infringement on the sovereignty of Pakistan. Such singing for the last 54 years and eight months was also hurting the feelings of more than 100-crore [one billion] people in India. He said the petition was to avoid any international dispute as such flaws in the National Anthem could bring dishonour and disrespect to the nation. He sought a direction for deletion of the word 'Sindh' and substituting it with the word Kashmir.[10]

Some months later, the Supreme Court dismissed the petition. The same newspaper reported:

> The judges said a national anthem was a hymn or song expressing patriotic sentiments. 'It is not a chronicle which defines the territory of the nation which has adopted the anthem....Nor is it necessary that the structure of the national anthem should go on changing as and when the territories in the internal distribution of geographical regions or provinces undergo changes'.[11]

The court then fined the petitioner Rs 10,000 (approximately $230) for 'wasting its time' over this matter and closed the issue. While the petitioner was acting upon a widely-held popular notion of territorial sovereignty, asking for the deletion of Sindh (now in Pakistan) and the inclusion of Kashmir (part of which is still contested territory between India and Pakistan and a symbol of popular nationalism on both sides of the border), the court's pronouncement radically challenges any organic relationship between territory and nationalism. It does so partly to prevent a precedent for amending the anthem to continually reflect the provincial re-organization of the nation-state, but also because of the vastly complicated relationship between Sindh and the Indian nation. This was alluded to in an earlier response to the petitioner, when the Home Ministry of the Government of India declared:

> The word 'Sindh' refers not merely to the province of Sindh but also to the Sindhi culture, which is an inalienable part of the rich and diverse culture of India. Moreover, the contribution of Sindhi people in the making of modern India has been extremely noteworthy and cannot be overlooked. It may not, therefore, be appropriate to delete the word 'Sindh' from the National Anthem.[12]

The above statement hints in part at the anxiety that surrounds the relationship between the Indian nation and the Pakistani province of Sindh. Even though Sindh is now territorially a part of Pakistan, a separate nation-state, large numbers of Sindhis live in India where they moved after the Partition of British India in 1947. Their territorial affinities and ties are bound to be more complicated than what is presented on a physical territorial map of the subcontinent. Further, unlike the two other provinces directly affected by Partition—Bengal and Punjab—Sindh was not bifurcated between India and Pakistan, so that migrants to either India or Pakistan still were able to participate in their regional cultures, broadly defined, if they were Punjabis or Bengalis. For Sindhis coming into India, all of Sindh was left behind in another nation-state.

Given this background, I will now proceed to discuss some of the tensions that inevitably arise between the political and legal iterations of 'region' or 'community' and counter-perspectives to these official definitions. For every 'legitimate' definition of these concepts there must be alternative imaginations that are, for a variety of reasons, not represented in the official discourse. An ethnographic analysis located among Sindhi communities in Kutch provides a privileged vantage point to explore some of the means—both rhetorical and practical—through which boundaries (whether they are perceived as territorial, religious, or linguistic) are produced, and then how these boundaries in turn create competing cultural subjectivities of space, region, religion, language, and community. I underscore that these boundaries are contingent and subjective; the definitions of 'inside' and 'outside', 'inclusion' and 'exclusion' are neither finite nor natural but are produced as a dialectical relationship among competing cultural discourses of place making, sovereignty, and belonging. In the following sections, I provide a quick overview of some historical entanglements that have contributed to the ambivalent nature of the relationship between the adjacent territories of Sindh and Kutch today. I am arguing here that from the perspective of many people who circulated between Kutch and Sindh prior to the merger of the princely state of Kutch with the Indian Union in 1948 and before the emergence of the province of Gujarat as a distinct entity in 1960, one could, arguably, say that Kutch and Sindh constituted—from the perspective of those who circulated between these areas—a region, even though they did not share the same political system. After 1960, Kutch became a constituent unit of the province of Gujarat and its relationship with Sindh became an ambivalent factor in the official discourse of Gujarat, which strove to render itself as a discrete and homogenous unit. Sindh was clearly on the 'outside' and every attempt was made to incorporate Kutch into its officially legitimate regional identity—one that lay within a larger Gujarati identity.

PERSPECTIVES ON A REGION: MODERN GUJARAT AND ITS *ASMITA*

In this section, I engage critically with Gujarat's contemporary official self-image, formulated in the idea of Gujarati *asmita* (pride or glory). The notion of Gujarati *asmita* goes back in time to long before the creation of Gujarat as a separate provincial unit within India in 1960. During the nineteenth century, questions on what constituted 'Gujarat' and 'Gujarati' were frequent subjects of intellectual debate and discussion. During the period of my research in Kutch during 2001–2004, it had become a regional variation of right-wing Hindu nationalist ideology based on a selective erasure of Muslims in the region. In this discourse, Pakistan is a Muslim state and a cultural and political 'other' for the region's self image. Cross-border relationships with Sindh occupy an uncomfortable position within a regional imagination that seeks to contain Gujarat within the idiom of its *asmita*, in this instance, premised on the celebration of a Hindu past.[13]

Modern Gujarat emerged in its contemporary territorial configuration on 1 May 1960 following an administrative reorganization of Indian states. The then bilingual state of Bombay was bifurcated into two states—Gujarat for predominantly Gujarati speaking sections and Maharashtra for the Marathi speaking areas. The modern state of Gujarat consists of three broadly identifiable divisions—a strip of 'mainland' Gujarat, the peninsula of Saurashtra, and the western arm of Kutch.[14] These three sub-units have unique cultural traits and historical antecedents. Through my ethnographic research in Kutch, I have attempted to examine the tensions that underlie the incorporation of these diverse territories into a homogenous and singular regional identity that is expressed in the contemporary idea of a Gujarati *asmita*.

I now examine the manner in which regimes of contemporary historical consciousness, (1) construct a Gujarati regional identity through *asmita*, and (2) what this historiography means for Kutch as it re-aligns Sindh as a cultural and territorial 'outside' for the region as a whole. As a frontier area between mainland Gujarat and Sindh, Kutch shares deep historical, cultural, and sociological ties with Sindh. Before it joined the state of Gujarat, Kutch was an independent princely state that had a long tradition of circulatory movement encompassing Sindh. In contrast with this former close relationship between these two regions, the terms in which the relationship between Kutch and Sindh is articulated from the perspective of a greater Gujarati nationalism in contemporary times is rather different.

In examining regimes of contemporary historical consciousness, I have isolated two key strands of historiography that correspond to the two points raised above. On the one hand, I shall analyze the writings of certain key Gujarati nationalist authors and historians who have written extensively on Gujarati history. Some of these writings are closely tied up with the movement for the state of Gujarat as they form the ideological justification for a separate state based on a distinct linguistic and cultural identity for Gujarat. These histories form the authoritative version of historical writing on Gujarat (in the absence of a more 'secular' corpus) and these nationalist histories are largely influential for the ways in which history is taught and internalized in contemporary Gujarat. I probe these histories for their stand on Gujarati regional patriotism and their perspective on Kutch as a unit within Gujarat.

Second, I examine officially canonized historical memory in Kutch for the ways in which it represents the relationship between the adjacent territories of Kutch and Sindh and of Kutch as a nested identity within Gujarat. In the following analysis of these two types of historiographical constructions (i.e., nationalist writings and oral histories), I follow the maxim that 'it is often in the process of delineating the past that societies construct their identities' in the present.[15] An analysis of both these sets of historical arguments reveals that the nationalist impulse is to seek to anchor territory in an imagined mythico-historical past. I argue that the core ambivalence that the Kutch-Sindh issue poses to Gujarati *asmita* is the latter's nationalist investment in the idea of an anchored and bounded territory. What are the implications of this investment in rootedness for a place like Kutch that has been articulated through mobility and cultural flows?

NATIONALIST HISTORIES

Although formally constituted in 1960, the ideological foundations for the Gujarat state go back many years before that. The movement for the creation of a separate Gujarat state derived a special boost from the writings of K.M. Munshi, a prolific Gujarati language writer and novelist who was also a prominent Hindu nationalist ideologue in post-Independence India. In 1955, he wrote that there were two ways in which Gujarat could be understood:

> In one, it denotes the mainland between Mount Abu and the river Damanganga, *distinguishing it* from Kutch or Saurashtra on the one side and Marwad and Malava on the other. In the second and wider sense it connotes the much larger linguistic zone in which the language known as Modern Gujarati is spoken at the present time. The boundary of this Gujarati speaking area touches Sirohi and Marwad in the north and *includes Kutch and Saurashtra as well as the districts of Thar and Parkar in Pakistan* [emphasis added].[16]

For Munshi, a predominantly territorial and, as I explain below, historical definition of Gujarat would exclude Kutch, but a more inclusive linguistic definition would embrace it. The linguistic sense prevailed in the eventual territorial demarcation of modern Gujarat as it did in the general reorganization of provincial units all over India along a linguistic basis.[17] From this account, Kutch and Saurashtra are already ambivalently positioned within the idea of a united Gujarat. They are included linguistically, as they are seen to constitute Gujarati-speaking areas but excluded historically.[18] It is to this historical imagination of a Gujarati territory that I now turn.

The Re-territorialization of Gujarat in *Asmita*: Patan and Somnath

A number of histories of Gujarat produced in the 1950s and 1960s are situated within a cultural-nationalist framework. This framework provides the blueprint of the idea of a Gujarati *asmita* as it is understood in the present. It is important to note that its present iterations do not exhaust the meanings of *asmita* but are too complex to go into for the limited purposes of this essay. The intellectual history of *asmita* is discussed elsewhere.[19] In this section I turn to two evocative and enduring symbols of Hindu nationalist pride in Gujarat that find expression in contemporary manifestations of *asmita*—the city of Patan in north Gujarat and the temple at Somnath in Saurashtra. Such nationalist histories attempt to re-territorialize Gujarat within a mythico-historical Hindu space, the symbolic centre of which lies in the medieval city of Patan, approximately 70 miles north-west of the modern state capital, Gandhinagar. In these narratives, the city of Patan epitomizes good governance and Hindu pride in an age where a 'pure' Hindu dynasty ruled Gujarat, before the period of Muslim rule. The area directly ruled by the medieval Hindu Chaulukya dynasty (tenth to thirteenth centuries) is referred to as 'Gurjara-bhumi or Gujarat'.[20] Their capital was established at Patan. The ruling clans are described as 'connected by blood, tradition and by the country of their origin Gurjaradesa,' ruling out immigration or cultural mixture.[21] The period of Patan's ascendancy between the tenth to thirteenth centuries is hailed by nationalist writers like Munshi, Majumdar, and Rajyagor as the 'golden age' of Gujarati Hindu rule when the kingdom is thought to have reached its zenith in the sphere of cultural achievement.[22] This is the kernel of Gujarat's *asmita* as celebrated today. In Patan is anchored a primordially imagined Hindu identity. The medieval city of Patan thus becomes the symbol of a territory that is primarily animated by a Hindu cultural-nationalist ethic; its past royal grandeur is associated with the pomp and splendour of what retrospectively emerges from these texts as an essentially Hindu state.

To further cement the symbolic importance of Patan, at the first Independence Day celebrations in August 2003 following his first election victory in 2002, the Chief Minister Narendra Modi decided that he would unfurl the national flag not in the state capital Gandhinagar, as protocol would suggest, but in the city of Patan. On this occasion he planned a series of cultural events with the cooperation of various Hindu temple committees and religious organizations.

Like the city of Patan, the medieval temple of Somnath has also become, over the years, a key symbol of nationalist pride in Gujarat. Sacked by the Muslim Afghan Mahmud of Ghazni in CE 1026, it has aroused Hindu nationalist passions for many decades. The temple is dedicated to the Hindu god Shiva and is situated on the southern tip of the Gujarat peninsula. Richard Davis argues that the shrine of Somnath is a site where multiple historical claims and counter-claims converge.[23] Destroyed in CE 1026, it was rebuilt several times in following centuries by different constituencies who wished to stake a claim to its grandeur and civilizational allure. Following Indian independence, it was Munshi who took up the task of its reconstruction with great fervour. From the perspective of Munshi, the ruins of Somnath were a potent reminder to Gujaratis of the loss of their former glory at the hands of invading Muslims. Reconstructing the temple became a matter of national pride for him. His novel *Jaya Somanath* describes his own personal and emotional attachment to the temple cause. Elsewhere, he describes the importance of Somnath:

> Somanatha was the shrine beloved of India....In maintaining it with magnificence, she felt a throbbing zeal to maintain the core of her faith, tradition, and collective greatness.... As often as the shrine was destroyed, the urge to restore it sprang up more vividly in its heart....That is why for a thousand years Mahmud's destruction of the shrine has been burnt into the Collective Sub-conscious [*sic*] of the race as an unforgettable national disaster.[24]

In Munshi's writings, there is a frequent slippage between Somnath being the key to the restoration of Gujarat's regional glory, its sovereignty, and identity, and on the other hand, the shrine's symbolic importance for the Indian nation at large.[25] Reclaiming the temple's desecration at the hands of a Muslim king serves the dual causes of restoring Gujarat's regional pride as well as healing national wounds. This latter concern is crucial, for the context in which Munshi wrote was conditioned by the experience of Partition and Hindu-Muslim violence still in vivid memory. In his quest to rebuild the temple, he enlisted the support of Sardar Vallabhbhai Patel, a prominent Gujarati nationalist leader in the newly formed national government.

The emotional power of Patan and Somnath—both enduring symbols of Gujarati *asmita*—derives from the basic ideological formulation of Hindu nationalism (i.e., a xenophobic fear and othering of Muslims and Christians as alien to the Indic cultural ethos). As with the destruction of the Somnath temple, the decline of Patan is also ascribed to incoming Muslims. The arrival of Muslim rulers after the decline of the Chaulukya dynasty is described in this cultural-nationalist historiography as the 'shameful' decline of a glorious Hindu past, 'the downfall of Hindu sway in Western India after more than thousand [*sic*] years.'[26]

Kutch and Sindh

In published histories of Gujarat such as the ones analyzed above, Kutch is generally absent, except when it is hinted that parts of it were encompassed within the Chaulukya dynasty's sphere of influence while they ruled at Patan. A glance at a map shows that Kutch is geographically an intermediary between Sindh and the rest of Gujarat. According to archaeologists, it is also a geological mediator between distinct zones.[27] Although discrete and bounded territorial entities are for the most part modern constructs, owing to its long coastline and formerly navigable northern boundary with Sindh, Kutch has been one of the more significant transit zones into Gujarat through which traders, pastoralists, and other itinerants have made their way into the region.

Kutch sits somewhat ambivalently within the regional historical narrative of Gujarat animated by the notion of *asmita* not only because it remained relatively marginal to the assumed centre of Gujarati Hindu court culture at Patan but also because it shares a long border with Sindh, across which waves of migration have taken place over the centuries. Nationalist histories of Gujarat are uncomfortable with these cultural flows across Kutch and Sindh, for they seek to ground Hindu identity firmly in space and time as 'indigenous' while Muslims are portrayed as the 'invaders' and quintessential 'outsiders'. Sindh is associated with Islam in this kind of nativist discourse not only because it is today a province in the Islamic state of Pakistan, but because Sindh was one of the main transit zones through which Islam was introduced into Western India. Following the Arab conquest of Sindh in the eighth century, incoming traders, mendicants, and pastoralists came into Kutch and Western India as the bearers not only of goods and services but also a new religious message for those who were receptive to it. However, it is important to note, as scholars have pointed out, that Islam was not the only proselytizing force in Gujarat. It is argued that Islam, Vaishnavite Hinduism, and Jainsim provided a range of possibilities in an increasingly variegated religious marketplace that was articulated by constant movement and migration.[28]

I have already indicated that one of the ways in which Hindu nationalist versions of history seek to present the nation is through essentialist constructions of indigeneity. This makes such historiography, manifest in the idea of Gujarati *asmita* for example, relatively uncomfortable with the idea of mobility and associated cultural flows. In such histories, movement threatens the bounded-ness of the collective imaginary as it seeks authentication in primordial fantasies of rooted-ness to construct essentialized dichotomies of insider and outsider. The following section discusses only one of the many types of cross border circulation that took place over time between Kutch and Sindh. Through the narratives of Hindus from Sindh who moved permanently into Kutch following Partition, I explore the tension between their experiences of migration on the one hand, and on the other hand, their desire to participate in regional discourses of authenticity and indigeneity that are ambivalently disposed to this kind of cross-border mobility.

ACQUIRING A NATIONALITY: SINDHIS IN KUTCH

Recent work in anthropology has tended to highlight travel and movement over contained immobility, focusing increasingly on the flexible and contingent rather than the fixity and stability that were taken to be the norm in classical ethnography.[29] These newly discovered 'flexible subjects' inevitably have to engage with the form of the nation-state and its legitimating strategies that may be, as argued above, uncomfortable with mobility.[30] One perspective on mobility has been to view it as explicitly 'postnational' where supposedly postnational spaces and alliances are sites where the perceived shortcomings of the nation-state may be overcome.[31] While scholarship influenced by Arjun Appadurai may be overly optimistic about the decline of the nation-state as a regulatory and invasive agent, work by Aihwa Ong perceives a more nuanced situation where flexible subjects engage creatively with a state that is always present.[32] Where both these perspectives fall short of providing a persuasive argument in favour of bringing mobility back into our analytical frame is in their over-emphasis on 'transnational' subjects.[33] For Ong, the nation-state remains strong, but it is one that in turn favours 'flexibility, mobility, and repositioning in relation to markets, governments, and cultural regimes'.[34] It is perhaps the limited context of late capitalism and capital accumulation that enables Ong to argue for this benevolence of state regimes towards flexibility. I suggest that we ought to bring this literature on mobility and cultural flows into dialogue with perspectives on nationalism. It would then seem that the mobility of certain populations in certain times and places become intractable problems for the self-image of the nation-state as it attempts to contain and preserve its authentically imagined (and fixed) core.

Prior to the postcolonial reorganization of space and the consequent valorization of certain regional ties as legitimate and others as illegitimate, there might be sufficient evidence to presume that Kutch and Sindh shared a close regional bond. For the average resident of Kutch or southern Sindh, the two spaces constituted a discrete region; one that was bound together by historical memory, social and economic ties, and cultural and linguistic affinity. With the reorganization first of Sindh within a different nation-state in 1947, and then Kutch within the state of Gujarat in 1960, this bond becomes a difficult one to sustain, especially given the context of the politics of *asmita* that have animated the cultural politics of Gujarat over the past couple of decades. This section attempts to unpack some of these dilemmas of identity as they play out among post-Partition Sindhi settlers in Kutch.

Once closely linked by travel and trade links, the Partition of British India in 1947 meant that Kutch and Sindh fell across a new kind of territorial and national divide. The rest of this chapter looks at particular individuals who have, in their lifetimes, lived on both sides of the border. These sections are based on in-depth interviews with Sindhis who were born and raised in Sindh before 1947 and who made the transition into Kutch following the Hindu exodus from that province after the Partition.[35] As Hindus who moved into India following the Partition, these Sindhis represent the dominant view of nationality and religious identity at the time. Pakistan was presented as a Muslim demand for a Muslim homeland. For Sindhis, Punjabis, or Bengalis who moved into India, as for those who moved in the reverse direction, religious identity was foregrounded at the expense of a regional identity. Further, unlike the provinces of Punjab and Bengal that were split into Eastern and Western constituents so that incoming and outgoing migrants could still participate in their regional cultures broadly defined, Sindhis coming into India did not have a territorial dimension of Sindh to inhabit. In other words, Sindhis who moved to India did so primarily as 'Hindus', less so as 'Sindhis'. This is an important distinction with respect to my argument about how these Sindhi migrants attempt to renegotiate their identities as residents of Kutch. The paradox of identity among Sindhis in Kutch is borne out of their desire to evade the status of an incoming minority and to stake claims to a majority status within the regional political situation of Gujarat. Their move from Sindh is thus tied into postcolonial identity politics of the region in ways that mark this border crossing very differently from the circulatory back and forth migration that characterized the region during earlier periods.

The post-Partition rehabilitation of Hindu Sindhis in Kutch tends to preclude an overt attachment to Sindh. As a territorial referent, Sindh is now part of another nation, and moreover one that is a prime 'other' for the dominant political discourse of the region. In the context of Sindhis who now live in Kutch, Sindh becomes an imaginary 'elsewhere'.[36] In her ethnography of Aru, an Indonesian archipelago, Spyer writes that a 'forgetfulness of one's past is, indeed, the price that many so-called indigenous peoples must pay for a legitimate place within the nation-state and a stake within a larger world'.[37] The memory of Sindh, for those who left it as refugees to start a new life in India, involves a similar forgetfulness of their past, an 'elsewhere' that cannot be celebrated in the manner of other displaced or diasporic populations. Their affectively constructed homeland is not always a publicly celebrated trope among the Sindhis in India as with other diasporic populations. Unlike Spyer's case, however, the Sindhis in Kutch are not a marginalized group. In contrast, I suggest that a public 'forgetfulness' of the territorial dimension of their homeland enables them to acquire full membership into the mainstream of the national community in India.[38] Thus it is not their marginality that becomes the condition of this amnesia, but rather its opposite. Yet, as I hope to show in later sections, 'forgetfulness' does not entail wiping the slate of memory clean. Even as it may be politically pragmatic for Sindhis to cultivate a public amnesia with reference to Sindh, for this empowers them within the elite political and cultural discourse of the BJP in Gujarat, Sindh remains central to the more intimate and personal memories of the Sindhi community in Kutch.

CIRCULATORY CONNECTIONS

Sindh came to be gradually dominated by Islam in the centuries following its conquest by the Arabs in the eighth century. Even though they were a minority, the Hindus of Sindh were prominent economically, especially the class of merchants and traders known as Bhaiband.[39] Sindhi Bhaibands have, from at least the eighteenth century, formed distinctive global merchant networks.[40] Shikarpur and Hyderabad—cities in Sindh—were the main centres for these trading families. Shikarpur became the established locus for overland trade with Russia and Central Asia while Hyderabad families moved globally and established family firms all over the British Empire. The city of Karachi in southern Sindh also developed into a strong regional financial centre for Sindhi merchants.

Sindhi and Kutchi traders and financiers moved back and forth between Kutch and the port city of Karachi in Sindh prior to Partition. Sindhi merchant families moved back and forth between Sindh and the Bombay Presidency throughout the colonial period and, similarly, people from Kutch also frequently lived and worked in Karachi.[41] British administration was established in Sindh in 1843, and in 1847 it was merged into the Bombay Presidency. Karachi and Bombay were developed as its major commercial and maritime centres.[42] A weekly steamer service connected Bombay with Karachi and docked overnight in Mandvi, the southern port of Kutch. This steamer ran continuously even after

Partition, until deteriorating political relations between the two countries led to its suspension in 1965 (it has never been reinstated). Kutchis today still talk of the 'good old days' of the steamer when it was a simple overnight journey by sea to the big city of Karachi and also when each side enjoyed the benefits of trade with the other. A Kutchi journalist recalled that as a young boy in the early 1950s he delighted in Monday mornings when his family would feast on delicious baked goods that had arrived from Karachi the previous night. At the time bakery bread and cakes were unknown in Kutch.

Although my ethnography addresses the movement of people from Sindh into Kutch after Partition, one would also need to establish the historical context within which this move occurred. A circulatory connection between Sindh and Kutch enables us to envision the larger landscape of movement that embraced these two territories long before the political events of the mid-twentieth century.[43] Rather than focusing on the moment of Partition itself, I suggest that we embed the movement of Sindhis into India after 1947 within a larger analytic of the 'experiences of migration and dislocation' where migration and movement between Sindh and Kutch had been institutionalized long before the political events of the Partition.[44] What changed in the post 1947 migration was that this movement became confined to the movement only of Hindus, and in one direction. With Pakistan's professed commitment to being an Islamic state, when Sindh became one of its five provincial units, Hindus of that province decided to move into India where they would not be a religious minority. In the following section, I present a biographical sketch that provides nuanced ways in which we might begin to think through the Sindhi experience of migration into Kutch after 1947.

BIOGRAPHY OF DISPLACEMENT[45]

Ram Malkani, in his early seventies, is a retired bank official living in Gandhidham, a Sindhi resettlement town in south-eastern Kutch.[46] His family moved to Bombay from Karachi in 1947, before the infamous Karachi riots of 6 January 1948 that constituted a decisive moment for many Hindus in Sindh who decided to leave for India. Although Malkani's family hailed from Larkana, a small town in upper Sindh, his father and grandfather before that had been living and working in Karachi for some years. Other than visits to the ancestral house in Larkana during school vacations, Malkani had stayed in Karachi for the greater part of his childhood until the family decided to move to Bombay at the time of

Partition because of the news of Hindu-Muslim violence that was trickling in from other parts of the country. Bombay was the logical choice for them as they had relatives there. At the time he was about twelve or thirteen years old. In Bombay, his father received a cash compensation of 8,500 rupees (approximately $195) for rehabilitation from the Indian government and this got them started on a new life. Malkani graduated from High School in Bombay in 1951 and the following year he arrived in newly established Gandhidham in search of a job and a future. He moved from one job to another. Starting out on daily wages at the Kandla Port, he then worked as a clerk in an office and eventually got a job at the Bank of India, a position he held until he retired. As soon as he began earning a regular salary, he sent for, first, his grandmother, and then his parents from Bombay and they settled down together in the new house they had been allotted by the Sindhu Resettlement Corporation (SRC) in Gandhidham.

By the time I met him, Malkani had lived in Gandhidham for just over fifty years. He admitted that the only time he talked about Sindh was occasionally when he went for an evening stroll with friends of his age. 'Most people are not interested in all this talk of the past', he said. 'My own children also get exasperated when I say something about Sindh; they think these stories are the ramblings of old men. They certainly don't talk to their own children about it. How can they anyway? They never listened to me in the first place'.

When I first met him he was surprised that I was interested in his childhood spent in Sindh. He claimed he did not think much about Sindh, and since he was a young boy when he left, there was not that much to remember anyway. Yet he made it a point to listen to the daily Sindhi language news programme that was beamed on a Pakistani television network, KTN. 'It is not very clear; sometimes the reception is bad, but on the whole I manage to tune in', he said. His initial explanation for this choice of news network was that even though there were dozens of news channels that beamed news all the time they were full of commercial breaks which were too annoying to sit through. 'Anyway, all the news networks basically carry the same news, so I just prefer to watch the one with the least disturbances'.

KTN (Kawish Television News) is a Sindhi language television station broadcast from Pakistan. By the time we had got to this point in the conversation and as the news started up, Malkani could not contain his excitement. 'Look at her [the newsreader's] language! That's the real reason I watch it. There is no other reason. Look at the speed with which she speaks such pure Sindhi. Even we can't speak like that any more. It's first-class...clear; our language has become adulterated over time as we live away from Sindh'.

Over time, as we talked of Sindh, Malkani became more and more animated. In response to my genuine hope that I was not being a nuisance, by dropping in to talk over tea and snacks, he admitted that it was pleasant for a change to have an appreciative audience as no one else of my generation had any interest in listening to him speak of Sindh. One day he was particularly voluble about Karachi:

> My memories of life really begin in Karachi. I still recall the *galiyan* [streets] of our old neighbourhood. The image of our apartment is also clear in my mind, playing with my friends. Actually now that you have begun talking about this, it's all fresh in my mind. *Nazar ke samne ghumti hai voh jagah* [the place moves before me in my field of vision]. It is like a picture now, our house, everything; where we used to sit, where we played, the place where I used to hide my toys and things; I recall everything.

By the end of our conversations, Malkani felt that perhaps he and his wife should go to Karachi once:

> Just for fun, to see our *janambhumi* [birthplace]. It is close by, by the grace of god we have the money and the strength to travel; perhaps we should go. I am keen to see if our old apartment is still there. It should be there, I am certain of it. If I do go, I will go laughing [in good cheer], into the streets of my childhood. Let me see if the house is there or not. I'm sure it is there, where would it go?[47]

SINDHI 'REFUGEES' IN INDIA: 1947 AND BEYOND

In August 1947, British India was partitioned and certain Muslim dominated areas in the northwest and east separated to form West and East Pakistan respectively. There followed an exchange of populations between the two newly created nation-states on a scale hitherto not encountered in the history of the region. In Punjab and Bengal, amid massacres and looting, Hindus and Sikhs moved into Indian territories and Muslims moved into Pakistan. Although Sindh has not received the kind of attention that Partition scholars have given to Punjab and Bengal, it did not remain unaffected by the violence, displacement, and population movements that took place in other areas.

Historiography that concerns itself with Sindh in the early years of its association with Pakistan emphasizes its marginalization within the new political culture of Pakistan dominated by Punjabis.[48] This feeling built on earlier historical tensions. A sense of marginalization under the British administration had led to demands within Sindh for the autonomy of the province from the Bombay Presidency, a movement that was for a while supported equally by both Hindus and Muslims, united in their attachment to a common homeland.[49] In 1937, Sindh was separated from the Bombay Presidency following the success of a Sindhi nationalist movement.[50] However, these same years were also crucial for the discourse on Partition and the 'Two Nation Theory' that held that Hindus and Muslims constituted two distinct nationalities, creating tensions among Hindus and Muslims of Sindh who had only recently argued with one voice for the autonomy of their province within British India.

Following Partition, Muslims from India began to stream into the cities of Pakistan as *muhajirs* or refugees. These refugees were typically drawn from the educated elite Muslim families of northern India. A full analysis of the position of Sindh within Pakistan is beyond the scope of this work. For the moment it is relevant to recount that with the arrival of Muslims from north India to bolster Muslim numbers in Sindh and the Islamization of the administration, it is argued that Sindhi Hindus began to feel more insecure.[51] Oskar Verkaaik refers to these processes as 'ashrafization', following Vreede de Stuers' use of the term referring to practices that aspire to upward social mobility in imitation of those higher in the social hierarchy, but specifically following an elite north Indian Muslim ethos.[52] Given this bias in the new state of Pakistan, such insecurity was not confined merely to the Hindu Sindhis, for the new policies in Pakistan also alienated Sindhi Muslims who were concerned at the large north Indian influx into their cities.[53]

Initially, only a few Hindu Sindhi families moved into India—those who already had family and business interests in Bombay. Hindus from Gujarat and Kutch who were settled in Karachi also began to think of moving, or sending their families back at this time, but again it was a relatively easy move to contemplate for their ancestral homes and families were back in Gujarat or Kutch. For the vast majority of Hindus living in Sindh at that time, however, any move outside of Sindh was simply unthinkable for Sindh was their homeland.

Sixth of January 1948 created the conditions when most of them realized that leaving Sindh was the only practical alternative. That day, Karachi witnessed riots that were instigated by the arrival of Muslim migrants from India into the city, and their scramble for houses and assets.[54] Following these events, the Hindus of Sindh, increasingly a minority in a new country that was justified as a homeland for Muslims, began to leave Karachi for India in hordes via airplanes, ships, and trains. The 1948 census of displaced persons in Bombay Province counted 231,710 refugees from Sindh.[55]

There are few detailed studies of Sindhis in India after 1947 and much of this has to do with their assimilation into mainstream Indian Hindu society instead of maintaining a distinctive ethnic identity as Sindhis.[56] Early literary production among the displaced Sindhi community displayed a nostalgic quality for a homeland torn asunder by political exigencies.[57] Aijaz Ahmad distinguishes between a political and literary community, arguing that as far as literature is concerned a shared community remained united long after the political community was partitioned in 1947.[58] His analysis, based on North Indian Urdu literature concludes: 'the "nation" was not, so far as Urdu is concerned, reorganised once and for all, at the moment of Partition'.[59] This argument suggests that there was a common imagination of community that, even when it was physically and territorially separated after Partition, continued to express itself through the medium of literature. The same might be argued for Sindhi literature in the immediate post-Partition years when Sindhis writing from India were drawing on literary metaphors and tropes that were immersed in a regional Sindhi culture that they had left behind.

One of the most potent signifiers of a unifying Sindhi culture that cuts across religious and class lines is the story of Sassi. Sassi is a mythological Sindhi heroine who wanders ceaselessly in search of her lover. She has inspired an entire genre of story telling in verse and prose and was a strong signifier for an uprooted community in flux in the immediate years following Partition as the Sindhi community in India was seeking a new home. There are innumerable *kafi* compositions based on the love story of Sassi and Punnu and I described my quest for some of them in the introductory vignette. Although she was invoked by Sindhis writing soon after Partition when the memory of the move from Sindh was still fresh, she no longer holds the same fascination for the Sindhi community of Kutch today, at least not in a public and everyday context.

I would suggest that Sindhi migrants in Kutch have negotiated a 'pragmatics of identity' that allowed them certain 'strategies of invisibility'.[60] These strategies are selectively invoked, however, for while invisibility is desired in some contexts, in other contexts Sindhis in Gandhidham are marked as a distinct demographic unit for they constitute a relatively elite and cosmopolitan class vis-à-vis the local Kutchi population. Invisibility on the other hand, becomes empowering when it renders them unmarked as 'refugees' or 'Pakistanis' or other similar othering forms of speech. In a context where Hindu nationalist politico-cultural discourse constructs Sindh as primarily a Muslim province, epistemologically outside of a Hindu civilizational rubric, it is productive for Sindhis in Kutch to remain well integrated as Hindu Indians. A discourse of autochthony and indigeneity becomes one way in which these migrants' claim to assimilation is articulated. The moral uncertainty that attaches itself to a rootless condition finds anchor and respectability through assimilation into the host community rather than a celebration of the homeland.[61]

SINDHI RESETTLEMENT IN KUTCH

Soon after the diasporic dispersal of Sindhis all over India, first in temporary refugee camps and then in countless towns and cities in every part of the country, it was decided to bring them together in a specially constructed township in Kutch. The chief architect of this plan was a Sindhi Bhaiband originally from Hyderabad, Sindh, Bhai Pratap Dialdas. Kutch was found to be most suitable for such large-scale rehabilitation because of its proximity to Sindh as well as its deep historical and cultural links with the area. The Sindhi language also bears a strong resemblance to Kutchi. In his *Linguistic Survey of India*, George Grierson categorized Kutchi as a dialect of Sindhi.[62] To facilitate this plan, in 1947 the ruler of Kutch donated 15,000 acres of land towards the cause of Sindhi resettlement in Kutch. This paved the way in 1952 for the establishment of the Sindhu Resettlement Corporation (SRC), a body that exists to this day as it oversees the development of Gandhidham (a new planned town for Sindhis).

Overtly at least, the Sindhis in Gandhidham assert that they have assimilated into the mainstream of life in Kutch. Recent Sindhi writing closely ties their fortunes with the idea of Kutch as homeland.[63] In 1996, the publishers of the local newspaper, *Kutch Mitra*, brought out a special edited volume that they named *Kutch Tari Asmita*. Literally this translates as 'Kutch, your *asmita*'. It is a good example of what Kutch is taken to mean, from the perspective of a certain stream of intellectual discourse in the region. In this collection of essays, Sindhis are acknowledged to be integral to the landscape of Kutch.

However, as argued above, the historical conditions post-1947 that produced Sindhi migration into Kutch and a contemporary efflorescence of Hindutva inspired ideologies in the region come together to render a certain dimension of Sindhi identity as 'illegitimate'.[64] This aspect of Sindhi identity is related to their historical and ancestral links with Sindh, a province that is now across the border in Pakistan. At times, this perceived 'illegitimacy' of Sindhi identity is sought to be overcome in their adoption of Hindu nationalist positions that enable them to merge with the political and religious majority position.

NARRATIVES OF AUTOCHTHONY

One of the ways in which Sindhis in Kutch selectively invoke a strategy of assimilation is their adoption of certain political positions on ideas of mobility and territory that are associated with mainstream Hindu nationalism. An overt identification with political and religious symbols associated with Hindutva ideology serves to highlight how an uprooted community attempts to align itself with nationalist histories in order to insert itself into a primordialist narrative of territorial belonging.

In the aftermath of the deadly earthquake that struck Gujarat on 26 January 2001, numerous geological changes were observed in Kutch, the earthquake epicentre. Among them, it was noticed that streams of water had temporarily emerged in the hitherto dry areas of the Rann. The Rann of Kutch is believed to have been covered with water at some point in the distant past, and the possibility of it being an inland arm of the Arabian Sea elevated due to ancient tectonic and geological activity has not been discounted.[65] I was, however, given a very particular interpretation of this occurrence by some Sindhi acquaintances and one that fit closely into a widely shared opinion among the nation's revisionist historians.

Earthquakes are frequent occurrences in Kutch, and in 2002–2003 they were discussed in every home in Kutch, especially in view of the new proposed 'town planning' that would rebuild the major cities. One day in Bhuj, I went to the internet café and office supply store that I visited frequently. It was owned and run by two Sindhi brothers whose families hailed originally from the city of Hyderabad in Sindh. Their father came to Kutch in his youth and settled down in Bhuj instead of Gandhidham hoping to develop a commercial business with less competition from fellow Sindhis in search of new opportunities. The reason for my visit was to photocopy an article on the Kutch earthquake of 1819. I handed over the article and settled down to wait for the young man to process it as the office boy scurried off to fetch us all a round of tea. The young Sindhi man was intrigued by the subject of the article and we were soon engaged in discussing his own views on the recent earthquake. He turned to me and said:

> Do you know that the River Indus is actually called the Sindhu? The Sindhu is the first river of India and we [the Sindhis] belong to this river. We lost this river to Pakistan when Sindh went to them but we will get it back. The Sindhu flowed with the Saraswati River, on whose banks the ancient Hindu texts were recited. The Saraswati disappeared underground, but this area was where it flowed through. Tell me, after the earthquake, how did fountains of water emerge miraculously from this desert? It is no accident; it is because the Saraswati River flows here, deep under this land. The earthquake is just the beginning; slowly the two rivers will meet once again, and they will meet here.

Revisionist history in India has for long been concerned with establishing the 'original' inhabitants of India. V.D. Savarkar, ideological architect of Hindutva, had identified the key terms of belonging to Hinduism and the Indian nation. In his writings on the subject, the river Indus (Sindhu in the vernacular) constituted the western boundary of the Indian nation. In Savarkar's rendition, subsequently the backbone of Hindu nationalist ideology, a Hindu is:

> [H]e who looks upon the land that extends from Sindhu to Sindhu—from the Indus to the Seas—as the land of his forefathers—his Fatherland (Pitribhu)... and who above all, addresses this land, this Sindhusthan as his Holyland (Punyabhbu), as the land of his prophets and seers, of his godmen and gurus, the land of piety and pilgrimage. These are the essentials of Hindutva—a common nation (Rashtra) a common race (Jati) and a common civilization (Sanskriti).[66]

The historian Romila Thapar has been at the forefront of secular scholars and academics who pose a direct challenge to Hindutva's version of history. She argues that Savarkar's definition of Hindu depends on a deliberate coincidence of *pitribhumi* (ancestral land) and *punyabhumi* (the land of one's faith). She concludes that, 'this definition of the Hindu excluded Muslims and Christians from being indigenous since their religion did not originate in India'.[67] As such, she argues that it is a politically driven construction of indigeneity.

In Kutch the debates over indigeneity are particularly charged, especially as some of the larger archaeological sites of the Indus Valley civilization have been located here. The Indus Valley culture has been appropriated by Hindutva ideologues as proof of an ancient 'Hindu' civilization. Early historical theories that had accounted for the demise of this civilization by an Aryan invasion from the north were revised by the

Hindu Right. They argued that this was an Aryan civilization and in making this claim, according to Thapar, they ignore all available archaeological evidence that suggests otherwise.[68] As she explains, '[S]ince Hindus sought a lineal descent from the Aryans, and a cultural heritage, the Aryans had to be indigenous…that there is a range of possibilities between the two extremes of invaders or indigenes does not interest them'.[69]

The revisionist view, since it holds that Hindus are descendents of the Aryans, had to now prove that it could not have been an Aryan invasion that destroyed the Indus civilization, for this would make Hindus exogenous as well. In their attempt to prove beyond doubt the autochthony of present day Hindus as an Aryan race and within the territorial boundaries of modern India, the Indus Valley civilization was renamed by the proponents of Hindutva history as the Sindhu-Saraswati civilization. Sindhu is the vernacular name for the Indus and the Saraswati is a mythico-historical river said to be mentioned in the Rig Veda, the foundational text for Hindu civilization in this view.

The narrative of the second generation Sindhi migrant in Kutch aligns himself and his antecedents as a Sindhi within the sacred 'geo-body' of India.[70] In Hindu nationalist narratives of Indian history, the fetishization of the geo-body occurs through a number of discursive tropes such as *akhand bharat* (undivided and inclusive India) and *bharat mata* (Mother India). In this instance, by referring back to the Indus civilization and linking it to the Saraswati, he is simultaneously reiterating contemporary and politically charged claims to autochthony. By aligning Sindhis with this narrative, they too become insiders and indigenous inhabitants of the Indian motherland, which is defined as the primordial home of Hindus.

Narrations of this genre play an important role in resolving some of the paradoxes of identity for Sindhis in Kutch. Sindh is automatically extended in the *longue durée* to include all of Vedic Hindu civilization by virtue of its association with the two rivers, Indus and Saraswati. The political fact of Partition and the separation of Sindh from India are glossed over here as a model of assimilation into a primordial Hindu civilization.

THE PROBLEM OF TERRITORY AND ATTACHMENT

The Sindhis of Gandhidham permanently reside in Kutch and would have as much claim to it as do other Kutchis who came through waves of immigration at various points in the distant past. Yet, unlike many other immigrants into Kutch who came from Sindh or elsewhere some generations ago, in popular imagination and recent historical memory, Sindhis are from Sindh, Pakistan. One way in which this problem is negotiated is illustrated by the anecdote above, where assimilation into the mainstream of Hindu society in India has entailed a full acceptance of Hindu nationalist arguments about authenticity and nationality. This tendency manifests itself in other less extreme forms as well. A Sindhi resident of Gandhidham who was a former journalist with the English language daily *The Times of India* narrated to me the story of Sindhi resettlement and declared that due to the efforts of Bhai Pratap in the establishment of Gandhidham they were spared the ignominy of life in refugee camps. 'Bhai made us Sindhis human beings', he said. He asserted emphatically and thankfully, 'we never had to see the inside of a refugee camp'. Earlier Malkani, the retired banker, had also reiterated the fact that after their displacement from Sindh they moved in with their family in Bombay and 'didn't have to see the face of a camp'.

The idea of exile or refugee status inevitably acknowledges the possibility of return, for to be exiled immediately conjures up the idea of home. By distancing themselves from the status of refugees, some elite Sindhis are able to suspend their past in a desire not to allow the past to define their present. By disclaiming their identity as refugees, they are simultaneously distancing themselves from the political fact of Partition and the creation of Pakistan. However, this distancing from Sindh as homeland is not predicated on an erasure or denial of the past so much as it is a suspension of it; the very existence of Pakistan is rendered illegitimate in such a view.[71] Even as this resonates with larger political discourse in Gujarat and Kutch that is caught up in the project of producing amnesic elisions on the shared past with Sindh, most Sindhis in Gandhidham negotiate a far more ambivalent relationship with it.[72]

In Gandhidham, there is a large temple dedicated to Jhuley Lal, the deity worshipped by many Sindhi Hindus. Every morning and evening it springs into life as devotees come from all over the city to offer their prayers. In the evening it doubles up as a social space, as friends and acquaintances meet and exchange their news. During the Sindhi New Year, celebrated as Cheti Chand in the summer month of Chaitra, this temple is the focus of all-night festivities and prayers. It sits in a large compound that is kept locked except during morning and evening visitation hours. Inside this compound is a row of water taps where devotees freshen up and wash if they desire before entering the temple. It bears a plaque with the names of the donors of this water tank. Under this is a dedication written in Sindhi, in the Arabic script under which is translated in Hindi, *Meri mitti amat, tum hamse bichdi hai. Bisri nahin hai.* In English, this literally translates into 'my un-erasable soil, you are separated from us. Not forgotten'.

The journalist waxed eloquently about the good life that the Sindhis were able to build up for themselves following their repatriation in Kutch: 'For being able to settle and prosper in Kutch, I am grateful to two people—Jadeja [the former ruler of Kutch] for donating the land and Bhai Pratap. Bhai was our hero'. When he spoke of Sindh, he clarified:

> Hindus and Muslims in Sindh were never bigots. All that started only after 1947....Muslims came in from other places and were encouraged to take over Hindu homes and property...cannot imagine what happened to our beautiful homes. This is why nobody would want to return even though we can easily travel now [the travel ban between India and Pakistan had recently been lifted].

Later he said that he was happy in his retired life; his sons were all living in the United States with their families and he had no desire to return to Sindh. After a long pause, however, tears poured down his face as he whispered, 'my ultimate desire is for my ashes to be taken to Shah Abdul Latif at Bhit'. Shah Abul Latif is a celebrated Sufi mystic of Sindh, rendered as a popular icon of *Sindhiyat* ('Sindhi-ness') that transcends particulars of class or religion to stand for Sindhis a whole. Even though he initially distances himself from a desire to return to Sindh to see his old home taken over by Muslims, later in the same conversation he breaks down when talking of his 'ultimate desire' to return in death, for his ashes to mingle with the shrine of Shah Abdul Latif, who, like the popular Sindhi figure Sassi, is a key symbol of Sindhi-ness.

Different interpretations of the past reveal some of the ambivalences that many Sindhis in Gandhidham negotiate in their everyday lives. Compelled on the one hand by the promise of citizenship and identifying with the religious majority in India, they are also haunted by traces of their past in Sindh. Ram Malkani lives in Kutch and his social world is constituted in the space between Gandhidham and Bombay where the rest of his family lives. His children display the cosmopolitanism of the new generation, educated in English and speaking in Sindhi only with their parents. Yet he watches the daily news bulletin on a Sindhi news network beamed from Karachi so that he can listen to the 'pure' Sindhi of his youth.

I have argued in this chapter that the history that informs the notion of Gujarati *asmita* is inevitably compromised by other accounts that bear the marks of other experiences and different histories. In the specific instance of Kutch, which shares a border with the Pakistani province of Sindh, official nationalism leads to a silencing of the connection with Sindh both in the past and present. Hindu Sindhis who moved into Kutch following Partition choose to highlight their identity as Hindus rather than as Sindhis. In so doing, they acquire symbolic political capital as members of a religious majority and an elite class, who can participate in the majoritarian discourse of the region that the notion of *asmita* is symptomatic of.[73] In the context of rhetorical invocations of indigeneity that have become a key marker of nationalism and territorial belonging, Hindu Sindhis who originate in Sindh are faced with the problem of negotiating an identity for themselves in Kutch that will allow them to participate in Gujarati political discourses in a manner that does not mark them as a minority. As the narratives from Sindhi migrants in Kutch reveal, however, traces of Sindh do remain and they interrupt the master narrative of assimilation that the Sindhis in Kutch have for the most part adopted.

In using narrative accounts of people, I do not intend to bring out a false dichotomy of memory versus history where the former is lodged in authenticity and the latter enmeshed in power and politics. I believe that both memory, whether it is individual or collective, as well as history, whether we deem it to be official or oppositional, are the products of the contexts that produce them.[74] However, in Lisa Yoneyama's study of the re-inscription of Hiroshima memories into the contemporary Japanese national imaginary, a case which parallels what I am suggesting is the official erasure of Sindh in Kutch, an attempt to loosen the grip of the past over the present 'paradoxically generates mnemonic sites that have the potential to interrupt the accelerating move toward the amnesic way of remembering'.[75] I suggest that individual and collective memory can conceal within itself an excess that has the potential to de-centre the official way of remembering. The production of the past is indeed an inherently political enterprise. Embarrassing associations that do not fit into a neat national past tend to get eclipsed and written out of the official historical record.[76] History becomes a crucial resource in the creation of community because forgetting or erasure is as crucial as commemoration.[77] Within Kutch's official history, the debatability of the past is not infinite, but set within the parameters of *asmita*. These parameters derive from the compulsions of territoriality, indigeneity, and sovereignty in contemporary nationalist ideologies. As a space on the border, Kutch must be distinguished from what lies beyond the border. Yet, the presence of a sizeable Sindhi population within Kutch constitutes a zone of ambivalence with regard to the construction of a regional identity for Kutch that is supposed today to nest within a larger Gujarati identity.

NOTES

1. This essay contains arguments made more extensively in Farhana Ibrahim, *Settlers, Saints and Sovereigns: An Ethnography of State Formation in Western India* (New Delhi: Routledge, 2009).
2. H.T. Sorley, *Shah Abdul Latif of Bhit: His Poetry, Life and Times* (London: Oxford University Press, 1940).
3. This was true at the time of writing; subsequently, the urban layout of Bhuj has changed almost beyond recognition, and the old markets within the walled city have been transformed.
4. Thomas Blom Hansen, *The Saffron Wave: Democracy and Hindu Nationalism in Modern India* (Princeton, N.J.: Princeton University Press, 1999).
5. Richard Handler, *Nationalism and the Politics of Culture in Quebec* (Madison, WI: University of Wisconsin Press, 1988); Brackette Williams, *Stains on My Name, War in My Veins: Guyana and the Politics of Cultural Struggle* (Durham: Duke University Press, 1991).
6. It must be added that this is also true within India as a whole as well.
7. Bernard Cohn, 'Regions Subjective and Objective: Their Relation to the Study of Modern Indian History and Society', in R.I. Crane, ed., *Regions and Regionalism in South Asian Studies: An Exploratory Study* (Durham, N.C.: Duke University Program in Comparative Studies on Southern Asia, 1967), 5–37.
8. E. Valentine Daniel, *Fluid Signs: Being a Person the Tamil Way* (Berkeley: University of California Press, 1984).
9. Ibid., 78.
10. *The Hindu*, 4 January 2005.
11. *The Hindu*, 14 May 2005.
12. *The Hindu*, 4 January 2005.
13. This was not the way *asmita* was presented in the past; the limits of inclusion and exclusion have varied over *asmita's* history and I have argued this more extensively in my monograph.
14. 'Mainland' because the two wings of Saurashtra and Kutch are separated from it by a marshy desert-like formation known as the *Rann*.
15. Shereen Ratnagar, 'Archaeology at the Heart of a Political Confrontation: The Case of Ayodhya', *Current Anthropology* 45.2 (2004): 239–259.
16. K.M. Munshi, *Glory that was Gurjara Desa, AD 550–1300* (Bombay: Bharatiya Vidya Bhavan, 1955), 10.
17. With the exception of Thar Parkar, already in Sindh, and by extension, in Pakistan by 1960.
18. This is a complicated claim for Kutch, for although standardized Gujarati is the language of schools and administration, as a spoken language, it dominates only in eastern Kutch, in the area known as Wagad. Elsewhere in Kutch, the spoken language is Kutchi, a language closely associated with Sindhi.
19. Farhana Ibrahim, *Settlers, Saints and Sovereigns: An Ethnography of State Formation in Western India* (New Delhi: Routledge, 2009).

20. Munshi, *Glory*, 9.
21. Ibid., 13.
22. Ibid.; M.R. Majumdar, *Cultural History of Gujarat: From Early Times to Pre-British Period* (Bombay: Popular Prakashan, 1965); S.B. Rajyagor, *History of Gujarat* (New Delhi: S. Chand and Company, 1982).
23. Richard H. Davis, *Lives of Indian Images* (Princeton: Princeton University Press, 1997).
24. K.M. Munshi, *Somanatha: The Shrine Eternal* (Bombay: Bharatiya Vidya Bhavan, 1976), 89.
25. He mentions that Somnath was the guardian deity of the Chaulukya rulers of medieval Gujarat and also of the people of Gujarat.
26. Rajyagor, 141.
27. Gregory Possehl, *Indus Civilization in Saurashtra* (Delhi: B.R. Publishing Corporation, 1980).
28. For example, see: Samira Sheikh, 'State and Society in Gujarat, c.1200–1500: The Making of a Region' (D.Phil. Thesis at Oxford University, 2003).
29. Pheng Cheah and Bruce Robbins, *Cosmopolitics: Thinking and Feeling Beyond the Nation* (Minneapolis: University of Minnesota Press, 1998); James Clifford, *Routes: Travel and Translation in the Late Twentieth Century* (Cambridge: Harvard University Press, 1997); Amitav Ghosh, *Antique Land* (Delhi: Ravi Dayal, 1992); Akhil Gupta and James Ferguson, 'Beyond "Culture": Space, Identity, and the Politics of Difference', in Akhil Gupta and James Ferguson, eds., *Culture, Power, Place: Explorations in Critical Anthropology* (Durham: Duke University Press, 1997); Aihwa Ong, *Flexible Citizenship: The Cultural Logics of Transnationality* (Durham: Duke University Press, 1999); Smadar Lavie and Ted Swedenburg, 'Introduction: Displacement, Diaspora, and Geographies of Identity', in Smadar Lavie and Ted Swedenburg, eds., *Displacement, Diaspora, and Geographies of Identity* (Durham: Duke University Press 1996).
30. Ong (1999).
31. Arjun Appadurai, *Modernity At Large* (Minneapolis: University of Minnesota Press, 1996).
32. Ong (1999).
33. Vinay Gidwani and K. Sivaramakrishnan, 'Circular Migration and Rural Cosmopolitanism in India', *Contributions to Indian Sociology* 37.1/2 (2003): 339–367.
34. Ong, 6.
35. 'Sindhi' is of course a regional referent that encompasses all those who are 'of Sindh.' Thus it includes both Hindus and Muslims. In this chapter, an unqualified 'Sindhi' indicates Hindu Sindhis who moved from Sindh to Kutch after Partition. This is also how the term Sindhi is used throughout India.
36. Patricia Spyer, *The Memory of Trade: Modernity's Entanglements on an Eastern Indonesian Island* (Durham: Duke University Press, 2000).
37. Ibid., 37.
38. At the time of this research, the right-wing political party BJP (Bharatiya Janata Party) was in power in the province of Gujarat and was also a core component of the ruling alliance at the centre in New Delhi. As mentioned above, the cultural nationalism of the BJP in general and in Gujarat more particularly imagines India as an essentially Hindu nation.
39. Claude Markovits, *The Global World of Indian Merchants, 1750–1947: Traders of Sind from Bukhara to Panama* (Cambridge: Cambridge University Press, 2000).
40. Ibid.

41. Ibid.
42. Mariam Dossal, *Imperial Designs and Indian Realities: The Planning of Bombay City, 1845–1875* (Delhi: Oxford University Press, 1991); Claude Markovits, *The Global World of Indian Merchants, 1750–1947: Traders of Sind from Bukhara to Panama* (Cambridge: Cambridge University Press, 2000); Asiya Siddiqi, 'The Business World of Jamsetjee Jejeebhoy', *Indian Economic and Social History Review* 19.3–4 (1982): 301–324. For Karachi, see Markovits (2000) and D.V. Maheshwari, 'Ek Or Kachchh Vase Pakistanma', in K. Khatri, ed., *Kutch Tari Asmita* (Bhuj, India: Kutch Mitra, 1997), 273–275.
43. 1947 was not the decisive moment for the rupturing of circulation between Sindh and Kutch. This did not happen until 1965, and the early post-Partition years witnessed considerable fluidity in population movements back and forth.
44. Shelley Feldman, 'Bengali State and Nation Making: Partition and Displacement Revisited', *International Social Science Journal* 55.1 (2003): 111–121.
45. This narrative synthesizes a series of long and repetitive conversations we had on the theme.
46. This is a pseudonym.
47. His choice of language is notable here for this term has acquired currency in Hindu nationalist political discourse after the destruction of the sixteenth century mosque that is believed to have been built on the birthplace of the Hindu god Ram in the north Indian town of Ayodhya.
48. Subhadra Anand, *National Integration of Sindhis* (New Delhi: Vikas Publishing House Pvt. Ltd., 1996); Theodore Wright, Jr., 'Center-Periphery Relations and Ethnic Conflict in Pakistan: Sindhis, Muhajirs, and Punjabis', *Comparative Politics* 23.3 (1991): 299–312; Oskar Verkaaik, *Migrants and Militants: Fun and Urban Violence in Pakistan* (Princeton, N.J.: Princeton University Press, 2004).
49. Rita Kothari, 'Crossing the Sea: Nineteenth Century Travelogues in Gujarat', in A. Singh, ed., *Indian Renaissance* (New Delhi, Creative Books, 2004), 145–155.
50. Verkaaik (2004).
51. Anand (1996).
52. Cora Vreede-de Stuers, *Parda: A Study of Muslim Women's Life in Northern India* (Assen: Van Gorcum, 1968).
53. David Lelyveld, *Aligarh's First Generation: Muslim Solidarity in British India* (Princeton: Princeton University Press, 1978); Verkaaik (2004).
54. See Markovits (2000) and Anand (1996).
55. Government of Bombay, *Bombay Legislative Assembly Debates, Official Report of Oct 13, 1949* (Bombay: Government Central Press, 1950).
56. Anand (1996).
57. For example, see: Anju Makhija and Menka Shivdasani, eds., *Freedom and Fissures: An Anthology of Sindhi Partition Poetry* (New Delhi: Sahitya Akademi, 1998).
58. Aijaz Ahmad, *The Mirror of Urdu: Recompositions of Nation and Community* (Shimla: Indian Institute of Advanced Study, 1993).
59. Ibid., 20.
60. Liisa Malkki, *Purity and Exile: Violence, Memory, and National Cosmology among Hutu Refugees in Tanzania* (Chicago: University of Chicago Press, 1995), 157.
61. For example, see: Malkki (1997); Hannah Arendt, *The Origins of Totalitarianism* (New York: Houghton Mifflin and Harcourt, 1973 [1951]).
62. George Abraham, *Linguistic Survey of India*, Volume 8.1 (Delhi: Motilal Banarsidass, 1968 [1919]), 11.

63. Nirmal Vasvani, 'Sindhion ane Kutch', in K. Khatri, ed., *Kutch Tari Asmita* (Bhuj, India: Kutch Mitra, 1997 [1996]), 110.
64. Harald Eidheim, 'When Ethnic Identity is a Social Stigma', in Fredrick Barth, ed., *Ethnic Groups and Boundaries: The Social Organization of Culture Difference* (Boston: Little Brown and Company, 1969), 39–57.
65. C.P. Rajendran and Kusala Rajendran, 'Characteristics of Deformation and Past Seismicity Associated with the 1819 Kutch Earthquake, Northwestern India', *Bulletin of the Seismological Society of America* 91.3 (2001): 407–426.
66. Vinayak Damodar Savarkar, *Hindutva: Who is a Hindu?* (Bombay: Veer Savarkar Prakashan, 1969), 115–116.
67. Romila Thapar, 'Hindutva and History', *Frontline* 17.20 (2000).
68. Ibid.
69. Ibid.
70. Winichakul Thongchai, *Siam Mapped: A History of the Geo-Body of a Nation* (Honolulu: University of Hawaii Press, 1994).
71. Malkki, 194.
72. Lisa Yoneyama, *Hiroshima Traces: Time, Space, and the Dialectics of Memory* (Berkeley: University of California Press, 1999).
73. Many Sindhis who came from Pakistan after Partition went on to long and successful careers within right-wing Hindu organizations in India such as the RSS and the BJP. K.R. Malkani and L.K. Advani are two prominent examples.
74. Michel-Rolph Trouillot, *Silencing the Past: Power and the Production of History* (Boston: Beacon Press, 1995); Yoneyama (1999).
75. Yoneyama, 65.
76. Shahid Amin, *Event, Metaphor, Memory: Chauri Chaura 1922–1992* (Berkeley: University of California Press, 1995); Ann Laura Stoler, '"In Cold Blood": Hierarchies of Credibility and the Politics of Colonial Narratives', *Representations* 37 (1992): 151–189; Harry Harootunian, 'Memory, Mourning, and National Morality: Yasukuni Shrine and the Reunion of State and Religion in Postwar Japan', in Peter Van der Veer and Hartmut Lehmann, eds., *Nation and Religion: Perspectives on Europe and Asia* (Princeton: Princeton University Press, 1999), 144–160.
77. Ernest Renan, 'What is a Nation?', in R.G. Suny, ed., *Becoming National: A Reader* (New York: Oxford University Press, 1996), 42–55; Prasenjit Duara, 'National Identity, or Who Imagines What and When', in R.G. Suny, ed., *Becoming National: A Reader* (New York: Oxford University Press, 1996).

CHAPTER 3

Unwanted Identities in Gujarat

RITA KOTHARI

Gujarat is home to one-third of the Sindhi-speaking population of India.[1] In the wake of the Partition, Gujarat was one of the four provincial governments, besides Maharashtra, Madhya Pradesh, and Rajasthan, to take charge of the relief and rehabilitation of migrants from Sindh. The physical contiguity between Gujarat and Sindh made both sea and land routes easy. Ships from Karachi arrived at the ports of Porbander, Veraval, and Okha on Gujarat's coast. Movement towards Gujarat also happened indirectly, especially via Rajasthan, when Sindhis arrived by Jodhpur Railways from Mirpurkhas to Pali in Rajasthan. Since Gujarat had more extensive arrangements for relief and also provided better business opportunities, many Sindhis gravitated to it from Rajasthan. Apart from the logistical convenience, Gujarat was also linked to Sindh in other ways: the regions of Kutch and Kathiawar have had cultural, mythological, and trade links with Sindh.[2] Thus, several factors made the region an obvious 'choice' for the Sindhi Hindus who left Sindh during and after Partition.

Although Gujarat proved to be a good option in economic terms, the Sindhi interaction with the host communities in the state has not been an easy one. I focus on the initial episode of settling down as one of the defining moments in this interaction. First, I will address issues surrounding Sindhi resettlement and rehabilitation. This process was formative for the development of stereotypes and set a permanent direction for subsequent exchanges between Sindhi immigrants and Gujarat's already established residents, both Hindu and Muslim. Sindhis came as traders determined to quickly overcome their displacement and disadvantage in what was essentially an already merchant-dominated region. This goal evoked economic resentment among Gujarat's trader groups, especially the Jains and the Vaishnavs. Sindhis also appeared to the mainstream Gujarati Hindus as 'Muslim-like'; influenced by their close proximity to Muslims over the centuries. The Hindus of Sindh were not quite the most suitable examples of orthodox Hindus, as they were a meat-eating community in a largely vegetarian region. The latter half of the chapter discusses this phenomenon and describes how the latest generation of Sindhis has reacted by seeking upward social mobility by denial of their own cultural background and identifying with the Gujarati-Hindu majority.

THE HISTORICAL PAST

Leaving behind their lands, homes, and businesses, the rich traders and *zamindars* of Sindh boarded trains and ships empty-handed, like migrant labourers, thankful to have escaped Partition unscathed. Once in India, poverty and dependence acutely dawned upon many Sindhis but they had neither the time to contemplate their miseries nor the luxury of returning home. Distracted by, and caught up in their immediate concerns, many didn't know whether to search for missing relatives, to earn a living, or to simply swallow their pride and live as refugees. When I asked my uncle, Udhavdas Makhija, whether he tried to look for his friends and family after he landed in Bombay, he said: 'Silly, who had the time?'

In contrast with my uncle's experience, a Sindhi mother of four sons wrote to the Maharaja of Baroda requesting simultaneously that her lost children be located and for money:

> I am a poor lady whose four sons have been lost in the past political disturbances and yet I have no news of them. They are somewhere in India but exactly it is not known where they are. I am giving you their names so that you can please find them. I am also sending you numbers of certain cash certificates I had bought in Sindh. If you can kindly issue new certificates from India, I will have some money with me.[3]

Very often, the tragic irony of arrival was far greater among the Sindhis than the moment of departure. The Sindhi story of Partition does not privilege the 'day of departure', although there are dramatic instances of people escaping disguised as Muslims. Instead, it is the hostility of the local population upon their arrival in India that gives them some of their most excruciating memories of this period:

> We waited in Hyderabad for three months before we could get tickets. Finally we left Hyderabad—11 families together. The train brought us to Marwar. People there did not let us get down at the Marwar junction. So we were taken to Barmer, or rather the desert-like outskirts of Barmer. We lived in a single tent. We were given free food but we felt too scared to eat. After the way the locals had behaved with us, we didn't know what to expect. We cooked our own food. One day, when the dust-storms were blowing and we could hardly see, one of the children fell into a sizzling kadhai. Those were the worst days of life.[4]

The owner of a well-known chain of sweet shops in Ahmedabad said to me about this period:

> I am so embarrassed about giving you details about how I was treated on coming here. First of all, there was the embarrassment about fleeing Sindh when we, Congress workers, were needed the most. But I already told you those circumstances. And when we came by train to Rajasthan, we first landed in Barmer and then moved to Ajmer. I remember going with my wife to a tea-stall in Ajmer. The *chaiwallah* gave me a cup of tea, but just when I was putting that cup down along with the others he shouted at me for 'polluting' other cups. Untouchability? In Sindh, we did not do that to *anyone* and the Jains and Oswals considered us low-castes here.[5]

This feeling of humiliation was far more common amongst the Sindhis who came to Rajasthan and Gujarat than those who arrived at Bombay. The strongly vegetarian Hindus and Jains of these states treated them with suspicion because they came from an 'Islamic' province, ate meat, and drank liquor. In parts of Rajasthan, the locals gave the Sindhis food in a humiliating manner, making them feel like the untouchables. In both Gujarat and Rajasthan, there are many examples of Sindhis who were not allowed to disembark their transport or enter into the heart of local cities.

Unlike Bombay, Gujarat had no record of refugee assistance from non-governmental or individual sources. In fact, letters received by Sardar Vallabhbhai Patel in 1948 contain a litany of complaints about how Sindhis intruded upon local life by creating dirt and disruption. Many complained that Sindhis only looked after themselves and had no concern for the Gujaratis of Karachi, who also had to repatriate:[6]

> I received your letter dated 21st. What you say does appear true, 'these days regional feelings are on the rise.' I feel that Sindhis have gone through a lot in recent times, seeing as what happened to Sindh. It is understandable that the Sindhi leaders would be sympathetic [to their own community]. If the assumption is that Gujaratis will manage anywhere else in India, it does not

> lead us to conclude that Sindhis leaders are provincial. It would not be proper to think that consideration for Sindhis is also injustice towards Gujaratis. The Sindhis have to leave a lot behind them, it is natural for Sindhis leaders to be considerate.... [7]

It is important to remember that Sindhis did not come as victims of Partition to a place that was rightfully theirs on this side of the border;[8] they were not a population in exchange but unwanted immigrants.

U.T. Thakur states that over 452,800 Sindhis were living in refugee camps in 1948.[9] Built at a 'safe' distance from the heart of most cities, one hundred camps (or rather, ex-army barracks built during the World Wars) housed Sindhis from 1947 to 1949. The Bombay government set up these camps away from the big cities so that the angry refugees would not excite the general population by their horror tales. The story of Sindhis staying in refugee camps in India hinges on a set of common problems faced by Sindhis. Quarrels over the limited resources of food and water, scrambling for employment, unhygienic living conditions, and the consequent infections and epidemics all angered and frustrated Sindhis living in those camps:

> Refugee Camp. Women pulling each other's hair for filling water from a single tap, swarms of flies outside latrines, drops of water leaking from the barrack roofs, gunny sacks held up as curtains with children sleeping behind them but watching parents, rationed grains on a skewed weighing-scale, a register with more names than people in the camp, sacks of wheat and rice grains bound from godowns to camps, 25% cut on amounts allocated for refugees....[10]

A gamut of social issues inform the refugee history of Sindhis in post-Partition India: state archives show letters asking for loans, requests for increased loan amounts, or applications for permanent employment in government offices. There are many letters about the use and abuse of power and relief resources in the camps. There are also complaints about discrepancies between the state policies for refugee-welfare and their implementation, between amounts that were sanctioned and what was finally disbursed as dole and so on. Such complaints were commonplace and evoked bitter acrimony between camp authorities and inhabitants. In the context of Gujarat, these letters also illustrate deep prejudices against the Sindhis. For instance, there is an obvious tone of distrust in a report by the Baroda State Refugee Officer. Issued in response to an application by Nihalchand H. Mahtani of Sindh, for resuming the maintenance of Rs 152 received from his son prior to Partition, the report states:

He [Nihalchand Mahtani] states that his son who was trading in Manila (Philippines) used to send to the applicant his maintenance expenses. During war, he could not send money to him for obvious reasons. He approached the Government of India who used to pay Rs 152/- a month for his maintenance. This allowance was continued to him from 1941 to 1945. Owing to the partition of the country, he states that the subsidy has been stopped. The applicant left Hyderabad (Sindh) on 17th December and came to Baroda with family member[s] on 4th January 1948. He requests that some amount may be given to him as maintenance allowance since his condition is very bad and it would not be possible for him to carry on....How could it be that an Indian is interned in Manila—unless he may have committed an offence against the state of the Philippines.[11]

The distrustful tone in the above report initially appears to lack grounds. Nonetheless, there were other exchanges where the issues of right and wrong were 'grey'. In a three-person application requesting a transfer to the refugee camp in Kalyan (located outside of Bombay) it is difficult to know the real reasons behind the request and whether the report's observations are accurate:

We [the applicants] have applied one application to your honour and again have to request that there is [*sic*] mosquitoes which are biting us seriously and my wife is sick and spent 50–55 rupees and medical treatment is going on and there is one child of 4 months is sick and have to sit for a whole night and there is a crowd of 1100 men in one camp and they have left the camp for the very reason and only 40 persons are there. Half in Andheri camp and half number in Kalyani camp is filled up by the camp refugees of Navsari. They are getting their rations. I have been to Kalyani (two men) in the camp no. 3 and 5. The camp officer refused to let me enter because ration is stopped for new persons. I returned for the very same reason to Navsari. At present I Ludu Kalumal is becoming sick and I am old and I have no one to look after me and my son is underage. So I beg to request your honour that you must order to the effect that we may be entered at Kalyani camp.[12]

In reply, the Refugee Officer states:

All three applicants Shri Ladumal, Acharmal Balumal, Alumal Tanumal are related to one another and are at present staying in Navsari, outside the refugee camp in a rented house for the last one month and a half. In their application it seems that they have misrepresented and exaggerated the actual facts in order to achieve their end of getting free rations and free railway facilities to go to Kalyan Camp. Free rations are only given to those refugee families who stay in the Camps. No facilities can be given to those who stay outside the camp. The applicants in spite of their staying outside the camps require free ration and all other facilities.

> The Navsari District being a damp area the trouble of mosquitoes and other insects is a general complaint not only of the camp people but of other people of the town too. Just about a month ago, the nuisance of bugs, mosquitoes, fleas and other insects was acute. It would be pointed out here at this stage that the refugees themselves are mainly responsible for increasing this nuisance as they never keep their rooms and blocks clean in spite of repeated instructions. They use vacant rooms, bath-rooms, open space, road as latrines and urinals even though separate arrangements are specially provided for. They were requested to cover their floor with cow dung coating, which was supplied to every room but none of them availed of it.
>
> As the climate of Navsari, they say, is not suitable, to them, many of the refugees go to Kalyan and other camps without informing the camp officer. The refugees, if they take up to labour, work and stick to one place, they would soon be rehabilitated and will have no difficulty for their absorption. But as these people have no liking for any labour they move from one place to another for a suitable and comfortable life. It would be seen from the application itself that their aim is to go to Kalyan camp with all the members of their families and their claim for their credit notes for free railway facilities.[13]

The use of phrases like 'these people' and references to 'free' things, 'unclean ways' and 'idle lives', to homogenously describe refugees are common in refugee reports and are a marker of local prejudice. At the same time, it is undeniable that refugees circumvented laws and rules in order to make quick money: documents illustrate the selling of rationed grains received in camps at higher prices on the open market; families claiming more members than actually existed, and/or people indulging in 'nefarious' activities. The frustration, anxiety, and greed of the refugees, along with the exasperation of the authorities who felt that they had more than met the needs of the migrants, were commonly reported by government departments working with Sindhis.

The refugee influx in places like Saurashtra was less systematic but the logistical convenience of Gujarat lay in its coastal belt, which made it possible for the Sindhis to board ships and small crafts from Karachi and land at any of the three ports of Veraval, Navlakhi, and Okha. The Sindhis began moving to Saurashtra before the arrangements for rehabilitation were formally handed over to the provincial governments in 1948. The states of Bhavnagar and Jamnagar each took in 10,000 refugees in September 1947.[14]

By mid-February 1948, twelve camps with a capacity to accommodate 32,000 refugees had been set up. Even so, the numbers of refugees exceeded expectations. A telegram dated 23 October 1948, discussed the 150,000 refugees who had arrived at Okha. In such a situation, the burden was shared between Baroda State and Saurashtra, with the latter arranging for temporary accommodation.

The poor conditions of relief, especially with regard to accommodation, resulted in severe discontentment amongst many refugees. In at least one instance, they complained to a Gujarati newspaper. This complaint resulted in the headline: 'Sindhis Are Not Accorded a Good treatment At the Port of Okha—The Authorities of the Post and Telegraph Refused to Send their Wires'. The same newspaper, *Sansar Samachar*, on 12 December 1948 reported:

> There are no adequate arrangements for the Sindhi refugees coming to Okha by steamers. The people coming here from Okha are complaining that the officers in charge of the Okha port and the contractors in charge of food behave in unmannerly way towards the Sindhi refugees who are fed with the food prepared two or even three days before. There are only ten or twelve tents for the refugees, the rest have to sleep in the open in this wintry cold, with the result those poor children and the aged persons are benumbed by cold and have been the victims of the various diseases. If anybody dares to make complaints the fellow is suppressed and bullied to the extent of using the military for the purpose. Is it a crime to make reasonable demands? Other complaints made by the refugees are also painful. Some esteemed and educated persons wanted to acquaint the Indian government, the Saurashtriya Government, and the Baroda Government with the above facts by sending telegrams but to their great astonishment the postal authorities refused point-blank to send their wires. The Indian government should make inquiries about the matter.

Historian and refugee officer, Shambhuprasad Desai, testifies to the poor conditions of reception in Veraval and Junagadh in Saurashtra. Speaking of his direct involvement at these places, Desai says that the Sindhis came to Saurashtra much against the will of the local populace. The grounds of opposition were both social and economic: local Gujaratis did not want Sindhis to occupy the evacuee properties left behind by Memons who had preferred to migrate to Pakistan once it was decided that Junagadh would merge with independent India. Local Gujaratis resented the government's decision to allocate evacuee properties to Sindhis. Also, as mentioned, they disliked Sindhis for being like Muslims, due to meat-eating. They appealed to Desai by asking him to oppose the Sindhi incursion in Kutiyana and Veraval. However, as the custodian of evacuee property and refugee officer, Desai ignored the local anti-Sindhi sentiments and took charge of the abandoned houses by sealing them. Due to a lack of local support and labour, Desai states that he had trouble managing makeshift arrangements for the Sindhis.[15]

Manubhai Bhatt, a Gandhian social activist from Bhavnagar who organized voluntary services, also made similar observations:

> The refugees were in a terrible state. They were full of anger. Each family was given a mere 10 feet space in the godowns [warehouses] and there were hundred such families. The picture of so many families living in a cellar like that was beyond imagination. What was surprising for us and even for the refugees was how different they looked from us. Their clothes, manners, appearance was [*sic*] a lot like Muslims. In fact they were not even used to thinking of themselves as Hindus, it must have occurred to them during partition that they were of a different religion. They seemed to have blended so much with the majority of the Muslim population in Sindh. The women could not stop saying, *Allah knows* every now and then, while the men would say *khuda khe khabar* [God knows].[16]

The evacuees' properties held a strong attraction for Sindhis. Since the procedure for requisitioning these properties to refugees (on both sides of the border) was slow and complicated, Sindhis in Saurashtra forcibly acquired many Muslim evacuee houses. On 28 February 1948, around 20,000 Hindus from Sindh arrived in Junagadh, hoping to claim the properties left behind by the Muslims after Junagadh's merger with India. In an interview, Chandra Asnani from Bantwa notes:

> We are from Lower Sindh. Our men were peasants. We lived in villages and never even visited Karachi or Hyderabad. Women in our families draw their veils down to their waists. I don't think my father-in-law even knew what I looked like. We were brought to Bhavnagar by country craft. From there we came to Bantwa. There were Muslim evacuee houses. I can't remember how, but we managed to live in one. It was a *dehla* [a large house]. I remember a woman used to visit our house and quietly walk up to one corner of the house and cry. We, women of the house, called her privately and asked her. She told us that her husband was killed in that corner.[17]

Parts of Bombay that included the districts of Godhra and Dahod (now in Gujarat) also beckoned Sindhis due to their availability of evacuee Muslim properties. Migrants to Godhra came from two different directions and socio-economic strata. A majority of the 15,000 Sindhis who live in Godhra are from Lower Sindh, the region of Lar. Peasants and fishermen by vocation, the Laris are considered among Sindhis coarse and poor. The second smaller group, one that is more powerful in terms of political representation, was from Upper Sindh and the regions of Larkana and Shikarpur. The Laris first disembarked at Navlakhi port in Saurashtra. They were then taken to the Katni camp near Jabalpur. Once the camp closed down, they were sent to Godhra. Of this smaller group, one interviewee (Tahilram Makhijani) said Sindhis were aware of the evacuees' properties but 'waited for our claims to come through and then bought them'.[18]

The subsequent communal history of Godhra, with its notorious series of riots between the Ghanchi Muslims and the Lari Sindhis has, at its roots, the issue of evacuee property. Harish Jethmalani, a lawyer from Vadodara, confirms this claim:

> The reputation of the Godhra Sindhis had spread to other parts of Gujarat. The Sindhi aggression against Muslims was seen as a special gift the Sindhis brought with them to Gujarat. The Maharaja of Baroda wanted us to put the Muslims of Baroda also in place. We were in Harni and Outram Camps, but the Maharaja wanted us to have townships next to Muslim colonies so they remain under control.[19]

Whether the assumptions communicated on behalf of the Maharaja have any grounds is a different matter. What is important, and here disturbing, is a new self-definition of Sindhis in Gujarat (the contexts and implications of which are discussed in the second half of this chapter). Ironically, the roots of this communalized self-definition lie not in a 'traumatic and violent' Partition experience, but in the circumstances of resettlement.

In addition to Baroda and Saurashtra, the city of Ahmedabad also accommodated a large number of Sindhis by providing transit camps and tents. The city was a transit point for Sindhis who shifted when the camps in Rajasthan or Madhya Pradesh were shut down. In 1947–1948, the camp of Kubernagar in Ahmedabad (now the second-largest Sindhi-township in India) could accommodate 100,000 Sindhis. It is difficult to know how many Sindhis live in Kubernagar now, but they probably form the largest component of the 400,000-strong Sindhi population in the city.[20] Apart from Kubernagar, Ahmedabad also had relief camps in the areas of Wadaj, Sabarmati, and Maninagar.

An event in the early history of Sindhi migration and rehabilitation that bears special mention is the establishment of Adipur-Gandhidham in Kutch, Gujarat. Bhai Pratap, a well-known Sindhi businessman and national activist, with the help of the Indian government, Mahatma Gandhi and the Maharrao of Kutch managed to get 15,000 acres of land near the port of Kandla for the purpose of building a new township (now called Gandhidham). Bhai Pratap founded the NGO, Sindhu Resettlement Corporation (SRC) with the aim of building the new township wherein lands were allotted to shareholders on 'easy' terms so as to promote and aid industrial, commercial, and public utility projects. Bhai Pratap managed to bring people who had not found any means of livelihood elsewhere in India to Gandhiham. The people of Gandhidham do not see themselves as refugees but as early settlers who created opportunities not only for themselves but also for others. This context of the Sindhi presence in Gujarat is somewhat different: it is an example of the community attempting self-rehabilitation without depending overly on state assistance.

Refugee camps were officially closed in 1949. By the end of 1948, only the disabled, the old, and/or children were given dole. The remainder of the Sindhis had to look out for themselves, which they often did better than other migrant communities. Despite this fact, many faced discrimination in Gujarat. Often pejoratively called *nirvasit* (homeless), Sindhis long battled the locals' prejudices. In other states, Sindhis were pejoratively labelled *sharnarthi* (refugees), which through the 1950s evoked images of dependence and being at the mercy of those who gave them shelter. Over the following decades, Sindhis would try to live down these labels by inventing new ones, like *purusharthi* (hard-working, or those making an effort), to suggest success and self-reliance. Apart from the ways in which their identity as refugees shaped the perceptions of others, it also created new cleavages within the community by separating those who lived in camps from those who did not. From my childhood I remember an offensive word, 'campi', which meant a 'coarse' or 'unrefined' Sindhi. It marked a class different from my family, who lived in a posh area of Ahmedabad. For people who continue to live in camps-turned-townships in cities such as Ahmedabad and Surat, condescension comes from all quarters, including their own community. Just as people from the Ulhasnagar Camps left and moved to Bombay, those from Ramnagar in Surat went to posh areas like City Light, and those from Kubernagar moved to Navrangpura in Ahmedabad. The movement out of the camp has been a traditional movement towards upward mobility. It also has been a concurrent movement away from a certain brand of 'Sindhiness' identified in Gujarat as negative. The upwardly mobile Sindhi rejects it, and in the process, rejects his own past and history.

A PRESENT WITHOUT A PAST

After fifty-seven years of re-settlement in Gujarat, Sindhis are one of the region's most affluent business communities. They dominate several forms of trade and businesses: they own bakeries, provisions stores, consumer goods businesses, readymade garments stores, hotels, and cinema houses. Sindhis often travel in sleek cars, wear diamond rings and build huge houses. They proudly declare that there is not a single Sindhi beggar anywhere in India. The Sindhis are 'model' migrants who now seem to show no traces of trauma. In fact, many claim to have done much better after Partition than before—all good reasons to be proud of one's community and its resilience. However, there is a sense of discomfort with the Sindhi identity amongst the younger generation of Sindhis. They refuse to speak their mother tongue and their parents co-operate with them in shedding not only their language but also their identity. This process has been a gradual one, beginning with a modification of external appearances and culinary habits and moving towards a relinquishing of an entire past and world-view. It has sometimes been conscious, sometimes not, and each generation has contributed in its own ways to the dissolution of the historical Sindhi identity. My purpose here is not to attempt to outline the various ingredients that make up what we call 'identity' and study them in a clinical framework. However, I do wish to provide a range of voices across age and space that speak of how they feel about being Sindhi, the negative perceptions about Sindhiness that they carry, and the various means of coping with them. Although there are many negative perceptions about the community all over India, the case of Gujarat holds a special significance. Perhaps it has to do with the fact that I was born and brought up there. Nonetheless, I believe that this negative perception in Gujarat has a special edge, almost a sense of stigma.

Gujarat's social geography divides its landscape between those who are 'like Gujaratis' and those who are not. The Sindhis occupy a peripheral zone by being neither 'proper' Hindus of Gujarat, nor *others* (i.e., Christians and Muslims). The people of Gujarat knew that Sindhis had left everything behind when they migrated to India because they were a Hindu minority in a Muslim-majority province. However, the Islamic influence upon the Sindhis, their pluralistic atypical Hindu practices and their blithe oblivion about ritual purity made the Hindu Gujaratis wonder if the Sindhis were Hindus like them. Some traces of this bewilderment persist even today.

Although the brunt of the negative perceptions was directed at the first generation, the pressures of resettlement helped deflect them. In the first twenty years following Partition, Sindhis were too busy making ends meet and lived in a self-enclosed world of either Sindhi townships or cheap *chawls* (a cluster of buildings, with single rooms each occupied by a family, comprising the lower to middle-class housing). Udhavdas Makhija, a first generation migrant who started his business on the pavement with less than a hundred rupees, has now retired from one of the best-known brassiere manufacturing firms in Gujarat. He moved from a camp to a *chawl,* and eventually, to an apartment complex that is exclusively Sindhi. According to him, 'Of course there was jealousy, but it didn't matter. Who had the time to bother with it?'[21]

As mentioned earlier, Sindhi settlers in the urban areas of Gujarat were largely traders coming to an already merchant-dominated region. Hungry for survival, no job seemed too menial and no work enough for them. They made inroads into the wholesale and retail trade of Gujarat, offering tough competition to the already well-established Gujarati dominated businesses. They made do with low margins, thereby undercutting the locals' business. They had no inhibitions, religious or otherwise, about working odd hours of the day and night. In a hurry to make ends meet and recover all that they had left behind, Sindhis adopted whatever means they could. They created tremendous local resentment and distrust, exemplified in the popular proverb, 'If you see a Sindhi and a snake, kill the Sindhi first'. Although the intertwining of commerce and ethics is rarely simple, the Sindhis draw attention to this aspect by being ubiquitous as a business community, with a negligible professional class. The emergence of the negative perceptions among the Gujaratis has roots in their hands-on market experience and the competition presented by the Sindhi.

Perhaps the pressures of earning quickly, immediately after Partition, may have governed some of the casual business practices among the Sindhis; regardless, the merchants of Sindh were always adept at maintaining mystifying accounts that neither the poor *haari* [peasant] nor the British colonial officer could understand. It is perhaps a continuation of the same trait, exacerbated by the pressures of survival, which the Sindhis are still unwilling to give up. It would seem that Sindhis have shed what seemed inconvenient to them and have continued with traditions that appeared to make commercial sense. According to Anita Thapan, the Sindhi businessman has his own particular concept of morality; for him, irregularities in business practices are occupational hazards.[22]

The other factor that led to this stigma was the Sindhis' non-vegetarianism. Gujarat as a state may have a large number of meat-eating communities but, in its upper social echelons, Brahmins, Jains, and Vaishnavs have always set the standards for 'acceptable behaviour'. These communities are strictly vegetarian and have led to the impression that Gujarat is a vegetarian state. The Jain-Vaishnav combine is both economically and culturally dominant and determines the 'purity' of the state and, by consequence, its social stratification. In such a context, it was understandable that the Sindhis' meat-eating habits did not make them popular. The stereotypes of Sindhis being 'dirty' helped the Hindu and Jain Gujaratis legitimize social distance, while creating in the Sindhis' minds a justifiable reason for that distance. On the grounds of 'cleanliness' and non-vegetarianism, the Sindhis are, even today, not sold homes in localities dominated by Jains and Vaishnavs. The latter's impact is particularly visible in cities like Ahmedabad, Surat, and Vadodara where urban trade is mostly in their hands.

In Ahmedabad, Sindhis live partitioned off from the social and psychological lives of Hindu Gujaratis. Although they may, on rare occasions, manage to stay in Gujarati-dominated colonies, they must comply with the Hindu Gujarati's norms of vegetarianism for eligibility to live there. In the late 1980s, when my parents were looking for a new house, I was shocked to find that Sindhis were not allowed to reside in certain localities. The sense of stigma is not uniform over all the sections of Sindhi society in Gujarat. The educated, westernized, and socially privileged upper-class Sindhis (e.g., Amils) may have encountered certain negative perceptions. But protected as they were and are by class and sophistication, the impact may not have been so comparatively deep. Also, this class did not generally come to Gujarat, preferring to go to Delhi or Bombay instead. Those who did usually, did not have to live in the camps since they often joined the Gujarat government directly as much-privileged government officers.

It was the second generation of this migrant community that, despite being materially well off, began to feel a sense of discrimination and felt affected by it. Shankarlal Ahuja, the owner of the chain of bakeries that produces 'Super Bread' has felt a tangible sense of exclusion. I met Ahuja at an elite club in Ahmedabad, of which he has been a member and where he has spent every evening during that period for over twenty years. In an interview, he told me:

> It was only in the last few years that I have been able to make friends here. They were not ready to give me membership in this club. They kept inventing excuses. I used to sit by myself, smoke and play cards. Nobody would come up to me and talk to me. Things have changed now.[23]

For the second generation of Sindhis born and raised in India, Sindh is an increasingly remote and irrelevant place. What was relevant to them was their respective place of settlement and the people that inhabited it. They have set their standards based on this knowledge, and in the process, internalised those of the society they were living in. Their ambivalence about being Sindhi did not allow them to pass on a legacy of pride in Sindhiness to the next generation. The absence of history and a past continued, and has now created a generation that operates in what Anita Thapan calls a 'cultural vacuum'.[24] For the third generation, Sindhiness is a cluster of undesirable traits, and the easiest way to distance oneself from it is to abstain from speaking Sindhi—the only historical marker of this linguistic identity. This phenomenon is evident in the self-perceptions of many urban, third generation, and college-going Sindhi boys and girls in Gujarat.

My first encounter with this self-perception was with a Sindhi student, Bhumika Udernani, in the college where I taught. One of my colleagues recommended her to me by saying, 'She is so smart looking, you would never be able to tell she's a Sindhi'. When I asked Bhumika what she felt when people told her she didn't look like a Sindhi, she smiled and said, 'I feel very happy. It's a compliment'. I was both pained and amused by the familiarity of this response: 'There are such misconceptions about Sindhis—they are not educated, they are fat, and [the] boys join business. I have had to work hard to establish myself and not be ignored because I was a Sindhi. I have had bad experiences'.[25] In a world that values a bourgeois brand of success, the lack of education, and what seemed like refinement among the Sindhis, left Bhumika apologetic. As a consequence, she has not only shed her language, but also finds it repulsive when a young Sindhi of her age appears ensconced in it: 'Nobody my age would like to be considered a Sindhi. When I see a girl of my age speaking in Sindhi, I feel, "Oh my God, what have her parents done to her!" I can make out that they are from Kubernagar or Sardarnagar. It's embarrassing'.[26]

It would seem from Bhumika's example, that Sindhis studying in westernized schools solely carry the burden of such prejudices. This, however, is not exclusively the case. Deepak Bhavnani, who studies in a Gujarati-medium college, also refuses to speak in Sindhi. He told me: 'People in my college think Sindhis are some kind of inferior people'.[27] When I asked him what the basis of that perception was, he replied: 'They say Sindhis are dirty, they eat meat and their homes stink'. Unlike Bhumika, Deepak is surrounded by middle-class and non-westernized Gujaratis, hence his share of stereotypes is different. Nonetheless, the response to social condescension in both cases is the same—the shedding of their language.

While the lack of comfort with Sindhiness among upwardly mobile Sindhis is quite visible, there is also a gradual erosion of confidence in the Sindhi heartlands, in what are condescendingly called the 'campi' Sindhis. The movement away from the camps, the aspiration of every Sindhi, is made possible by denying one's origins. Vidya Tewani and Krishna Ahuja are two of my students who lived in Kubernagar. Both studied in Sindhi-medium schools there and came to St. Xavier's College to continue their studies. The shift was almost like moving from a village to a city, destabilizing and disorienting. Krishna was not fluent in either Gujarati or English and found it excruciating to go on with her education. She made no claims about not knowing Sindhi, for that is all she had. However, in her conversation with me she said: 'I have to keep giving explanations of who I am. My classmates ask me why I look like a Muslim. Why do I wear such shiny clothes?'[28] Krishna started wearing a cross around her neck during her days in college and found herself suddenly very 'interested' in Christianity. Vidya, on the other hand, retreated into a shell and made sure she read many English books to overcome her sense of inferiority. She told me: 'No Sindhi girl in this college has come up and spoken to me. She wouldn't want to admit me as one of her own because I am after all a Kuberi girl'.[29]

The above examples are from within the city of Ahmedabad. When I extended my investigations to other parts of Gujarat (such as Kalol, Bhavnagar, Surat, and Rajkot) the results were not vastly different. The only exception was the region of Adipur-Gandhidham in Kutch because the Sindhis who live there do so in a close-knit community and in a location that is culturally and historically close to Sindh.

FINAL THOUGHTS

When third generation Sindhi migrants to Gujarat listen to Abida Parveen (a Sufi singer from Sindh, Pakistan) or when my second generation peers hear Runa Laila (a Bangladeshi who was originally a Pakistani) sing a rendition of '*Damadam Mast Qalandar*', it hardly occurs to them that these voices connect Sindhis with their past. The discontinuation of this Sufi and devotional aspect of Sindhi life may be seen as a manifestation of an anxiety to become a part of the mainstream in a new situation and relinquish all that one associates with a distant, irrelevant, and a 'Muslim' past. In a state that is historically divided along religious lines, the increasing Sindhi loss of religious syncretism in Gujarat becomes one more context which contributes to and results from anti-Muslim sentiment.

The trajectory of the ethno-religious choices exercised by Sindhis in Gujarat demonstrate both their movement towards the 'Hindu fold', and away from their past. As a symbolic statement of this new Hindu affiliation, Sindhis in Gujarat prefer to support Hindu fundamentalist organizations that feed into anti-Muslim sentiment (e.g., the Bharatiya Janata Party [BJP]). As one interviewee, Shankarlal Ahuja, said to me: 'You will find 90 per cent Sindhis with the BJP'.[30] Udhavdas Makhija also mentioned to me proudly: 'All my sons and my grandsons vote for the BJP. Now with L. K. Advani [a Sindhi migrant as its leader], it is our own party'.

It might be argued that this so-called 'hardened identity' has its origins in the history of pre-Partition Sindh, with its socio-economic disparities and various Hindu-revivalist organisations in the run up to Partition.[31] However, it is undeniably true that this movement owes its impetus, in no small measure, to the interaction of Sindhis with Gujaratis in the process of resettlement. The mainstream Gujaratis' lack of social acceptance of Sindhis appears to have affected the Sindhis of Gujarat deeply. Sometimes Sindhis, especially the third migrant generation, may not be aware of the covert forms of Gujarati dislike for him/her. Members of this generation may not have an immediate explanation for why they do not prefer to unqualifiedly and simply state that 'I am a Sindhi'. They may also not know that their desire to remain a vegetarian is perhaps a response to vegetarian friends who find meat-eating repulsive. Additionally, they may not want to wear 'Sindhi-type' clothes that are 'gaudy' and thus have their true identity on display. Sadly, but not in all cases, they may have internalised the Gujarati dislike for Sindhiness to such an extent that it would appear only 'natural'. Consequently, they may blame their own community for burdening them with an identity that only has negative stereotypes attached to it. A corollary to this process is a willed distance or unconscious alienation from 'Sindhiness', which is considered an unwanted identity in Gujarat and, to a lesser extent, elsewhere in India.

NOTES

1. Government of India, *Census of India* (New Delhi: Government of India Publications, 1991).
2. Rita Kothari, *Burden of Refuge: The Sindhi Hindus of Gujarat* (New Delhi: Orient Blackswan, 2007), 125–126.
3. Baroda State Archives, Refugee Files (1948–1949).
4. Radha Lilani. Personal Interview. 9 March 2003 (Kalol, Gujarat).

5. Chellaram Rochwani. Personal Interview. 12 September, 2005 (Ahmedabad, Gujarat).
6. Jaysinghbhai, *Gujarat No Rajkiya Ane Sanskriti Itihas*, Vols. 5 & 9 (Ahmedabad: Vidhyabhawan, 1977). This text states that, during Partition, Sindhis and 200,000 Gujaratis from Sindh migrated into Gujarat. What we see in the letter above is these people competing for refugee resources.
7. Sardar Patel's letter dated 25 July 1948 to Purushottam Bhatt in *Sardar Shree Na* (Ahmedabad: Sardar V. Patel Smarak Bhavan, 1975), 139.
8. Sarah Ansari, *Life after Partition: Migration, Community and Strife in Sindh 1947–1962* (Karachi and Oxford: Oxford University Press, 2005). Also, see: Amar Jaleel. Personal Interview, 3 September 2005 (Karachi, Pakistan).
9. U.T. Thakur, *Sindhi Culture* (New Delhi: Sindhi Academy, 1997), 31.
10. B. Atlani, 'Virhange jo Kahar', in Motilal Jotwani, ed., *Virhango* (Delhi: Sindhi Academy, 1998), 130–131.
11. Baroda State Archives, *Report by Refugee Officer* (*Submitted to the Refugee Minister Baroda, file no. 13*), 11 March 1948.
12. Baroda State Archives, *Letter from Ludimal, Alumal, Tanumal*, 19 January 1949. File no. 13.
13. Baroda State Archives, *Report by Refugee Officer*, File no. 13.
14. Ibid.
15. J. Relwani, *Sindhu Pravaaha* (Ahmedabad: Laxmi Pustak Bhandar, 2002), 67–80.
16. J. Relwani, *Shmane Sindhu Neer* (Ahmedabad: Laxmi Pustak Bhandar, 1996), 177.
17. Chandra Asnani. Personal Interview. 12 January 2004 (Adipur, Kutch, Gujarat).
18. Tahilram Makhijani. Personal Interview. 24 December 2004 (Godhra, Gujarat).
19. Harish Jethmalani. Personal Interview. 27 April 2004 (Vadodara, Gujarat).
20. Kubernagar is Ahmedabad's equivalent of the Ulhasnagar Camp in Kalyan, Maharashtra.
21. Udhavdas Makhija. Personal Interview. 8 September 2002 (Ahmedabad, Gujarat).
22. Anita Raina Thapan, *Sindhi Diaspora: Manila, Hong Kong and Jakarta* (Manila: Anteo De Manila University Press, 2002), 40.
23. Shankarlal Ahuja. Personal Interview. 18 January 2003 (Ahmedabad, Gujarat).
24. Thapan, 131.
25. Bhumika Udernanai. Personal Interview. 31 January 2002 (Ahmedabad, Gujarat).
26. Ibid. Kubernagar and Sardarnagar are erstwhile camps, now turned into townships. Bhumika lives away from such places, in a posh locality in the western part of Ahmedabad.
27. Deepak Bhavnani. Personal Interview. 8 March 2003 (Ahmedabad, Gujarat).
28. Krishna Ahuja. Personal Interview. 7 January 2003 (Ahmedabad, Gujarat).
29. Vidya Tewani. Personal Interview. 1 March 2004 (Ahmedabad, Gujarat).
30. Shankarlal Ahuja. Personal Interview. 18 January 2003 (Ahmedabad, Gujarat).
31. For additional detail, see: Kothari *Burden of Refuge: The Sindhi Hindus of Gujarat* (New Delhi: Orient Blackswan, 2007).

CHAPTER 4

Recreating Sindh: Formations of Sindhi Hindu Guru Movements in New Contexts

STEVEN RAMEY

In 1954, Sufi Sant Dr Rochal Das encouraged Sindhi Hindus in Lucknow to install the Guru Granth Sahib in Kasturbai Nari Shala, the Sindhi Hindu social service centre in Lucknow.[1] This organization provided vocational training and social support for indigent women, mostly Sindhis widowed during Partition. Rochal Das, a Sindhi Hindu disciple of a Muslim Sufi from Sindh, wanted the community to foster spiritual development alongside technical training. The best source of spiritual guidance for them, according to Rochal Das, was the Guru Granth Sahib. The community followed his suggestion by establishing a small room for the Guru Granth Sahib, which they placed under a canopy (as is common in Sikh gurdwaras). They called it the Harmandir, thus connecting it with the Harmandir (Golden Temple) in Amritsar, Punjab.

Over the next few decades, this little room became a focal point for the Sindhi Hindu community in Lucknow. Because community functions had outgrown the small room that housed the Guru Granth Sahib, another Sindhi guru—Dada J.P. Vaswani—laid the foundation stone in 1977 for a separate Harmandir with the Guru Granth Sahib placed in the central shrine. Later, the community added *murtis* [sculptures] of Hindu deities, the Bhagavad Gita, and images of six gurus/sants (including J.P. Vaswani's guru and Rochal Das) to the Harmandir.[2] The development of Rochal Das's initial suggestion into the centrepiece of the Sindhi community of Lucknow clearly demonstrates his recommendation that the Guru Granth Sahib be connected with the community's self-understanding and heritage. It also illustrates the nature of Sindhi Hindu traditions that place the Guru Granth Sahib—as well as a variety of Sufis and gurus—in central positions along with deities and sacred texts commonly recognized as Hindu.

Maintaining that heritage presents a serious challenge for contemporary Sindhi Hindus. Although many Sindhis have asserted to me that the Guru Granth Sahib, Sufi *fakirs*, and various deities all fit within the boundaries of Hinduism, many non-Sindhis demur. The dominant understandings in India and other parts of the globe associate these elements with three distinct religions, Sikhism, Islam, and Hinduism. Following Partition, when the region of Sindh became a province of Pakistan, many Sindhi Hindus immigrated to India and other places around the globe and immersed themselves in societies that rejected Sindhi understandings of the boundaries of Hinduism. As Sindhis struggle to re-establish their lives in diaspora, whether in India or elsewhere around the globe, they face the challenge of recreating their regional heritage in an environment where the larger society identifies Sindhi practices as aberrant. A prominent scholar on Sindhi Hindus has even suggested that these challenges will result in the assimilation of Sindhi Hindus into mainstream Hinduism and the diminution of the uniqueness of Sindhi traditions.[3]

As the prominence of Rochal Das and Vaswani in the formation of the Harmandir and the addition of guru/sant images to the institution demonstrate, spiritual teachers remain important in Sindhi Hindu communities. Comparing the development and contemporary form of Sindhi guru movements reveals the vitality and diversity of Sindhi Hindu communities in the face of the challenges of diaspora.[4] Immersed in a non-Sindhi environment, Sindhi Hindus and the various movements in their communities respond to those challenges in a variety of ways. The movements surrounding three Sindhi gurus, Sai Chandu Ram Sahib (whose predecessor, Kanwar Ram, is among the six figures installed in the Harmandir), Rochal Das, and Vaswani represent starkly different formations of Sindhi traditions in diaspora. Therefore, while Sindhi traditions challenge narrow understandings of religions that do not recognize the contestation that surrounds the definition of any religion, they do not comprise a monolithic tradition as Sindhis themselves maintain a range of understandings and practices.

This recreation of Sindhi heritage is a continuing process.[5] In the process of recreating practices, guru movements differ from other organizations that diasporic communities create. While organizations like the Harmandir in Lucknow must respond to various interests among leadership committees, the guru provides authoritative direction for the development of the guru movement. The guru's heritage, spiritual insights, and vision of how to reach followers combine to influence the form of their practices. As each guru has a distinct heritage, insight, and vision, their movements follow different paths that (like all living movements) proceed from their previous traditions. Comparing the hagiographical and didactic literature of each movement to their contemporary practices provides a sense of the progression of each movement within a historical context. While Sindhi temples and other organizations likewise develop in diverse ways, these guru movements highlight particularly well the different choices that Sindhis make in diaspora. These three different paths, moreover, do not exhaust the variety within these specific movements. The followers of each guru, despite their deep commitment to the movement and its influence on them, have the capacity to create their own emphases that differ from the official guru movement since they balance their particular background and individual experiences as part of a diasporic minority with their commitment and respect to their guru. As sociological theory has emphasized more fully in the past two decades, the forms of the guru movements are not deterministic for the practices of the followers, whose potential capacity for agency always remains present.[6]

Beyond providing historical context and an understanding of diversity among the movements, the written and oral representations of each movement reveal additional aspects of the challenges that Sindhis face. The gurus and their followers must represent their traditions to sceptical neighbours who draw boundaries separating the elements common to Sindhi traditions. The different ways that each movement explains Sindhi traditions and their own recreation of practices reveal further their understanding of themselves and their negotiation of issues in diaspora. This process of communication also faces the challenges surrounding language, as some of the vocabulary that Sindhis use to explain their traditions (especially terms derived from Sufi traditions) have different connotations to Sindhis than they have to non-Sindhis who are familiar with the religions of South Asia. The trauma of Partition and related strife has also influenced these representations, which reveal discontinuities between contemporary attitudes among some Sindhis and their idealized images of pre-Partition Sindh and their guru lineages. The variations that exist between and within the guru movements are a testament to both the vitality among Sindhi Hindus and the challenges that they face in diaspora.

DUAL FOCI: SAI CHANDU RAM SAHIB'S MOVEMENT

Chandu Ram was born in the village of Panno Akil, Sindh, in 1947 as the son of a Sindhi Hindu guru known as Asuda Ram. While many Sindhi Hindus left Sindh in the years following Partition, Chandu Ram remained with his father and many of his father's devotees. After his father's death in 1960, Chandu Ram stayed in Panno Akil. He continued to serve at his father's *Samadhi* [shrine commemorating cremation] while travelling, like his father had, to visit followers who had immigrated to India. In 1977, almost two decades after his father's death, Chandu Ram migrated to India and selected Lucknow as the location to build a new centre, which he named the Shiv Shanti Ashram. In his new home, Chandu Ram began the process of creating Sindhi traditions in a different environment, much as many Sindhi Hindus had been doing since Partition.

In the ashram's complex of buildings, Chandu Ram's movement conducts a vibrant array of activities. Followers come from other parts of India and from Sindh to serve in the ashram and sit at the feet of their guru. Besides *satsangs* [gatherings of devotees] every morning and evening, the community in 2002 provided housing for destitute women, sponsored a weekly free homeopathic clinic and an annual free eye clinic, established a cow shelter, and provided marriage arrangements for poor families among other charitable programmes. Leaders in the movement frequently connected these charitable activities to the example of Asuda Ram and his gurus, Kanwar Ram and Satram Das.

The community also emphasizes a range of ritual activities at the ashram, including the celebration of various festivals in addition to daily *satsangs*. These rituals perform the dual foci of the ashram, honouring both the Guru Granth Sahib and the lineage of gurus in which Chandu Ram is the living master. Perhaps the largest festival at the ashram is the *urs* commemorating the death of Asuda Ram, Chandu Ram's guru and father. The festival in 2001 involved much devotional music, an *akhand path* [continuous reading] of the Guru Granth Sahib, and teachings from Chandu Ram and other spiritual figures who visited the ashram for the occasion.

At the conclusion of the *akhand path* on the climactic evening of the three-day festival, one of the visiting gurus walked across the stage to a canopy containing the Guru Granth Sahib and presented a cloth to the sacred text. While devotees continued chanting '*Saccho Saccho Ram Hai* [Ram is Truth]', others on the stage began passing brocaded cloths to the guru as offerings to be placed on the honoured text. After these cloths had been presented, devotees in the audience began to line up to offer cloths to the Guru Granth Sahib as well. Later that night, devotees lined up for a second time. Instead of expressing devotion to the Guru Granth Sahib, the lines took devotees forward to have a brief audience with Chandu Ram and the visiting gurus and Sufis. The response of devotees during these two parts of the festival demonstrated the depth of their devotion to both the Guru Granth Sahib and their living guru Chandu Ram.

In the ashram's *satsang* hall, where the daily gatherings occur, the dual foci were evident when I visited as the end of the hall was divided into two shrines. The smaller of the two shrines honoured Chandu Ram's lineage with a painting of Asuda Ram in the centre and paintings of Kanwar Ram and Satram Das, Asuda Ram's two gurus, on either side. In the centre of the larger shrine was a canopy divided into three sections, each containing a copy of the Guru Granth Sahib; one in Gurmukhi, one in Hindi, and one in Sindhi. A smaller canopy along the side of the larger shrine contained the writings of other Sindhi gurus, including J.P. Vaswani's predecessor Sadhu T.L. Vaswani.

During the *satsangs* themselves, the focus of devotional activities shifted between Chandu Ram and the Guru Granth Sahib. Chandu Ram sat on a divan on the main floor of the *satsang* hall, with devotees continually approaching him to touch his feet, offer him sweets, and receive his advice and blessings. Whenever devotees arrived they typically bowed before Chandu Ram and then entered the larger shrine to pay obeisance to the Guru Granth Sahib, though some only venerated one or the other of these two foci. Several devotees venerated the smaller shrine also as a second representation of Chandu Ram's lineage.

The attention of devotees during the rituals also shifted between Chandu Ram and the Guru Granth Sahib. At the start of one evening *satsang* in February 2002, devotees faced Chandu Ram as he led the recitations of *Rehrasi* [evening hymns/prayer] and *Ardas* [requests] (both related to the Guru Granth Sahib), which most people knew from memory. The ashram's version of *Ardas* listed the ten Sikh gurus and various elements of Sikh traditions but eliminated references to the Khalsa that are typical in *Ardas* at Khalsa Sikh gurdwaras. With devotees still turned towards Chandu Ram, musicians started singing '*Jaya Jagadish Hare*' [Victory to Hari, Lord of the Universe]. Though ritualized activities at most Hindu temples dictate that devotees stand and wave lamps before *murtis* during this song, no one stood or waved a lamp. Several musicians led the community in singing a composition by Sami (a Sindhi Hindu poet saint), several *bhajans* devoted to Hindu deities, and a devotional song focusing on Sikh gurus with the refrain, '*Waheguru, Waheguru, Waheguru*' [splendid guru]. The intensity of the group's singing increased with each subsequent song.

After the devotional songs, everyone, including Chandu Ram, faced the Guru Granth Sahib for *arti* [ritualized offerings of devotion], which involved singing a different devotional song and honouring the texts and images in the shrine by waving an oil lamp. One leader of the ashram then sat behind the Gurmukhi Guru Granth Sahib and read a portion, while other men closed and properly wrapped the other Guru Granth Sahibs and two of the texts that were housed in the second canopy. During the reading, Chandu Ram repeatedly corrected the pronunciation and commented on the verses. Another leader then read from the Nuri Granth of T.L. Vaswani that was also housed in the second canopy (with similar commentary from Chandu Ram). When the readings from the two texts were complete and all of the texts were closed and wrapped, everyone stood, and the main reader faced the central canopy and recited the concluding *Ardas*. Afterwards, most devotees turned their attention back to Chandu Ram, who lingered for a moment to bless devotees and receive gifts from them that he passed on to others.

Beyond devotees shifting their attention between Chandu Ram and the Guru Granth Sahib, the way that the readings were conducted reinforced the dual foci of the ashram. Chandu Ram's interruptions to correct the readers revealed his respect for the texts, as he knew them well and wanted to ensure their proper recitation. This deep commitment was not something new to Chandu Ram and his lineage. Asuda Ram's guru, Kanwar Ram, learned Gurmukhi and passages from the Guru Granth Sahib and other Sikh recitations.[7] The biographer of Asuda Ram describes Asuda Ram's daily routine as including the circumambulation of the Guru Granth Sahib and recitation of its poetry.[8] However, these interruptions, including Chandu Ram's insertion of his own commentary, also demonstrated his priority over the texts. Although he turned to face the Guru Granth Sahib at this stage of the *satsang*, he maintained the final authority over the progress of the *satsang* and could interrupt or pre-empt any activity.

The relationship between the Guru Granth Sahib and other elements in the movement has shifted significantly. At the ashram in Lucknow, the three copies of the Guru Granth Sahib were not originally together in the central canopy. The Bhagavad Gita and Ramcharitmanas (which Chandu

Ram had studied as a child along with the Guru Granth Sahib) had been enshrined in the main canopy on the right and left of the Gurmukhi Guru Granth Sahib.[9] In early 2001, Chandu Ram decided to replace the Gita and Ramcharitmanas with translations of the Guru Granth Sahib in Hindi and Sindhi. The Gita and Ramcharitmanas were placed in a cabinet, where they could be used when desired. However, they no longer received the honoured treatment that the community accorded to the texts in the canopies. Explaining the changes, one volunteer leader in the ashram solely attributed it to Chandu Ram's directive. He then justified the change by asserting: 'Our base is the Guru Granth Sahib'. Whatever the explanation, the change removed any doubt that the Guru Granth Sahib was the sole text that, along with the lineage of gurus that Chandu Ram embodied, remained central at the ashram.

The changing of the enshrined texts reveals several aspects of the formation of traditions at the ashram beyond Chandu Ram's position of authority. First of all, the selection of Hindi and Sindhi translations is significant. Chandu Ram clearly wanted to maintain a connection to the Sindhi language, but he also recognized the dynamics of living in a Hindi speaking region, where businesspeople, professionals, and students all must be fluent in Hindi to succeed. Second, the switching of the texts challenges some common assumptions about Sindhis in diaspora. While the political tensions between Sikhs and Hindus in the 1980s pushed some Sindhi Hindus away from gurdwaras, the example of the texts in the ashram demonstrates that the experience of diaspora has not resulted in the wholesale homogenization of Sindhi Hindus into mainstream Hinduism as some scholars and many Sindhis have feared.[10] Third, this selection also clearly differentiates the ashram's formation from the understandings of Khalsa Sikhs in that Khalsa Sikhs typically do not recognize translations of the Guru Granth Sahib as being sacred texts alongside the traditional Gurmukhi version.

The treatment of the three texts composed by other Sindhi gurus, including Vaswani's Nuri Granth, demonstrated another unique component of Sindhi traditions at the ashram. Placing each text in a canopy with the proper ritualized actions, such as the formal opening and closing of the texts every day, raised the status of the Sindhi Hindu granths (and previously the Gita and Ramcharitmanas) to a level similar to the Guru Granth Sahib and thus diverged from the sole emphasis on the Guru Granth Sahib in Khalsa Sikh practices. Nevertheless, some distinctions remained between the Guru Granth Sahib and the other granths. Most of those who approached the main shrine gave greater reverence to the Guru Granth Sahib. I never observed an individual sit behind one of the side texts to read it silently, like some devotees did with the Guru Granth Sahib. Similarly, at the end of the *satsang*, the man who led the final *Ardas* faced the Guru Granth Sahibs and bowed before them with no consideration given to the texts in the side canopy. Therefore, the community maintained a hierarchy between the Guru Granth Sahib and the writings of other gurus despite raising those texts to a status close to that of the Guru Granth Sahib.

The increasing emphasis on the Guru Granth Sahib did not mean that other aspects of Sindhi traditions were neglected within Chandu Ram's movement. An *Om* [symbol representing the sacred syllable in Sanskrit] in raised brass adorned the top of each section of the central canopy, emphasizing the Hindu identification directly above each copy of the Guru Granth Sahib. Each section of the canopy also revealed the previous arrangement of texts, with raised brass letters under each Om praising Krishna, Nanak, and Rama, respectively. Similarly, three framed and garlanded paintings rested against the base of this canopy, Radha-Krishna on the left section, Nanak in the middle, and Ram, Sita, Lakshman and Hanuman on the right section. Other images of deities, including Shiva, Jhuley Lal, and Durga, were displayed both in the shrines and on the exterior of the main building.

The festivals celebrated in the ashram further demonstrate the continued importance of Hindu deities and rituals despite the increasing importance of the Guru Granth Sahib. In addition to the *urs* for Asuda Ram, the community holds significant events for Nanak Jayanti, Ramnaumi, and the Sindhi Hindu festival of Cheti Chand (which focuses on the Sindhi deity Jhuley Lal). In 2002, the festival of Cheti Chand coincided with commemorations of the birthdays of Kanwar Ram and Teoon Ram (another Sindhi guru). In addition to processions displaying images of Kanwar Ram, Asuda Ram and Jhuley Lal, the ashram commemorated Cheti Chand with a mass *Upanayana* [ritual investiture of the sacred thread for boys], organized for families who could not afford to conduct the ritual themselves.

Chandu Ram's recreation of Sindhi traditions in Lucknow also maintains a different connection to the land of Sindh than most diasporic Sindhis, including Rochal Das and J.P. Vaswani. While most Sindhi Hindus emphasize the difficulties of visiting Sindh, and few have actually made the trek, Chandu Ram and his followers maintain consistent connections across what is now an international border. Because of his three decades in Sindh following Partition, Chandu Ram maintains a larger following in Sindh than many Sindhi gurus in diaspora. Except when conflicts between India and Pakistan close the border, these followers often visit the ashram in Lucknow. Chandu Ram also makes trips to Sindh, as well as to other centres around India, when he is not maintaining a vow of solitude.

These connections make Chandu Ram's movement uniquely trans-national. Unlike most trans-national religions that conjure images of wealthy devotees flying around the world to connect with their guru, Chandu Ram's devotees in Sindh are not particularly affluent and the ashram provides housing for visitors and assists them with the necessary documents for Pakistani citizens to visit India. This trans-national component, rather than connecting Chandu Ram to Europe and America, keeps Chandu Ram grounded in the land of Sindh and the *Samadhi* of his father. While most diasporic groups must negotiate the memory of their ancestral land and the diasporic context, the physical contact that Chandu Ram maintains gives those memories a more tangible character. However, the contacts exist with a region that itself has not remained static like diasporic memories tend to do. He also continues to emphasize the Sindhi language to a degree that other gurus do not, a decision compounded by this continued connection to people in Sindh.

Hagiographical Representations

The hagiographies of Chandu Ram's lineage reflect the harmony that the lineage emphasized and some of the tensions that many Sindhis have experienced between that harmony and the traumatic nature of Sindhi experiences of Partition. Leaders at the ashram gave me two books about the lineage. Dr S.K. Punshi, a Sindhi dermatologist in Maharashtra, published an English biography of Kanwar Ram in 1985. The ashram published the Hindi biography of Asuda Ram, entitled *Jeevan Darshan* [View of Life]. The volume provides no date of publication but, based on some of the information it contains, was clearly produced sometime between the late 1990s and 2001 (when I received a copy of it).

Like many other Sindhi Hindus, Punshi, in his account of Kanwar Ram's life, represents Sindh in general as a land of communal harmony: 'Hindus Muslims lives [*sic*] as brothers, with friendship, and respect, affection and love for each other'.[11] However, the biography also reveals a tension between that harmony and communalism, both in Sindhi history and in Punshi's self-understanding. While Punshi praises Kanwar Ram for his respect for all Sindhi religious communities, he implies the superiority of the Hindu community and reveals some bitterness against Muslims.

According to Punshi, Kanwar Ram (like most saints) was beyond the communal divisions that have troubled South Asian society. After declaring Kanwar Ram a 'true saint in the real sense of the word', Punshi asserts, 'Saints proper do not belong to any religion. They belong to humanity and the welfare of humanity has been their goal'.[12] Throughout the biography, Punshi reiterates that Kanwar Ram had Muslim as well as Hindu followers. He even suggests that Kanwar Ram's followers asked him why he served Muslims more than 'the people of your own caste and others'.[13] Such a declaration suggests a sense of competition between Kanwar Ram's followers and 'Muslims'. However, the reference to caste, rather than a parallel religious identification makes it less clear whether that competition reflected ethnic and social distinctions or differences in belief and practice.

Punshi also discusses the breadth of Kanwar Ram's activities. He writes: 'He would sing song of Lord Krishna, Lord Rama, Guru Nanak, Kabir, Farid, Ravidas, Shah Sachal, Sami, Rohal and others even he would sing the songs in praise of Martyrdom of Hasan and Hussain'.[14] Punshi earlier had identified Shah and Sachal as Sufis and Sami as a Hindu.[15] In a chapter titled 'Communal Harmony', Punshi further emphasizes the extent of Kanwar Ram's acceptance of Muslims by asserting, 'Such was the greatness of Kanwar he even went to the *Mazar* (Sufi shrine) and tombs of Muslim *Pirs* and *Fakirs* with due respect so Kanwar was also great Sufi Saint'.[16]

Despite this emphasis on harmony, Kanwar Ram, according to Punshi, maintained a Hindu identification. For example, Punshi relates Kanwar Ram's investiture with a sacred thread and specifically emphasizes how that ritual 'is a must for a Hindu'.[17] However, as a Sindhi Hindu, this identification did not preclude the veneration of the Guru Granth Sahib. In fact, following Kanwar Ram's death, according to Punshi, he was cremated 'with Vedic mantras' and his ashes were 'submitted to the bed of Mother Ganga—the holy river of Hindus' (after the ashes were bathed in both the Indus River and the tank at the Harmandir in Amritsar).[18]

In contrast to the trope of harmony, Punshi emphasizes a communal identification as he praises Hindu and Sindhi culture throughout the biography. In the first chapter, he quotes portions of the Rig Veda that praise the Sindhu River, and then refers to the 'darkest day in the History of Sindh' when Mohammad bin Qasim defeated the 'great Hindu warrior' [presumably Raja Dahir], thus spreading Islam in 'the nook and corner of the pious and holy land of the Vedas'.[19]

This tension between praising communal harmony and emphasizing Hindu superiority is clearest in Punshi's account of the murder of Kanwar Ram. In 1939, the followers of a Muslim *pir* murdered Kanwar Ram after the *pir's* son had been attacked, presumably by Hindus. Punshi declares that the *pir* was 'fanatic and bigoted' and 'openly incited the Muslims against the Hindus' (although Punshi never addresses the identification of those who attacked the *pir's* son, whom the *pir* understood to be Hindu).[20] Discussing the murder, Punshi uses motifs of the Battle of Karbala [when Prophet Muhammad's grandson was martyred in 681] and the justice of the Prophet to demonstrate that Kanwar Ram was unjustly attacked. By associating Kanwar Ram with central figures in Islam, he implies that the *pir* and his followers failed to follow Islam fully.[21]

The quotes Punshi included in the text also diverge from the trope of harmony. Despite Kanwar Ram's appreciation of the Guru Grant Sahib, sixteen of the approximately 50 quotations in the book come from the Bhagavad Gita. The remaining sources include the Vedas, European and American authors, Indian religious leaders, and the Gospel of Matthew. The absence of quotes from Sikh gurus and Sufi Muslims ironically disregards Kanwar Ram's anti-communal sensibilities that Punshi otherwise praises. Punshi's biography of Kanwar Ram therefore reinforces some of the tensions within the Sindhi Hindu community between communal harmony and the superiority of Hindus, particularly in relation to Muslims. Their losses during Partition and the communal context of North India remain in tension with the communal harmony of Sindh that many Sindhis idealize. Such feelings complicate the formation of traditions in Chandu Ram's movement, as well as other Sindhi Hindu movements.

Addressing readers in the diasporic context of North India, Pursvani's Hindi biography of Asuda Ram maintains the clear Hindu identification that Punshi assumes. Nevertheless, it more carefully reflects the inclusion of the Guru Granth Sahib and occasionally Sufis that the rituals at the ashram incorporated. Pursvani's insertion of poetic material into the book, for example, more clearly reflects Sindhi Hindu traditions than Punshi's quotations did. Pursvani's selections come almost entirely from Indian, and often Sindhi, religious figures or texts. Based on Pursvani's direct attribution of about half of these quotes, the Guru Granth Sahib appears most often with the Bhagavad Gita and the Ramayana slightly less frequently. Pursvani also incorporates verses from a range of poets, such as Meera, Tulsidas, and Sami who are commonly identified as Hindu, and Islamic Sufi figures—including Shah Abdul Latif, Sachal, and Bulle Shah.

Throughout the biography, Pursvani assumes that his readers (as well as Asuda Ram and his lineage) identify as Hindus. Most directly, in a chapter tellingly titled '*Gao Seva*' [Cow Service], Pursvani explicitly connected respect for cows to Hindu traditions and then admonishes his readers, '*Aj ham gauon ke prati apane karttavya se vimukh ho cuke hain*' [Today we fall short being indifferent towards our duties towards cows].[22] His use of the plural first person explicitly connects Pursvani and his readers together as Hindus.

Despite this Hindu identification, Arabic terms appear in the biography, reflecting the Sindhi adaptation of Arabic. In several lists of holy figures, Pursvani includes *fakir* and *dervish* as separate terms from *sant*, implying a distinction that might relate to an Islamic heritage.[23] However, Pursvani does not use the terms consistently throughout the text so he may not intend to connote a clear communal identification. When discussing love, Pursvani also interchanges Hindi terms derived from Sanskrit with Arabic terms. When describing Asuda Ram's desire for Satram Das, Pursvani uses various terms for love; '*Prananath*' and '*Mahbub*' (from Sanskrit and Arabic respectively) in one section.[24] Pursvani also refers to Asuda Ram as an '*Ashiq*' (another Arabic term for a lover) because of his extreme devotion to Satram Das, Kanwar Ram, and the divine being.[25] In another section, Pursvani includes a poem from Sachal Sarmast, a Sindhi Muslim Sufi, in which Sachal uses '*Muhabbat*', an Arabic derived term for love to describe an unbreakable desire for the divine.[26] In the next paragraph, Pursvani builds on the ideas of Sachal by using '*Prem*' repeatedly for love.[27] This exchange reflects the interchangeable nature of the Arabic and Sanskrit derived terms for Pursvani. The Sindhi acceptance of Islamic Sufi masters and their poetry immersed Sindhis in such Arabic-derived vocabulary of Sufis.

While both hagiographical sources emphasize Hindu-Muslim unity as an ideal element of Sindhi culture, and support that ideal with references to the relationships between this lineage and Muslim Sufis, they illustrate two compounding challenges that Sindhis face as they form traditions outside of Sindh. In contrast to the ideal of harmony, Punshi expresses the estrangement of Sindhi Hindus from Muslims following the events surrounding Partition as he specifically emphasizes the superiority of the Hindu community. Pursvani's acceptance of the multiple strands of Sindhi traditions seems sincere but demonstrates the challenge of language in diaspora. The terms that he uses in his Hindi text reflect the significance of Sufis and Arabic in Sindhi culture, but non-Sindhis in North India often associate those terms specifically with non-Hindu traditions. The use of such terms reinforces doubts among some non-Sindhis about the identification of Sindhis as Hindus and conflicted feelings among Sindhi Hindus such as Pursvani about Muslims.

Contemporary Descriptions

Personal representations of Chandu Ram's movement and its formation of practices reveal challenges similar to the issues that the hagiographical accounts raise. Being immersed in a culture with different understandings of the boundaries defining religions and different associations with particular labels, Chandu Ram and his followers must explain and defend their practices. In the process, they reveal their own difficulties with the traditions that they have formed.

The increased centrality of the Guru Granth Sahib forced Chandu Ram's followers to defend its significance in the movement. In one interview, N. Ahuja (a young Sindhi man who served Chandu Ram in the ashram) confidently switched roles to make a point about the Guru Granth Sahib. When he asked me, 'What is the meaning of Sikh?', I referred to the outer symbols of the Khalsa. He looked chagrined and asserted that 'sikh' means disciple, that the first nine gurus were Hindus, and that the tenth guru was also a Hindu. He continued vigorously: 'The tenth guru restarted the Khalsa Panth; before that it was Hindu. Therefore, the Guru Granth Sahib, the Adi Granth is related to Hindus. If Sikhs say, "This is ours", they are wrong. If a Hindu says that it is not Hindu, they are wrong'. Ahuja's confidence in raising the definition of Sikh suggests that this question was prominent in his experiences. It also reflects his vehemence in asserting that Sikhs and Hindus who disagree are 'wrong' and suggests that he, or the community as a whole, had faced opposition from both Sikhs and Hindus concerning the inclusion of the Guru Granth Sahib in their activities.

With the tension in the tradition surrounding connections to Islam and the term Sufi, which some of Chandu Ram's followers used to identify him, I began asking leaders in the movement about the meaning of that term. A volunteer leader at the ashram identified various Hindu, Sikh, and Muslim holy figures as saints whom they followed but deferred to his guru when I asked about the term Sufi. At my request, he asked Chandu Ram about the meaning of 'Sufi saint' during one of Chandu Ram's brief daily audiences. (Chandu Ram had limited contact with people outside of the *satsangs* due to his practice of solitude.) Chandu Ram began his explanation with a reference to *Sanatan Dharm*, which, he explained, came from the Vedas and Shastras. *Sanatan Dharm* focused on the *murtis* of deities and ranged from very deep spiritual concepts to very easy practices. These preliminary statements clearly emphasized Chandu Ram's association with Hindu traditions that non-Sindhis would recognize.

However, as he continued, he revealed some of the tensions within Sindhi self-perceptions. Sufism, according to Chandu Ram, was separate from *Sanatan Dharm*, which he described as attaining a direct connection to God through the guidance of a guru. Chandu Ram then characterized Sufis as having '*Allah ka ishq*, [love of God (Allah)]'. His use of Arabic terms for both love and God, specifically in relation to Sufis, implied that Sufism derived from Islamic origins and reinforced his assertion that Sufism differed from *Sanatan Dharm*. As he concluded, however, he added that he and his followers were also Sufis in some ways, although following a *Sanatan Dharm* form. His descriptions clearly diverged from the discourse of Hindutva which recognizes Sufism as an Indian tradition separate from Islam. Instead, he implicitly connected Sufism with an Islamic heritage while also using the term as a sign of a person's deep religious commitment that extends beyond any specific religion. In practice, this conception meant that the activities at the ashram occasionally incorporated a few Sindhi Muslim Sufis but more frequently honoured non-Muslims who maintained '*Allah ka ishq*, [love of God (Allah)]'.

When I also asked Ahuja what the term Sufi meant, he became flustered: 'Sufi means those saints, or you can say Arabic saint. Muslims say that Sufi, I can't explain this word. Sufi means those who love god, their girlfriend or boyfriend is god'. In his answer he attempted to explain the term three times, stopping whenever he began to associate Sufis with Islam, as in his reference to Arabic and then to Muslims. His restatements reveal the connection between Sufism and Islam within his world-view and his reluctance to associate his guru with Islam. Such discomfort demonstrated the implications of the prominent definitions in Lucknow and perhaps, some animosity similar to Punshi's feelings. His final reference to love, as it coincided with some of Chandu Ram's teachings, suggested that he had heard Chandu Ram's definitions before I raised the issue, even though he had not fully internalized it.

Ahuja attempted another explanation of Sufism that same evening. He asserted: 'In Sindh, Sufi saints, they were Sindhi by religion'. He concluded his statements with the assertion that the saints were beyond definition. Highlighting their regional identification as opposed to any religious identification, Ahuja reiterated another common Sindhi explanation. Sindhi Sufis differed from Muslim saints from other places so defining them as Muslim was incorrect. Nevertheless, Ahuja implied the connection to Islam in the same conversation as he used Arabic-derived terms, such as '*kalam*' and '*ghazal*', for the teachings of Sindhi Sufis.

Chandu Ram's movement illustrates several of the difficulties that Sindhis face in diaspora. Developing rituals in a new context requires choices between elements of their heritage and the dominant ethos of the surrounding community. Chandu Ram has established a centre that honours his lineage, the Guru Granth Sahib, Sufis, and Hindu deities along with increasing emphasis on two primary centres of sacredness, the guru lineage which Chandu Ram himself continues, and the Guru Granth Sahib. Because the majority community among whom the Sindhis live do not recognize all of these elements as Hindu, Chandu Ram and his followers must defend these practices as appropriately Hindu. Moreover, the influence of Muslim Sufis on the language of the movement and Chandu Ram's continued identification as a Sufi 'in a Sanatan way' creates internal tensions for some Sindhis because of their animosity towards Muslims, especially following the inter-religious trauma of Partition and the continuing Hindu-Muslim tensions in India. However, these choices and challenges represent only one aspect of Sindhi Hindu traditions as other guru movements respond to these issues differently.

HINDU SUFIS: SUFI SANT DR ROCHAL DAS' MOVEMENT

Although Rochal Das suggested the installation of the Guru Granth Sahib in the Harmandir in Lucknow, that text is not as prominent in Rochal Das's movement as in Chandu Ram's movement. While Rochal Das's movement faces some of the same issues of labels and terminology in diaspora, their responses to those challenges and their formation of Sindhi traditions have differed considerably. Rochal Das's title itself demonstrates this difference. While some of Chandu Ram's followers referred to him as a Sufi, the title for Rochal Das within the larger Sindhi community is consistently rendered as 'Sufi Sant' in both English and Hindi. This terminology highlights his connection to Sufism while suggesting a relationship to the North Indian poet-saints—such as Nanak and Kabir—commonly referred to as *sant* movements. The practices and teachings of Rochal Das and his successors maintain both a Hindu identification and an acceptance of Islamic Sufi principles, thus moving in a different direction than Chandu Ram's movement.

Although Rochal Das identified himself as a Hindu, not a Muslim, he took initiation into the Jahaniyan lineage through his Sufi master, Qutab Ali Shah. Various works discussing Rochal Das's life highlight this Islamic lineage. S. Gajwani, a follower of Rochal Das, titled his book about the lineage *A Sufi Galaxy*. Gajwani traces Qutab Ali Shah's Jahaniyan Sufi lineage back to Jalaluddin Hussain and his grandfather Jalal Surkh Bukhari, who 'belonged to the sixteenth generation after Hazrat Ali,' the son-in-law of Prophet Muhammad.[28] Qutab Ali Shah himself was born in Hyderabad, Sindh in 1810. He emphasized *ishq haqiqi,* the Sufi concept of 'Divine love', and recited *kalam* primarily in Sindhi (although he frequently used Persian, Hindi, and Sanskrit terms in his poetry).[29]

Adopting an inclusive philosophy, Qutab Ali Shah did not view his Islamic heritage as a barrier to other traditions. He practiced yoga (occasionally even in a Hindu goddess temple) and placed special emphasis on *pranayama* [breath control].[30] Both Gajwani and Rochal Das's son and successor, R.M. Hari, identify several 'Hindu scriptures' that Qutab Ali Shah enjoyed hearing: the Bhagavad Gita, Japa ji and Sukhmani Sahib.[31] The inclusion of Japa ji and Sukhmani Sahib, which are commonly related to Sikh traditions as 'Hindu scriptures', demonstrates a Sindhi understanding of Sikhism as a branch within Hinduism (as stated within Chandu Ram's movement). Qutab Ali Shah also accepted Hindu followers and provided separate housing and eating arrangements for them to accommodate their different dietary practices.[32]

Rochal Das met Qutab Ali Shah while Rochal Das was completing his training to become a homeopathic doctor in Hyderabad, Sindh. According to the tradition, the guru of Rochal Das's eldest brother appeared to Rochal Das in a vision to encourage him to take initiation from Qutab Ali Shah.[33] With Qutab Ali Shah's inclusiveness, Rochal Das did not need to change his Hindu identification or reject Hindu texts or practices when he took initiation. Throughout his life, Rochal Das taught about the Bhagavad Gita and the Guru Granth Sahib among other texts. Moreover, when Rochal Das died in 1957 his followers cremated his body, thus further confirming his Hindu identification.[34]

Nevertheless, Rochal Das clearly exhibited the influence of his master's Islamic heritage. Rochal Das followed the Sufi practices and terminology of annihilating the self through concentrating on various figures. Rochal Das used the term '*fana-fi-al-Sheikh* [absorption in the master]' for his experience of merging into his master Qutab Ali Shah. Following Qutab Ali Shah's encouragement to strive for absorption in various religious figures, Rochal Das described his experience of '*fana-fi-al-Rasool* [absorption in the prophet]' as including merging with Nanak, Krishna, Ram, Buddha, Jesus, and Muhammad.[35] For the final two stages, Rochal Das used Vedantic concepts and described the process as 'the jiva becomes the Self' along with the traditional Sufi terms '*fana-fi-Allah* [absorption in god]' and '*baqa-ba-Allah* [merging with god]'.[36]

After the upheavals of Partition, Rochal Das and his successors (his son and grandson) established an ashram in Ulhasnagar, a major Sindhi settlement outside Mumbai. In Ulhasnagar, they continued to follow a range of practices, including reciting the *kalams* of Sindhi Sufis and passages from the Guru Granth Sahib, Bhagavad Gita, and other texts.[37] Their celebration of holidays such as *Janmasthami* [the birthday of Krishna] revealed the connections Rochal Das saw between Sufism and Hinduism. During a discussion about Krishna as a figure of divine love on Janmasthami in 1954, Rochal Das repeatedly used the Arabic term *ishq* for love and instructed musicians to sing the poetry of Muslim Sufis such as Sachal and Bedil.[38]

The veneration of Rochal Das's Sufi heritage increased after Partition. In 1957, a follower of Rochal Das had a dream in which Qalandar Lal Shahbaz, a Sufi from twelfth century Sindh, declared: 'You have forgotten me but I continue to look after you'.[39] Qalandar Lal Shahbaz then directed them to celebrate Lal Shahbaz's *urs* in Ulhasnagar as it is celebrated at his tomb in Sehwan, Sindh.[40] When Rochal Das discussed Lal Shahbaz with his followers, the stories included Imam Hussain foretelling Lal Shahbaz's birth, Lal Shahbaz memorizing the Quran and Lal Shahbaz's observance of Ramadan thus placing Lal Shahbaz within an unambiguously Islamic heritage.[41] Rochal Das proceeded to identify himself and his followers as the 'spiritual progeny' and 'the great-grandchildren of Qalandar Lal Shahbaz'.[42] When Rochal Das was on his deathbed a few months later, he placed each of his followers in the care of Qalandar Lal Shahbaz.[43] Two year after Rochal Das's death, his followers began commemorating the *urs* of Lal Shahbaz in Ulhasnagar.[44] In title and in practice, the Sufi component of Rochal Das's background continues to be prominent after resettling in India.

Literature in Rochal Das's Movement

The literature that Rochal Das's successors have published retains much of his inclusive philosophy. According to translations of various discourses that Rochal Das gave at the ashram in Ulhasnagar between 1952 and his death, Rochal Das used concepts and terms typically associated with Hindu, Sikh, and Sufi traditions interchangeably. For example, in explaining a quote from Nanak's composition Sukhmani Sahib, Rochal Das said: 'Better if a jiva remembers Allah than his own name.'[45] A moment later, he connected the Sanskrit term '*ananda*' with Allah by saying: 'The entire creation seeks ananda (bliss). Human beings, birds, beasts, plants, etc. want bliss, because Allah permeates everything and Allah is bliss'.[46]

Works that his followers have composed similarly equate terms that non-Sindhis commonly identify with separate religions. Gajwani equates the Arabic terms '*talib* and *murshid* [disciple and master]' with the Sanskrit terms '*shishya* and *satguru* [student and true guru]' and later uses 'satguru' and 'murshid' interchangeably.[47] Hari explicitly equates terms from Vedanta and Sufi traditions. He states that Rochal Das 'attained to the state of Oneness or non-duality which the Sufis call the state of *baqa-ba-Allah* and the Vedantists call the state of *turiya-atit*'.[48]

Hari also presents his own interpretations of texts based on Rochal Das's teachings and in a manner that defends Hindu Sufi practices. In his commentary on the Bhagavad Gita, his primary objective is to demonstrate that Vedanta and Sufism are the same. In bold on the front inner flap of the book jacket Hari declares: 'Truth is one and the same everywhere, at all times, and in all religions, because Truth is that which has no changeableness. The apparent differences between various religions are because of semantic reasons'.[49] Throughout this commentary, Hari places Arabic terms in parentheses after Sanskrit terms to demonstrate their equivalence. Hari uses 'Atma' for the universal form of Krishna and frequently follows it with '(God—Haq)', '(Zaat—Haq)' or '(Allah)'.[50] Explaining the fifteenth chapter of the Gita, he asserts: 'There is nothing excepting Atma (La illaha ill Allah)', thus equating the Islamic profession of faith with this principle in the Gita.[51]

While emphasizing these Arabic terms, Hari repeats the tendency of some Sindhis to broaden Sufism beyond Islam. Hari specifically asserts:

> Sufism is not a cult, or a sect, or a religion, or a school of thought followed by a select few; it is the spirit and the way of life that has influenced the people irrespective of caste, creed and religion.[52]

He continues with the claims that Sindhi literature and folk music are almost entirely 'Sufistic in content' as well as including some Hindus in the list of 'brilliant' Sufis from Sindh.[53]

A Contemporary Disciple

A prominent follower of Rochal Das, Dr V.L. Advani was especially interested in the Sufi component of my research on Sindhi Hindus. His relation to Sufism began before taking initiation from Rochal Das. Advani remembered his morning walks with his paternal grandfather, who took him to pay obeisance to Muslim and Hindu saints in their village in Sindh. Advani recounted his early experiences in our first interview:

> VLA—He [Rochal Das] was a sant, so had lots of spiritual disciples. He was the first homeopath in Sindh, a pioneer in Sindh and, um, I received my inspiration from him to study homeopathy.
>
> SR—How did you hear about Dr Rochal Das?
>
> VLA—He was spiritual guru of my father, belonged to the same birthplace, Rohri, where first homeopathic clinic [was]. He was a disciple of Sufi saint Sayyid Qutab Ali Shah in Hyderabad, Sindh, but because he had medical education in Hyderabad, came in contact with that, what you call, *murshid* or guru. So apart from his charitable homeopathic dispensaries, he was devoted to preach religion and to godly virtues. At his place there was discourse of religious books at 4 o'clock in the morning for about 2 hours, and the evening also. The rest of the time he used to attend patients but without remuneration.

Advani's representation demonstrated the significance of his mentor, who inspired him to practice homeopathy as well as follow his spiritual teachings. Before Partition, Advani had managed one of Rochal Das's homeopathic clinics in Sindh. His use of both 'murshid' and 'guru' in this quote to designate Rochal Das's relationship with Qutab Ali Shah reflects the use of Arabic and Sanskrit-derived terms in the literature about Rochal Das.

Later in the same interview, he described in more detail Rochal Das's teachings and philosophy:

> He had knowledge of Guru Granth Sahib, Gita, Upanishads. He used to explain even a single word of Gita and Guru Granth Sahib in such a minute explanation [that you] can understand relations with God. He was devotee of Islam, Sikhism, Hinduism, used to teach [that] in every religion, one and the same things, how should be one with God. No hatred for Christianity, Muslims, Hinduism, Sikhism. Always remember God in whatever religion you want, the oneness of God. Apart from godly things, he taught how to be helpful with mankind. If you have money or energy, if you have abundance of anything, give to your neighbour or the needy.

These assertions displayed the emphasis on service to humanity and an inclusive philosophy that equated various religions, much as Hari's writings argued. In making that argument, a recognition of the prominent understanding of the distinctiveness of each tradition arises as Advani labels Sikhism and Islam separately from Hinduism.

As he listed texts important to Rochal Das, Advani did not include the Quran or anything specific to Muslim Sufis, even though he listed Islam as a tradition that Rochal Das honoured. The closest that he came to a Sufi text was his assertion that Rochal Das used *bhajans* and *kalams*, which he explicitly connected with Hindus and the followers of the Prophet Muhammad respectively. When I specifically mentioned the Quran in an interview, Advani directly stated that Rochal Das did not use the Quran. Though Sufis frequently use the Quran, Advani's distinction between the Quran and Sufi elements distanced his use of the term 'Sufi' from Islam.

Towards the end of our first interview, Advani explicitly universalized Sufism beyond Islam, much as other Sindhis did:

> Sufi means love. In Hindi we use Prem, Pyar, Mahbub, Ishq. This is the main idea behind Sufism. They say it is only love in Bible. God is love, love is God.

The balance between two Hindi and two Arabic-derived terms subtly highlights the universal nature of love and reflects the Arabic influence on Sindhi Hindu statements that was visible in Pursvani's biography of Asuda Ram. Advani then expanded Sufism's main concept further by invoking Christianity, clearly assuming that I would resonate with the reference to the Bible.

This universalized definition of Sufism became particularly important for representing Rochal Das outside of Sindh. It neutralized the apparent contradiction, based on dominant understandings, of following a Muslim Sufi while remaining Hindu. He also dismissed any difference between Hindu and Muslim saints by asserting: 'The names may change; the intention, motive, purpose are the same'. Apparently responding to concerns from non-Sindhi Hindus about Islamic influence on Sindhi traditions that he had heard from others, he also dismissed the significance of Islamic influences on Sindhi traditions by explaining that it was natural since the majority of the province was Muslim.

On a personal level, Advani reflected broader Sindhi Hindu traditions. In his apartment, he and his wife had created a shrine with the Guru Granth Sahib with photos of Rochal Das, Qutab Ali Shah, and various other gurus and deities. His wife conducted the daily rituals of opening, reading, and closing the Guru Granth Sahib. They were also active at Sindhi Hindu institutions in Lucknow and visited various pilgrimage temples (most recently Tirupati) whenever they travelled to other parts of India. Advani also visited Rochal Das's Samadhi in Ulhasnagar occasionally.

While the term Sufi remained deeply important to Advani, his regular practices and pilgrimages placed as much importance on the Guru Granth Sahib and Hindu temples as Sufi traditions. Being separated from his master's home in Ulhasnagar, Advani connected with other Sindhi Hindu traditions in Lucknow, including Chandu Ram's ashram. Moreover, his family's devotion to Sufis generally did not transfer to non-Sindhi Sufis. Through Advani's experience of diaspora, the universalized definition of Sufism became particularly significant as his ritualized practices incorporated less specifically Islamic Sufi elements than his ancestors and guru did.

The formation of traditions within Rochal Das's movement led in a different direction than the increasing emphasis on the Guru Granth Sahib in Chandu Ram's movement. Islamic Sufi terminology and the Sufi label itself are particularly important in the teachings of Rochal Das and his successors, while other elements in the Sindhi Hindu heritage (including the Guru Granth Sahib and various Hindu texts), remain significant. To maintain this outside of Sindh, their explanations emphasize the equality of religious terminology, the unity of all religions, and the universal definition of Sufism.

COSMOPOLITAN HINDUISM: THE SADHU VASWANI MOVEMENT

In contrast to the centrality of the Guru Granth Sahib and the Sufi label in the previous two movements, the contemporary Vaswani movement has increasingly presented itself as a mainstream Hindu movement with an emphasis on respect for all religions. Much more than Rochal Das and Chandu Ram, the Vaswani movement has become a global Sindhi movement with centres around the world. This trans-national character has taken on a very different form than the trans-nationalism of Chandu Ram and has pushed the movement towards a different formation of Sindhi Hindu heritage by applying the principles of inter-religious harmony and respect to a broader diasporic situation.

The life story of T.L. Vaswani, the founder of the movement, demonstrates both his Sindhi heritage and the influence of elements beyond Sindh. Vaswani was born in Hyderabad, Sindh, in 1879.[54] His mother had instilled in him a respect for the Sikh texts, which becomes evident in his writings about Guru Nanak. As a teacher in Calcutta, he became a disciple of Promothalal Sen, a nephew of Keshub Chandra Sen, which placed him in a non-Sindhi lineage. After he resigned his educational posts, he travelled across Sindh and other parts of India emphasizing spiritual truths from the Gita and other texts while also supporting Indian nationalism. In his travels, he visited numerous shrines associated with Hinduism and Islam and spoke before various religious organizations, including groups identified as Hindu, Muslim, Parsi, Sikh, and Jain. In contrast to Chandu Ram's almost exclusive emphasis on Sindhi, T.L. Vaswani, with his experiences outside Sindh even before Partition, wrote numerous books in Hindi and English as well as Sindhi. Many of these draw on the teachings and examples of figures such as Shah Abdul Latif, Nanak, and Meera.

His successor, J.P. Vaswani, was born in 1918 in Hyderabad, Sindh. His father, who was T.L. Vaswani's elder brother, revered Sindhi and Persian Sufi poets. In his early twenties, J.P. Vaswani completed a Masters degree in Physics and then immediately forsook a career in education to devote himself fully to his uncle. Both of the Vaswanis moved to Pune following Partition and established the Sadhu Vaswani Mission there. Since T.L. Vaswani died in 1966, J.P. Vaswani has led the movement as it has expanded, developing centres around the world and significant charitable activities centred in Pune.[55] J.P. Vaswani's experiences with his parents and his uncle, as well as his education and international travels, fostered his familiarity with and respect for wisdom from a wide range of sources.

Despite this common Sindhi heritage of veneration of Sufis, the Guru Granth Sahib, and Hindu deities, the form of the Vaswani movement at the turn of this century primarily emphasized the Vaswani lineage as a mainstream Hindu guru movement. Based on visits to centres in Pune, Singapore, and Atlanta (and discussions with Vaswani's followers elsewhere), the regular *satsangs* at Sadhu Vaswani Centres around the world honoured the guru lineage while enacting a clearly Hindu identification. They generally began with a few devotional songs (some of them coming from the Nuri Granth that T.L. Vaswani composed) and continued with recitations from sacred texts associated with Hinduism, such as the Gayatri Mantra from the Rig Veda. Unless J.P. Vaswani himself was present, the group typically watched a video-taped discourse by him, in Sindhi, Hindi, or English. After the video, they performed *arti*, honouring pictures of J.P. Vaswani and T.L. Vaswani by singing '*Jaya Jagadish Hare*', waving a lamp and presenting food. The events concluded with the distribution of the food as *prasad.* Such a programme differed from the *satsangs* that T.L. Vaswani led in the first half of the twentieth century only in the omission of recitations from the Guru Granth Sahib.[56] This exclusion of the Guru Granth Sahib placed the regular *satsangs* within the borders of Hinduism as many non-Sindhis understand it.

When J.P. Vaswani visited Lucknow in 2001, his series of discourses and the ritualized actions surrounding them similarly venerated the guru lineage in a mainstream Hindu idiom with a cosmopolitan flair. Vaswani gave a discourse in Sindhi at the Shiv Shanti Ashram seated next to Chandu Ram. The following two nights, Vaswani gave one discourse in English and one in Hindi on the field of the City Montessori School in a suburban section of Lucknow. The range of languages in which Vaswani presented his discourses, much like the writings of his guru, highlights both his continued concern for the Sindhi language and his competing desire to reach Sindhis and others who do not understand the Sindhi language (in contrast to the virtually exclusive emphasis on the Sindhi language in Chandu Ram's movement).

Each evening's ritual included musicians singing Hindi *bhajans*. The demeanour of the musicians, who wore different coordinated outfits each night, the décor of the stage, and the closed circuit broadcast of the events on large projection screens created a professional image for the movement. Following the Hindi *bhajans*, an older woman sang compositions from the Nuri Granth that T.L. Vaswani had composed.

On the second night, a non-Sindhi businessman from Lucknow introduced Vaswani. Reflecting the cosmopolitan tone of the event, he emphasized Vaswani's international stature, including his speeches at the United Nations, Kyoto, and Chicago. He characterized Vaswani's message as drawing together people regardless of caste, creed or colour and emphasized Vaswani's use of both the Sermon on the Mount and the Bhagavad Gita.

After lighting a lamp before his guru's image, Vaswani sat in the solitary chair on the central stage to begin his English discourse, which he presented entirely from memory. Vaswani's discourse was neither a typical Hindu nor Sindhi presentation. He combined a variety of anecdotes and quotes with very practical suggestions about how to be happier by altering one's perceptions and attitudes. His clear English and the breadth of his stories and quotations revealed his broad education and experience, as well as his respect for the wisdom that he saw in various Indian and non-Indian cultures. In this one lecture, he discussed Krishna's advice to Arjuna from the Bhagavad Gita, the Bahai prophet Bahaullah, the Prophet

Muhammad, as well as American figures including Benjamin Franklin, Mark Twain, and William James.

In fact, the version of Hinduism expressed in this discourse was so inclusive that it excluded most symbols of Hinduism beyond the veneration of images of the gurus, some devotional songs, and the brief reference to Krishna. This recreation of ritual also ignored the Guru Granth Sahib and Sufi elements that were central in the other movements. The incorporation of anecdotes from sources around the world reflected an emphasis on a universal spirituality and when combined with the emphasis on dignitaries, multiple languages, and the professionalism of the production, created a cosmopolitan image geared towards the affluent trans-national segment of the Sindhi community which functions in multiple cultures and has family members living throughout the world. Among these three Sindhi gurus, Vaswani, with his Western-style education and breadth of experiences, was uniquely suited to lead this type of transnational movement.

Despite the emphasis on the Vaswani lineage, the treatment of the Nuri Granth during Vaswani's discourses demonstrated the reduced importance that ritualized actions played in the Vaswani movement generally. Although J.P. Vaswani's sister asserted that the Nuri Granth 'occupies the same importance as the Guru Granth Sahib in the case of Sikhs',[57] the text was only treated with the ritualized actions associated with the Guru Granth Sahib at Chandu Ram's ashram where they placed the Nuri Granth in a canopy on the stage with Chandu Ram and Vaswani. The following nights, the singer sang compositions from the Nuri Granth entirely from memory. The professional arrangements of the activities on those nights suggested that they could have arranged for a canopy to honour the Nuri Granth if they felt that it was important. The placement of the Nuri Granth in a canopy at the ashram reflected Chandu Ram's priorities which the Vaswani Mission did not consider necessary to repeat elsewhere.

Literature in the Vaswani Movement

A review of the literature in the movement displays a similar shift from the breadth of Sindhi traditions to the dominance of mainstream Hindu and cosmopolitan elements. The bookstall at Vaswani's discourses in Lucknow promoted a recent publication, *Dada Answers*. In the section on Hinduism, J.P. Vaswani asserts the uniqueness of Hindu traditions by maintaining that other traditions are 'tributaries' of Hinduism.[58] He then refers to the Hindu religion as the 'hope of the world' while also reiterating his opposition to proselytizing.[59] The epigraph of this section presents a quote from Ramakrishna Paramahansa, 'The Sanathana Dharm, the Eternal Religion declared by the Rishis, will alone endure'.[60] Including such a quote, without any contextualization, reinforces the superiority of Hinduism. When the Sadhu Vaswani Centre in Singapore reprinted much of this section on Hinduism in a pamphlet titled 'Hurrah!!! I'm a Hindu!' the editor repeats the combination of Hindu inclusivity and superiority. According to the editor, J.P. Vaswani 'believes in the unity of all races and religions in the One Spirit,' but the editor concludes by admonishing youth to recognize Hinduism as 'the right way'.[61] If all traditions provide routes to the divine, Hinduism, according to this material, has the lone superhighway.

Beyond specific assertions of Hindu pride, much of the material from the movement emphasizes texts and other concepts typically recognized as Hindu. T.L. Vaswani's English paraphrase of the Bhagavad Gita holds a prominent position in the publications of the Mission. In the Introduction, T.L. Vaswani singles out the Gita as 'India's richest gift to humanity'.[62] Among the other topics discussed in *Dada Answers*, J.P. Vaswani addresses karma, yoga, the Gita, and vegetarianism, as well as referring to the Gita extensively in a section on duty.[63] A biography of J.P. Vaswani that the movement publishes also emphasizes Hindu conceptions as it discusses Vaswani's previous births and the power of the stars to indicate—though not compel—events.[64]

However, like his discourses in Lucknow, the variety of materials that appear in the Mission's publications extends beyond a narrow emphasis on Hinduism to include many non-Indian sources. Like the discourses in Lucknow, a series of J.P. Vaswani's devotional books, entitled *Snacks for the Soul,* draws spiritual truths from various sources, including anecdotes about Abraham Lincoln, the Prophet Muhammad, a *fakir* named Abu Hassan, Vivekananda, and others.[65] The publisher's note in another book by J.P. Vaswani, which a leader of the Vaswani centre in Lucknow recommended to me, highlights Vaswani's position as a scientifically educated Hindu as it declares that the book 'combines the wisdom of the best Indian traditions with the well-proven and scientific approach of western thinkers and philosophers'.[66]

The older literature and historical works in the movement reveal a different inclusivity that reflects more common expressions of Sindhi heritage. Biographies of both Vaswanis refer positively to their reverence for Muslim Sufis.[67] One of T.L. Vaswani's books, appropriately titled *Lights from Many Lanterns*, presents Vaswani's translations from a range of texts and traditions that have ties to South Asia. It includes selections from the Quran, the Vedas, and the Guru Granth Sahib, as well as the poetry of Gautama Buddha and several Hindu and Muslim figures (such as Chaitanya, Mira, Rumi, Rabia, and the prominent Sindhi Sufis Shah Abdul Latif and Sachal).[68] Another publication from T.L. Vaswani, *Guru Nanak: Prophet of Peace,* compiles several of T.L. Vaswani's discourses on elements commonly identified as Sikh. The 'Publisher's Note' attests T.L. Vaswani's devotion to the Guru Granth Sahib and his significance as an interpreter of Nanak's teachings to Sindhis.[69] Throughout these discourses T.L. Vaswani asserts that Nanak loved both Hindus and Muslims and worked against the divisions of creed, caste, and race.[70] Much like Pursvani's biography of Asuda Ram, T.L. Vaswani's use of terminology also suggests an absence of barriers as he uses the Arabic-derived term *fakir* for Muslims, Nanak and the Buddhist emperor Ashoka.[71]

Sufis are not entirely excluded from more recent expressions of the Vaswani movement, as noted above in the variety in *Snacks for the Soul.* Sufism was particularly prominent in a recorded lecture that J.P. Vaswani gave in the United States in 1996 which I watched on video-tape at a *satsang* in Atlanta several years later. In this presentation, he admonished his listeners to be Sufis, which he defined as loving God and others. However, in the course of his discourse he repeatedly referred to Islamic figures as examples of Sufis. In that sense, much like Chandu Ram's statements about Sufis, J.P. Vaswani connected Sufis with Islamic traditions historically but used the identification more broadly to connect to concepts of love and devotion to God.

Nevertheless, the shift within the movement from a South Asian inclusiveness to a global inclusiveness is still evident. The prominence of Sufis and Sikh gurus has declined in the past few decades as T.L. Vaswani devoted more of his writing to figures commonly identified as Sikh and Sufi than J.P. Vaswani has. Similarly, while T.L. Vaswani visited various Sufi and Sikh sites, the biography of J.P. Vaswani referred to participation in other ritualized activities as a theoretical or exceptional activity.[72] For example, in his presentation to the 1993 World Parliament of Religions, J.P. Vaswani highlighted the inclusive ideals of Hinduism, meaning that Hindus have no compunction with participating at a mosque, Zoroastrian fire temple, or Christian church.[73] The clearest reference to J.P. Vaswani practicing this ideal, however, highlighted the exceptional nature of his participation in *namaz* (Islamic prayers). 'Dada promptly knelt down and joined them in their *Namaz*! Dada's spontaneous gesture of devotion created such a beautiful bond of brotherhood and love....'.[74] The exclamation point and adjectives like 'spontaneous' suggest that the biographers consider this participation exceptional, which creates a different image than the characterization that T.L. Vaswani's biographers present.

The overall representation that these publications create, when taken together, highlights an inclusive Hindu philosophy that has shifted over the century. T.L. Vaswani honoured the truths within a variety of traditions from India, especially emphasizing the Bhagavad Gita, Guru Granth Sahib, and Sindhi Sufis while participating in related ritualized activities. As the movement has become more global and related to the successful trans-national Sindhi diaspora, J.P. Vaswani has increasingly emphasized American and European material in his discourses while limiting his references to Sufis, Guru Nanak, and the Guru Granth Sahib. These shifts, combined with his glorification of Hinduism in recent publications, increasingly highlight a mainstream Hindu identification with a trans-national focus.

Contemporary Followers

A follower of J.P. Vaswani and a leader of the Sadhu Vaswani Centre in Lucknow, P. Jashnani emphasized reformist critiques of Hindu practices as she described her experiences following Vaswani. She asserted:

> After believing in Dada, I became less superstitious. Hinduism has too many superstitions and too much idol worship. Dada emphasizes karma....His main philosophy comes from the Gita. At the satsang we recite a few verses from the Gita. His teachings are all about the Gita.

When I asked her to explain further what superstitions she left, she refrained from specifying activities, describing instead how she became more accepting of her life and more focused on the needs of others. Although she refrained from specifying 'superstitions', she implicitly connected image worship with that pejorative category. While other Sindhis connected the ideas of reformed Hinduism—especially the rejection of faulty rituals and image worship—with Nanak, Jashnani highlighted instead J.P. Vaswani's emphasis on the Gita. This assertion kept her critique of Hinduism within a mainstream Hindu identification and coincided with the movement's de-emphasis on some ritualized elements. A Vaswani follower in Singapore expanded on Jashnani's rejection of certain rituals with a common Hindu reformist conception by stating 'Brahmins promote the superstitions of the uneducated'.

Another exchange in my interview with Jashnani highlighted this diminished role of ritualized activities. Jashnani had recently acquired a copy of the Nuri Granth for her home to facilitate hosting *satsangs*. However, when I asked her if she opened it each morning like a Guru Granth Sahib, she said that she had not begun that practice yet 'but I am going to', she declared. While many Sindhis considered a failure to perform the proper actions when keeping a copy of the Guru Granth Sahib to be a serious lapse, her stated intention to begin similar actions confirmed my interpretation of the absence of a canopy at Vaswani's discourses at City Montessori School, Lucknow. Ritualized restrictions were not strictly applied to the Nuri Granth.

While Jashnani's discussion of the Vaswani movement emphasized reformed Hindu elements, Jashnani maintained some of the ritualized activities of her childhood in Indonesia, most notably visiting a gurdwara:

> I go [to Naka Hindola Gurdwara] for 10-15 minutes, just to pray, but I do not stay for a long time, listening to all the words. I don't believe in pleasing the gods or wasting time sitting there.

While she had earlier rejected visiting temples, this exchange clearly suggested that she considered praying in the largest gurdwara in Lucknow to be worth the effort to go there. After that admission, she quickly reiterated her de-emphasis on ritualized activities by noting the brevity of her prayers. This exchange further suggests the decreased importance of the Guru Granth Sahib in the Vaswani movement since a follower who personally venerates the Guru Granth Sahib does so only outside the guru movement.

Having heard J.P. Vaswani identify himself as a Sufi, I asked Jashnani if a Sufi identification was appropriate for him. After she assented, I asked her what the term meant and she referred to the 'special qualities' that distinguish a Sufi. Since the only specific trait that she mentioned was the celibacy of both Vaswanis, she never connected it explicitly with Islam as Vaswani did in the discourse. She did not struggle with answering the question as much as N. Ahuja at the Shiv Shanti Ashram did but her answer never revealed a familiarity with Vaswani's definition of Sufism, further suggesting the lack of emphasis on Sufism within the contemporary Vaswani movement.

In the activities and representations of the Vaswani movement, its focus on affluent and trans-national Sindhi Hindus becomes clear. The literature and the ritual recreations in the movement stress the veneration of a guru, social service, and the inclusion of wisdom from many sources, while de-emphasizing certain ritualized activities. Such an emphasis has led the movement away from the primacy of the Guru Granth Sahib in Chandu Ram's movement and Sufi elements in Rochal Das's movement and towards a particular Hindu identification that matches prominent understandings of a reformed and inclusive Hinduism.

DIVERSE FORMATIONS IN DIASPORA

The experiences of Partition and rebuilding lives and communities in diaspora have been disruptive, even traumatic, for many Sindhi Hindus. While continual change is a common element in the history of religious movements, the tensions between nostalgia for the remembered traditions of Sindh and desire for acceptance in a different environment—which dismisses aspects of that nostalgia—have increased the pressures of change on Sindhi identity and religious practices. While Sindhi Hindus commonly maintain an identification with Sindh, they have responded to these pressures in a variety of ways.

The three movements that I have described have adjusted their ritualized activities and representations in different ways to address their current concerns and the unique character of each movement. While Chandu Ram specifically increased the centrality of the Guru Granth Sahib alongside the veneration of his own lineage, he emphasized a different aspect of Sindhi traditions than Rochal Das and his successors, who highlight the centrality of Sufi rituals and a Sufi identification even as they argue for the unity of all religions and use the Guru Granth Sahib, and Hindu texts to teach spiritual truths. Following a different path, J.P. Vaswani has increasingly emphasized a mainstream Hindu identification that expands its inclusiveness beyond Sufi masters, the Guru Granth Sahib or any of the traditions of Sindh and South Asia to develop a global and cosmopolitan perspective.

While collectively these guru movements challenge homogenizing definitions of religions that ignore the contestations that occur within any religion, they do not convey fully the variety among Sindhi Hindus. Even the personal practices and understandings of their committed followers differ from the elements that each guru emphasizes, as in Jashnani's continued visits to gurdwaras. Moreover, the varied emphases in these three movements do not exhaust the variety of choices made in other Sindhi Hindu movements.

This broad range of practices throughout the Sindhi Hindu community should not result in simply an atomistic view of the community, where each group and individual does their own thing. Clear connections maintain the ties between these movements and within the Sindhi Hindu community more generally. The common pride among Sindhi Hindus about their ethnic identification and homeland remains palpable, even as the tie of a common language diminishes in diaspora. The common veneration of Sindhi elements is evident in the inclusion of each movement within the six guru/sant images in the Harmandir described at the beginning of this chapter. More directly revealing the larger sense of a Sindhi Hindu community, during J.P. Vaswani's first lecture in Lucknow in 2002 at Chandu Ram's ashram, Chandu Ram and Vaswani sat on the platform together. They specifically praised the work and teachings of each other, even though these two leaders have pushed the emphases of their movements in clearly different directions. Similarly, most Sindhi Hindus on an individual basis not only claimed that identification but also found community and meaning in a variety of Sindhi Hindu groups. For example, Advani, the follower of Rochal Das described above, attended *satsangs* at Chandu Ram's ashram occasionally.

Beyond these expressions of community through joint participation common elements unite these movements and Sindhi Hindus in general, despite their individual expressions of agency. Considering these three movements, each of them has emphasized both a Hindu identification and their Sindhi heritage. A concern about preserving the Sindhi language and identity has clearly influenced each movement. On a more specific level, all three use elements that are significant in many accounts of Sindhi traditions, most notably the Bhagavad Gita, Hindu deities, the Guru Granth Sahib, Guru Nanak, and Sindhi Sufis, though each movement has its own emphasis among these elements.

A final uniting element is the dynamic vitality that these movements and their followers express. Facing the challenge of recreating their heritage in a sometimes hostile environment, many Sindhi Hindus have developed actively their community practices and individual expressions in a variety of ways to address their diverse needs and concerns. As these three examples illustrate, their recreations have maintained some specific elements of Sindhi Hindu traditions, belying concerns about the wholesale assimilation of Sindhi traditions into mainstream Hinduism. Because of these dynamic recreations, generalizations about Sindhi Hindus—whether focused on the nature of ethnic identification, ritualized practices, or a specific movement among Sindhis—can be dangerously distorting. Only a contextualized representation that recognizes the vitality in Sindhi traditions and religious expressions can begin to approximate the complexity that comprises Sindhi Hindus in diaspora.

NOTES

1. Another version of this chapter appeared in Steven Ramey, *Hindu, Sufi or Sikh: Contested Practices and Identifications of Sindhi Hindus in India and Beyond* (New York: Palgrave Macmillan, 2008) and is reproduced with permission of Palgrave Macmillan. Primary research for this project was made possible by a Junior Dissertation Fellowship from the American Institute of Indian Studies (AIIS) in 2001–2002. I gratefully acknowledge the assistance of Purnima Mehta, Pradeep Mehendiratta, and the other staff members of AIIS and Dr Abha Avasthi of Lucknow University. I am even more deeply indebted to the gracious assistance of Sindhis in Lucknow, Pune, and other parts of India, as well as Singapore and Atlanta for their willingness to share their experiences with me and answer my interminable questions. To protect their privacy, I have changed their names within the text. All quotes from interviews in this study took place in 2001 or 2002.
2. Sant refers to religious leaders in North India, including Guru Nanak and Kabir, who, beginning in the thirteenth century, emphasized egalitarianism and devotion to an often nameless divine and have been recognized as challenging the boundaries dividing Hinduism and Islam. Some Sindhis use this label for some of their religious leaders.
3. Claude Markovits, *The Global World of Indian Merchants, 1750–1947: Traders of Sind from Bukhara to Panama* (Cambridge and New York: Cambridge University Press, 2000), 285.
4. As I demonstrate later, terminology is a continuing problem for Sindhi Hindus. They variously referred to the leaders of these movements as Sufis, gurus, *murshids*, *sants*, etc. For simplicity and consistency, I will use the term guru for these figures generally, inserting other terms when they reflect a specific statement in a particular context.
5. Richard Schechner, *Between Theater and Anthropology* (Philadelphia: University of Pennsylvania Press, 1985), 35–55.
6. William H. Sewell, Jr., 'A Theory of Structure: Duality, Agency, and Transformation', *American Journal of Sociology* 98.1 (1998): 2.
7. S.K. Punshi, *A Biography of Saint Kanwarram* (self-published on behalf of Amar Shahid Saint Kanwarram Birth Centenary Celebration Committee of Amravati, 1985), 33.
8. Gul A. Pursvani, *View of Life: Perfect Sant Baba Asuda Ram Sahib* (Lucknow: Shiv Shanti Sant Asudaram Ashram, n.d.), 71–76.
9. Ibid., 170–171.
10. Raymond Brady Williams, *Religions of Immigrants From India and Pakistan: New Threads in the American Tapestry* (Cambridge: Cambridge University Press, 1988), 241; Markovits, 285.
11. Punshi, 6.
12. Ibid., 17–19.
13. Ibid., 77.
14. Ibid., 65.
15. Ibid., 7–8.
16. Ibid, 67 (italics and parenthetical definition added).
17. Ibid., 31.

18. Ibid., 87–88.
19. Ibid., 2–3 and 5.
20. Ibid., 77–78.
21. Ibid., 78.
22. Pursvani, 56.
23. Ibid., 49 and 177.
24. Ibid., 28–29.
25. Ibid., 62.
26. Ibid., 58.
27. Ibid.
28. S.L. Gajwani, *A Sufi Galaxy: Sufi Qalandar Hazrat Qutab Ali Shah, His Spiritual Successors and Select Disciples—Sufi Saints of the Present Times* (Ulhasnagar, Maharasthra: H.M. Damodar, 2000), 4.
29. Ibid., 8–49.
30. Ibid., 39.
31. Ibid., 41; R.M. Hari, ed., *Some Moments with the Master: Spiritual Dialogues with the Sufi Saint Sai Rochaldas Sahib* (Ulhas Nagar, Maharasthra: H.M. Damodar, 1995), 10.
32. Gajwani, 41.
33. Ibid., 147–149.
34. Hari, *Moments with the Master*, 418–419.
35. Gajwani, 166; Hari, *Moments with the Master*, 303.
36. Hari, *Moments with the Master*, 310.
37. Ibid., 58 and 222.
38. Ibid., 190–218.
39. Ibid., 363.
40. Ibid.
41. Ibid., 364–366.
42. Ibid., 374.
43. Ibid.
44. Ibid., 374–375.
45. Ibid., 92.
46. Ibid., 92–93 (parenthetical phrase in original).
47. Gajwani, 8.
48. R.M. Hari, *Sri Yoga Vasishtha: The Spiritual Dialogue Between Sri Ramachandra and Sri Vasishtha, Abridged and presented in Questions and Answers* (Ulhasnagar, Maharasthra: H.M. Damodar, 1992), vi–vii.
49. R.M. Hari, *Shrimad Bhagwad Gita (Ilim Ludani-Va-Tohid): The Knowledge that Draws Towards Spirituality—The Oneness* (Ulhasnagar, Maharasthra: H.M. Damodar, 1982), book jacket.
50. Ibid., 141, 168 and 179.
51. Ibid., 209.
52. Hari, *Moments with the Master*, 4.
53. Ibid.
54. For his life story, consult H.P. Vaswani, *A Saint of Modern India* (Poona: Meera Union, 1975).
55. For more about J.P. Vaswani's life, see Krishna Kumari, Prabha Sampath and Gulshan Gidwani, *Love is Never Blind: Life and Message of Dada J.P. Vaswani* (Pune: Gita Publishing House, 1998).
56. H.P. Vaswani, *A Saint of Modern India*, 228.

57. Ibid.
58. J.P. Vaswani, *Dada Answers: Questions You Have Always Wished to Ask* (New Delhi: Sterling Paperbacks, 2001), 120.
59. Ibid., 124.
60. Ibid., 119.
61. J.P. Vaswani, 'Foreword', in J.P. Vaswani, *Hurrah!!! I'm a Hindu!* (Singapore: Sadhu Vaswani Centre, 1990).
62. T.L. Vaswani, *The Bhagavad Gita: The Song of the Supreme*, 2nd Edition (Pune: Gita Publishing House, 2000), 17.
63. J.P. Vaswani, *Dada Answers*.
64. Kumari, et al., 27, 86 and 101.
65. J.P. Vaswani, *Snack for the Soul: An Inspiring Story for Every Day of the Year, January–June* (New Delhi: New Dawn, 2000), 225, 218 and 254.
66. J.P. Vaswani, *Burn Anger Before Anger Burns You* (Pune: Gita Publishing House, 1992), back cover.
67. Kumari et al., 90; H.P. Vaswani, *A Saint of Modern India,* 159.
68. T.L. Vaswani, *Lights From Many Lanterns* (Pune: Gita Publishing House, n.d.).
69. Gangaram Sajandas, 'Publisher's Note', in T.L. Vaswani, *Guru Nanak: Prophet of Peace* (Poona: Mira Publications, n.d.), 7–8.
70. T.L. Vaswani, *Guru Nanak: Prophet of Peace* (Poona: Mira Publications, n.d.), 15 and 18.
71. Ibid., 21–22.
72. H.P. Vaswani, *A Saint of Modern India,* 159, 199 and 246.
73. Kumari, et al., 297.
74. Ibid., 320.

CHAPTER 5

Code Switching Among Sindhis Experiencing Language Shift in Malaysia

MAYA KHEMLANI DAVID

John Gumperz, in *Discourse Analysis*, defines switching as the 'juxtaposition within the same speech exchange of passages of speech belonging to two different grammatical systems or subsystems'.[1] Code Switching is the simultaneous use of two languages at the word, phrase, clause, or sentence level.[2] Linguists have addressed the social meaning of code switching in different contexts.[3] Gardner–Chloros describes language competency, or the lack thereof, as a reason for code switching.[4] Blommaert writes that code switching indicates 'they-ness' and 'other-ness' in language.[5] In the Malaysian courtroom context, David analyzes how Malay/English code switching can influence and coerce courtroom participants.[6] Jariah Mohammed Jan views code switching as a strategic tool for wielding power in official government meetings.[7] She analyzes how an organization's head, who is an ethnic Malay, uses her mother tongue, i.e., the national language, to demonstrate power over non-Malay subordinates. While Jariah Mohammed Jan notes how English/Malay code switching in formal government meetings expresses status and power, Zuraidah argues that Malay language/dialect code switching is a tool used by members within a community to signal rapport, intimacy, and regional identity.[8]

In multi-linguistic settings, code switching can act both as an accommodation strategy (especially in encounters with members from different ethnicities), as well as an alienation strategy that excludes participation in conversations (particularly when one cannot speak the language code selected). For example, Kow maintains that English/Hokkien/Mandarin/Malay code switching, among Malaysian children between the ages of four and six, is an innovative linguistic strategy by which children consider efficient and effective ways to communicate, especially when compensating for a limited vocabulary. A similar conclusion has been reached by Kuang, who worked with an under-two-year-old bilingual child who used Mandarin and English to communicate his needs to speakers of different languages.[9]

In Malaysia, code switching is an effective linguistic option in spoken language and achieves several objectives. In formal and informal settings it signals speech convergence and divergence, achieves a number of strategic goals (including that of power and control), and marks regional allegiance. For young Malaysians growing up in multilingual settings, code switching aids in meaning making, as well as the development of efficient and effective forms of communication. Code switching is a language option open to and increasingly used by Malaysians for a range of tactical reasons in multiple settings (e.g., during in-group and out-group encounters). In social practice, it is increasingly 'normative' linguistic behavior to code switch in spoken language.[10] Code switching in Malaysia results in a distinct language variety that is becoming increasingly entrenched as a linguistic option for achieving a wide-range of spoken objectives.

In contrast to most contemporary studies which focus on the use of mixed discourse in spoken language, this chapter investigates the reasons for and functioning of code switching among the Sindhis of Malaysia, a minority community, currently experiencing a language shift.[11] As communities move away from the habitual use of a community's language, they gravitate toward new language functions that are redistributed differently within the group. The function of a code switch can vary depending on whether it is used by younger or older community members. The focus of this study is to describe the aims of code switching among different age groups and generations of Sindhis living in Malaysia.

CODE SWITCHING AMONG SINDHIS IN MALAYSIA

Studies illustrate how code switching is a step in the process of language shift: an intermediary stage in the move away from one language toward adopting a replacive language.[12] Lieberson, while investigating language shift among Gujaratis in Nairobi, found that many parents used both Gujarati and English to address their children. Leiberson concludes that the shift from Gujarati to English is explained by code switching.[13] In South Australia, Smolicz shows that the decline in Italian-speaking among immigrant children involves a tendency to mix Italian dialects with

English.[14] Hashim's study of the choice of language between standard and regional Malay in Perak, a state in Peninsular Malaysia, also addresses how people use more than one language within a single utterance. All these studies emphasize how code switching can be symptomatic of a language shift. Different reasons and circumstances can trigger people's code switching. For example, code mixes by older members of a community can be interpreted as an accommodation to the community's younger members.[15] Code switching by younger members of a community can be viewed as a strategy to 'camouflage' reduced language proficiency. Code switching can be seen as a symptom of linguistic shift when it is triggered by an imperfect knowledge of a community's mother tongue.

Malaysia is a multi-ethnic country with a population of 23.27 million which uses at least a hundred languages. Of the total population, Bumiputeras, who are Malays and other indigenous groups, comprise 65.1 per cent, Chinese 26.0 per cent, and Indians 7.7 per cent.[16] While the Malay majority consider themselves 'indigenous', non-Malays, such as the Chinese and the Indians are described as non-Bumiputras, or more controversially, 'immigrants' since most of them arrived and settled in Malaysia during the colonial period. Within each group, a variety of languages and dialects are spoken.

Less than six hundred people make up the Malaysian Sindhi community. Within the community, approximately twenty to twenty-five per cent have exogamous marriages to non-Sindhis.[17] The first members of the community initially arrived in Malaysia during the British period to trade, principally in textiles. During the Second World War, the Sindhis established themselves on a more solid footing in the country. The permanence of their stay was further consolidated by Partition, when Sindh, their original homeland, became part of Pakistan. Many Sindhi Hindus residing in Malaysia, known as Malaya at the time, lost their homes back in Sindh and decided to remain in Malaysia as well as in other areas where they had settled earlier. With the passage of time, children of the first generation entered, in contrast to their merchant-parents, more professional and skilled jobs.

Since settling in Malaysia, Sindhis have experienced a language shift.[18] The majority of the first generation Sindhi women were not (and still are not) fully proficient in English. Sindhi remains their primary language. In contrast, the first generation Sindhi men, who were largely merchants, are competent in English. A variety of Malay, known as Bazaar-Malay, has generally been the language of preference for cross-cultural and local encounters; Bazaar-Malay is widely used by Sindhi men (as well as many first generation women). This variety of Malay is usually not formally learnt but acquired through service encounters. Second generation Malaysian Sindhis, who attended English-medium schools during the colonial era, are proficient in English (which has increasingly become a dominant language among Sindhis). Most second generation Malaysian-Sindhis generally use Sindhi to communicate with older, non-English speaking community members. They also use Malay with non-English speaking domestic help, which may include Tamil or Indonesian domestic servants. As Malay is the medium of instruction in schools for many third generation Malaysian Sindhis, they use standard rather than the bazaar form of Malay in active discourse and service encounters. They are generally additionally proficient in English, which is often spoken by their second generation parents as well. So, when second and third generation Sindhis from English-speaking homes interact, they generally make little use of the Sindhi language.

The use of different languages within the same conversation occurs frequently within the Malaysian Sindhi community. During the process of shift, use of the Sindhi language, although it is no longer the dominant language for communication among them, can be continued for vestigial purposes. The sequential analysis of turn-taking in spoken language reveals that peer interaction among members of the first generation, especially for first generation women, entails code mixes from English that integrate Sindhi speech. In contrast, second generation Malaysian Sindhi code mixes appear in English-dominated speech, both with peers and younger community members, such as the third generation. Although Sindhi is not the usual language for communication in peer interaction for either the second or the third generation, my language transcriptions and field observations reveal that there is a strong tendency to continue using Sindhi terms for particular types of social and speech interactions. Use of Sindhi is usually maintained for the following functions: while referring to religious and cultural items; for issuing directives; for negative responses; for quotations; and for both teasing or social exclusion of outsiders and non-Sindhi speaking insiders.

Social practices that relate to religion are entrenched in the Malaysian Sindhi community. Sindhi lexicon, in reference to these practices, is often invoked, even in contexts where English is the dominant language. In religious ceremonies, which are often held in an individual's home in Malaysia, Sindhi is habitually used to refer to different types of prayers (such as, come for the *arti*), religious observances (such as, when somebody is fasting, he/she says, 'Today I am keeping *virith*') in references to God (such as, do *sheva* or husband is *Bhagwan*), to objects used in religious ceremonies (such as *diyo* and *degro*). It is also used to refer to particular ceremonies. Dowry and weddings play a strong role in the life of the Sindhi community. There are thus many lexical references associated with these social phenomena, especially weddings. These wedding-associated references include statements such as: they did *kachi misri,* or today is the *satharo. Kachi misri* is best understood within the context of arranged marriages. It is a quick and simple engagement ceremony, attended only by close family members, which aims to formally present and formalize the social commitment between the two families involved in a marriage. *Satharo* is the culmination event, which follows the various ceremonies and festivities that constitute Sindhi weddings.

Since Sindhis are bound historically by close networks of kinship, the Sindhi language has a multitude of special terms that refer to a wide variety of relationships. The younger generation may not know the entire range of kinship terms but utilize the more common ones. *Chachi*, *bhabhi*, *didi,* and *beta* are terms used by all generations of Sindhis.

Social networks and relations are often maintained through the exchange of food. Sindhis in Malaysia have not forsaken their ethnic dishes and Sindhi cuisine still forms a major part of the community's diet. Young Sindhi children usually know the Sindhi names for traditional dishes like *mani saal, tikki, thelabadi, papar,* etc. The retention of Sindhi terms, with regard to food items, even when speaking in English is clearly evident in the speech of the younger Sindhis. Phrases like 'make *malpro* for me', 'I want to eat *jamu*', 'My mother made *miti loli*', and 'I ate *palao*', are common.

Many examples from my data illustrate instances of Sindhi being used for directives. In a recorded exchange between a second generation mother (who uses English more often than Sindhi) and her 17-year-old son, the former shifts to the community's mother tongue when she directs him. Sindhi is used here for a directive to lower the radio's volume:

Son: Talk *lah* what whatever you say you want to talk ['lah' is a multifunctional particle in Malaysian style English].

Mother: No nothing. Slow *kar awaaz* [i.e., reduce the volume].

Despite historically strong families, Sindhi society in Malaysia is experiencing radical change with the increasing break-up of its traditional and extended family structure. The impact of greater educational opportunities provided for female children, movement away from the textile trade and towards professions like doctors, lawyers and engineers, and women increasingly working outside homes and family businesses, have all played a role in this process. A further reflection of this change is that the primary language used by the second and third generations at home is no longer Sindhi.

In such a changing linguistic environment, Sindhi is sometimes utilized to negatively reinforce role relationships, as well as the authority that accompanies asymmetrical relationships within the family. There is evidence that members of the second generation use Sindhi to regularly give negative responses. The use of a non-habitual language for negative responses operates as a social distancing strategy that can be face-saving for both speech-partners. When a reprimand is issued in the non-habitual language, the chastiser is 'distanced' from the actual act of chastising. This is reflected in conversations when an older second generation member, who normally uses English with the third generation, shifts to Sindhi to withhold permission (for example, when being asked by a youth for consent to see a movie). Similarly, single Sindhi words that refer to unpleasant matters are also commonly found in English-dominant linguistic structures or utterances. These often take the form of pejoratives in which the speaker disassociates with the act of speech by utilizing language that is normally not used by the speaker. Examples of this type of code switching includes phrases like: 'Don't be a *bhangi*', 'She is so *kanjus*', 'He is *badmash*', and 'He is a *mathe jo sur*'.

The Sindhi language is also used by second generation speakers to quote elders of the first generation who generally use the community's language, e.g., 'Anywhere I have to live, even when I go to India, my sister will always tell me, "*Cha khaindia*?" [What will you eat?]'. Additionally, when members of the second generation relate narratives to peers they make use of Sindhi to quote what they said to a first generation speaker. In one example, a second generation Sindhi states: 'What I told the old lady, *Asi achoo pia* [we are coming]'.

In addition to quoting, Sindhi is reserved for the function of intimacy, kinship, and friendship, as well as teasing and joking. When the second and third generations use Sindhi for teasing and joking, the amount of mother-tongue they use is usually nominal compared with the dominant use of English. For example, the tease and joke function may be limited to a single word. For instance, an English-speaking eighteen-year-old teased her sister with the word *paapi* [sinner] when the sister did not maintain a vegetarian diet on a day of religious observance. In another instance, when a member of the third generation who is about to graduate from law school, asked a peer: 'What are all the lawyers doing here?', the latter teasingly provided a two-word Sindhi response: '*Vando vakil*' [i.e., idle lawyers].

On a number of occasions, I observed that, although English dominates peer interaction, the second and third generation Sindhis used their community's mother-tongue to socially and linguistically exclude non-Sindhis, especially the English-speaking Filipino domestic servants and non-Sindhi salesmen. Public settings, like restaurants, are spaces in which the Sindhi language is regularly employed to exclude non-Sindhis:

> Sindhi Customer#1: to Waiter: Can I have the spaghetti with some cheese?
> Sindhi Customer#2: X *chavai suto kone* [X said it was not good].
> Sindhi Customer#3: *Yesah* [Malaysian English for 'Is that so']?
> Sindhi Customer#4: *Mu* try *kayo aahe sutho kane* [I tried it, it was not good].

Sindhi is not only used by the second generation to exclude non-Sindhis but also the third-generation children from 'private' conversations. For example, a second generation female recalled to me an event largely in English, however, since the conversation was in the presence of her children she resorted to Sindhi when she talked about an affectionate embrace, a *bhakhi*, with her husband. Just as Sindhi is used to exclude outsiders and Sindhi children, I also observed second generation Sindhis using English to exclude those of the first generation who did not know English.

SUMMARY

Despite their dominant use of English, many second and third generation Malaysian-Sindhis do utilize their community's mother tongue in a limited way. This is most evident in the linguistic domain of kinship terms use of quotes and pejorative referents. Sindhi is also employed for specific speech acts like directives, teasing and joking and providing negative responses. At times, Sindhi plays the role of a private language that excludes others. It is also popularly used to refer to food, culture, and religion by members of the second and third generation who may have otherwise shifted to using English mostly.

While the use of Sindhi appears to have a wide range of functions among the second and third generations of Sindhi immigrants, it is never used in linguistic isolation. It is habitually part of code switching that includes English as the dominant language. As a result, the extent to which Sindhi is used is limited vis-à-vis the total language use. Nonetheless, it is generally found in code switch utterances with English as the unmarked language.

With less then six hundred members, who straddle three generations, and growing incidents of exogamous marriages, use of the Sindhi language in Malaysia is becoming increasingly limited. The decreasing use of the language results not only from the community's current linguistic needs but is also due to limited attempts by Sindhis themselves to maintain the language as a marker of identity. Although some parents do try to teach Sindhi to their children, their task is an uphill one since Sindhi is not taught in schools. Similar declines and difficulties in the use of the Sindhi language can be noticed in other Sindhi communities around the world as well. As linguistic minorities in the countries they have migrated to from India, the community has difficulties in the continued maintenance of its mother tongue outside Sindh in the newer generations. Nonetheless, since the community, at least in Malaysia, is generally conscious and proud of its Sindhi identity, its members are likely to retain elements of their mother tongue, through limited to specific types of speech acts and social contexts.

NOTES

1. John Gumperz, *Discourse Strategies* (Cambridge: Cambridge University Press, 1982), 59.
2. Guadalupe Valdes, 'Code switching as a Deliberate Verbal Strategy: A Microanalysis of Direct and Indirect Requests among Bilingual Chicano Speakers', in Richard Duran, ed., *Latino Language and Communicative Behavior* (Norwood, N.J.: Ablex, 1981), 95–107.
3. J.P. Blom and John Gumperz, 'Social Meaning in Linguistic Structures and Codeswitching in Norway', in John Gumperz and Dell Hymes, eds., *Directions in Sociolinguistics: The Ethnography of Communication* (New York: Holt, Rinehart and Winston. 1971), 407–34; Monica Heller, *Code-switching: Anthropological and Sociolinguistic Perspectives* (Berlin: Mouton de Gruyter, 1988).
4. Penelope Gardner-Chloros, *Language Selection and Switching in Strasbourg* (Oxford: Oxford University Press, 1997).
5. Jan Blommaert, 'Codeswitching and the Exclusivity of Social Identities: Some Data from Campus Kiswahili', *Journal of Multilingual and Multicultural Development* 13.1–2 (1992): 52–70.
6. Maya Khemlani David, 'Selling in an Intercultural Context: The Case of Malaysia', *International Scope Review* (www.internationalscope.org [accessed 5 June 2002]).
7. Jariah Mohammed Jan, 'Code-switching for Power Wielding: Inter-gender Discourse at the Workplace', *Multilingua* 22.1 (2003): 41–58.

8. Mohammed Don Zuraidah, 'Language-Dialect Code-switching: Kelantanese in a Multilingual Context', *Multilingua* 22 (2003): 21–40.
9. Ching Hei Kuang, 'Code Switches: A Measurement for Language Shift? A Case Study of a Malaysian Chinese Family', in Maya Khemlani David, ed., *Methodological and Analytical Issues in Language Maintenance and Shift Studies* (Frankfurt: Peter Lang, 2002), 91–111.
10. Nancy Dorian, *Language Death: The Life Cycle of a Scottish Gaelic Dialect* (Philadelphia: University of Pennsylvania Press, 1981).
11. Maya Khemlani David, 'Language Shift among the Sindhis of Malaysia' (PhD Dissertation in Linguistics at the University of Malaya, 1996).
12. R. Appel and Pieter Muysken, *Language Contact and Bilingualism* (London: Edward Arnold, 1987); Marilyn Martin-Jones, 'Sociolinguistic Surveys as a Source of Evidence in the Study of Bilingualism: A Critical Assessment of Survey Work Conducted Among Linguistic Minorities in Three British Cities', *International Journal of the Sociology of Language* 90 (1991): 37–55.
13. Stanley Lieberson and Edward McCabe, 'Domains of Language Usage and Mother Tongue Shift in Nairobi', in Stanley Lieberson and Anwar Dil, eds., *Language Diversity and Language Contact Essays* (Stanford: Stanford University Press, 1981), 249–262.
14. Jerzy Jaroslaw Smolicz, 'Modification and Maintenance: Language Among School-Children of Italian Background in South Australia', *Journal of Multilingual and Multicultural Development* 4 (1983): 313–37.
15. Maya Khemlani David, 'Language Shift Among the Sindhis of Malaysia' (PhD Dissertation in Linguistics at the University of Malaya, 1996).
16. Government of Malaysia Statistics Department, *Population and Housing Census of Malaysia 2000* (Kuala Lumpur: Government of Malaysia, 2001).
17. Maya Khemlani David, *The Sindhis of Malaysia: A Sociolinguistic Study* (London: Asean Academic Press, 2001).
18. Maya Khemlani David, 'The Sindhis in Malaysia-Language Maintenance, Language Loss or Language Death?', in Gary Jones and Conrad Oxog, eds., *Collected Papers from the Conference on Bilingualism and National Development* (Darussalam: University of Brunei, 1991), 368–380.

CHAPTER 6

Sufism, Hinduism, and Social Organization in Sindh: The Forgotten Tradition of Pithoro Pir

MICHEL BOIVIN

Pithoro Pir is a Muslim saint believed to have lived in fifteenth century Sindh. His hagiography describes him as a renunciant and a warrior who did not hesitate to fight against the local *raja* who harassed him. Today, Hindu Rajputs manage Pithoro Pir's cult while his followers are mainly Untouchables from the Menghwar caste and Muslims. This chapter presents the first results of an on-going study of this previously unexamined cult.

In south-eastern Pakistan, close to the Indian border, there is a temple devoted to Pithoro Pir. The temple is in an arid area on the fringes of the Thar Parkar desert. The sources used to examine the history of the Pir and his temple are from different collections. First, I utilized reports completed by British officers during colonial rule. Second, I drew on the official tradition as reported to me by the present head of the sect and by a local historian. Third, the chapter contains personal observations from fieldwork. The main purpose of the chapter is to decipher the contribution of the Pithoro Pir tradition to the relationship between Sufism, history, and society. It seeks to make sense of this religious tradition by examining the interplay between historical dynamics and social factors.

I maintain that, despite the spread of Islamization in Pakistan, there are still communities who express discourses (through narratives and rituals) that are located beyond the categories of 'Muslim' and 'Hindu'. I initially give a brief survey of 'Sufi Culture' in Sindh before discussing sources, both oral and written. The second half of the chapter will focus on the legend of Pithoro Pir. It will demonstrate that, although it is not possible to re-construct the making of its narrative process, Pithoro Pir's tradition incorporates different levels of historical narratives. I devote the final part of the chapter to the study of ritual narratives. It examines to what extent the 'communitas' concept reinforces social domination while claiming that the master-disciple system fits well into regional caste hierarchies.

THE 'SUFI CULTURE OF SINDH': CONTEXTUALIZATION AND SOURCES

Many British officers, soon after arriving in Sindh, observed the spirit of toleration which encompassed the province. Despite the centuries old reputation of Sindh as 'the land of the Sufis', only a few studies are devoted to this topic.[1] Nonetheless, the topic of 'Sufi culture in Sindh' was developed by Gulraj Parsram in his 1925 book entitled *Sindh and its Sufis*. What did Gulraj mean by the expression 'Sufi culture'? Gulraj stated that religion in Sindh was not orthodox because Muslims in the region were influenced by Sufism and the Hindus were essentially Sikhs. The implications of the Sufi culture were that the caste system was virtually absent: The Brahmans were not particularly powerful, the Shashtras were little known, and finally, 'the problem of the depressed castes is non-existent'.[2] Religious bigotry was, therefore, little known in the province. According to Gulraj, this 'Sufi culture' was best described as a 'marriage' between 'the Indo-Aryan Sanatana Dharma and the Arabic-Persian mystic culture'.[3] What I shall try to demonstrate here is that this 'Sufi culture' still pervades Sindhi society and that it encompasses a broader spectrum of beliefs, including the cult of Pithoro Pir. Along the way, some insights will be proposed, in the context of my particular case study, for understanding the achievement of such a 'marriage'.

Although the oral tradition of Pithoro Pir affiliates him to Sufism, no traditional sources of Sufism quote him as a Sufi. He cannot be traced among the 382 *awliya* quoted with a short individual note in a recent *tazkirah* devoted to the saints of Sindh.[4] The first mention of Pithoro Pir is found in the work of Richard Burton, who published a book on him in 1851. Surprisingly, Burton wrote that the disciples of Pithoro Pir are mainly Menghwars (i.e., Untouchables) and that they had scriptures in the language and the writing of Malwa.[5]

The mention of these scriptures, which Burton qualifies as *pothis*, raises questions. According to the present *pir*, the tradition of Pithoro Pir is mainly oral and confirmed by disciples who meet in various places. However, this does not contradict the fact that Pirpanthis could have *pothis*. In nineteenth century Sindh, Burton described *pothis* as *vade mecum*, and consequently, of private use. Groups like the Lohanas and

Khojas have such scripture. They are generally handwritten texts concerned with various and varied literary categories but most importantly include divination books (*fal namos*) and devotional poetry.[6] In the case of Pithoro Pir, two main categories of devotional poetry are *bhajans* and *kafis*. Each pious person can make a choice of texts dear to him from various titles. The choice is always personal. It is consequently difficult to assimilate them to the sacred writings of a normative religion like Hinduism or Islam.

The tradition of Pithoro Pir primarily remained an oral tradition until 1955 when Raichand Sartani, himself a Menghwar by caste, published a booklet on Pithoro Pir.[7] Sartani's book represents the official version of Pithoro Pir's tradition at the time of Partition. Sartani was a schoolmaster in the village of Chelhar and he travelled extensively in Thar Parkar collecting legends and traditions. Sartani is better known as Raichand Harijan and it is under this name that he published a reference book on the history of Thar Parkar.[8] The most interesting point is that Sartani locates Pir Pithoro's religious knowledge in two sources: Baha al-Din Zakariyya and Gosain Birnath Swami.[9] The author portrays the official version of the Pithoro Pir tradition in terms of service (*shevak*), wisdom (*haqiqat*), and miracles (*karamat*). He also provides basic insights into the temple (*mari*), guardian (*mujavar*), and annual fair (*melo*).

The devotional literature of the Menghwars appears to be in Sindhi, both in Sindh and Kutch.[10] In a work devoted to the folk literature in Sindhi of Kutch, Jetho Lalwani collected three *bhajans* devoted to Pithoro Pir. These *bhajans* are sung in various Sindhi dialects but most frequently in Thareli (which prevails in Thar Parkar). The *bhajans* of Pithoro Pir, which can either contain a refrain or not, are weaved on the pattern of devotional poetry. The saint is described as a protective figure and as a provider of happiness: he is called upon in particular for his miraculous capacities (*karamat*). His disciples, called *murids* in the poems, address many requests (*sowal*) to him. Sartani's booklet ends with *bhajans* and *kafis* devoted to Pithoro Pir.[11] Eight *bhajans* and seven *kafis* are presented. Pithoro Pir is praised as a spiritual master (*murshid*) who provides the milk (*kiro*) of his mystical love (*pyar*), but also as the inner *avtar* of the Essence or *Dhat* (*Dhat desu me andar avtar*).[12] The most striking aspect of the devotional literature is the lack of reference to the Sodhas (i.e., Rajputs). Pithoro Pir often refers to himself as a Sodha while his temple is usually described as the *mari sodhi*.[13]

Although the title of *pir* generally refers to a Muslim saint, it is used by Hindus as well. For example, the Kanphatas in Kutch designate their living spiritual guide with this term. In the Sindhi context, there are examples where a Hindu saint can be described as *shah*, as well as *pir*. This is the case with Rama Pir or Janda Pir, another name for Udero Lal.[14] The *gaddi nashin* of Pithoro is himself called a *pir*. At all events, nobody disputes that Pithoro Pir was a Muslim.

PITHORO PIR AT THE CROSSROADS OF LEGEND AND HISTORY

In 1926, J.W. Smyth notes that it is difficult to draw conclusions from the history of the legend of Pithoro Pir.[15] To what extent do the sources allow us to re-construct Pithoro Pir as a historical character? In an initial attempt to address these questions, I will explore Pithoro Pir's hagiographical legend.

According to the legend of Pithoro Pir, a man called Maadan (Madan according to Burton) asked for the intercession of Baha al-Din Zakariyya (d. 1267) to have a son during a visit to the famous Sufi of Multan in Sindh. Baha al-Din offered him the small end (*pithu*) of a dried date. When his wife tasted the blessed date, she fell pregnant. The son they had was named Pithoro, after the name of the date end. Pithoro became thereafter a disciple of Baha al-Din. The legend of his birth is almost always identical despite some people, including the *gaddi nashin*, stating that the request for a son was made not of Baha al-Din Zakariyya but Shah Rukn al-Din (d. 1335)—another later saint of Multan. It should be stressed that both Sufis were members of the Sohrawardi order and that Shah Rukn al-Din was no other than the grandson and successor of Baha al-Din Zakariyya.

Pithoro settled in Thar Parkar, not far from Umarkot and his wisdom soon attracted disciples: he became a venerated saint with many followers (*murids*). Their number steadily increased day after day. Hamir Rano, the local *raja* (*rano*) of Umarkot, took umbrage at the success of the *pir*. The *rano* became convinced that the final objective of Pithoro Pir was to seize power. The *rano* gathered an army and decided to attack Pithoro Pir. But a miracle turned the situation in favour of the *pir*: an invisible army came to help him and the *rano* could not do anything but pay homage to him. The *rano* asked for forgiveness. From this moment on subjects of the *rano* offered gifts to the *pir* and even the *rano* himself sent him a tribute.

The legend of Pithoro Pir thus has two main components: (1) the spiritual formation, and (2) the fight with the *rano*. Baha al-Din Zakariyya is a central character of thirteenth century South Asian Sufism and meeting with him is commonplace in Sufi-related narratives in the Indus Valley. This episode even exceeded the framework of Sufism: the meeting is described in a devotional song (*ginan*) credited to Pir Shams (an Ismaili saint) and in the tradition of Guru Nanak, the founder of Sikhism in the sixteenth century.[16] Although the meeting with Baha al-Din Zakariyya is a recurring topic, it should be noted that the context in which it occurs varies. For Pir Shams, the meeting is a confrontation during which each one wants to prove their superiority during a contest of miracles. Lal Shahbaz for its part is described during a time of mystical hearing (*sama*) in company of Baha al-Din. No mention is made of an unspecified competition.[17] Quite to the contrary, the two saints are represented as friends.

While devoting a significant part of his booklet to the meetings between Pithoro Pir and Baha al-Din, Sartani mentions another charismatic figure who is supposed to have played a key role in Pithoro Pir's life. This figure is named Gosain Birnath Swami.[18] This enigmatic figure is honoured near Pithoro Pir's temple with a small *ashram* standing in front of the main entrance of the *mari*. The inscription gives the name as Goswami Virnathji. Inside the small building, there are Shivaite emblems including the trident. The figure of Birnath or Virnath is shrouded in mystery although he could be a figure belonging to the Nathpanth since he reminds us of Viranatha, one of the twelve wise men to whom the doctrine of the Kapalikas was revealed. Viranatha should have been initiated later than Gorakhnath himself, the master of the Kanphatas.[19]

As regards the second component of the legend, the name Pithoro Pir deserves special attention. Besides the local explanation of the word 'pithoro', from *pithu* meaning end, Pithoro Pir's name connects him to an important character of Indian history and through him to key historical events related to confrontations between Muslims and Hindus. There is a very important historical character with the name of Rai Pithora in Muslim sources. In other sources he is named Prithvi Raj but all agree he was the last sovereign of the Chauhan dynasty, which was superseded in 1193 by Muhammad Shihab al-Din of Ghor following the second battle of Tarain. This character is at the core of several legends. Amir Khwurd reports in *Siyar Al-Awliya* (i.e., biographies of the saints) that Muin al-Din Chishti, the famous Sufi of Ajmer, captured Rai Pithora alive thanks to a miracle before delivering him to the sultan of Ghazni, Muizz al-Din.[20] Rai Pithora appears in another legend relative to Goga Pir. Gorakhnath is said have sent an invisible army to help Goga Pir against Rai Pithora, despite another tradition where Goga Pir perishes in a battle against Firuz Shah Tughluq (d. 1388).[21]

Moreover, the socio-political trauma provoked by Muslim invasions in the eleventh and twelfth centuries gave birth to what Aziz Ahmad called 'counter epic'. He stated that the invasion began a Muslim epic of conquest and also, in return, an epic of resistance or 'counter-epic' from the Hindu side.[22] The counter-epic was not expressed by the Brahmanic tradition but by the Bardic one. This literature embodies two levels: (1) Rajput resistance against Muslim invaders, and (2) internecine rivalries between Rajputs, which are generally neutral to Muslims. The most famous counter-epic of the first type was *Prithvi Raj raso*, attributed to the authorship of Chand Bardai (who is reported to have been Prithvi Raj's minister and poet). Even if the nucleus of the epic was composed soon after the events it reported, additions and interpolations continued until the seventeenth century. This bardic literature embodies tales of Rajput struggle against Muslims and this is the reason why the Chauhan dynasty is often celebrated. The last hero of the Chauhan is named Hamir, the raja of Rathambore. In the epics related to internecine rivalry between the Rajputs, interpolations also occurred but a common feature is an attitude of reconciliation 'which has its historical basis in the assimilation of Rajput chivalry in the composite machinery of the Mughal Empire by Akbar'.[23]

At the local level, the area of Umarkot where Pithoro Pir lived had been the object of violent fights between two Rajput clans: the Somras and the Sodhas.[24] In 1439, the *rano* Hamir Sodha inflicted a defeat to Hamir Somra that finalized the reign of the Somras in the area. Although the Somras were defeated by the Sammas in 1351, after the death of the Delhi Sultan Muhammad Shah Tughluq, they retained control of the Eastern part of Sindh. Their resistance was facilitated by the arrival of Muhammad Shah Tughluq, while pursuing a rebel. The sultan died a little later in Sonda, on the banks of the Indus, and was buried in Sehwan Sharif, near Lal Shahbaz Qalandar's mausoleum.

After some time, in 1355, the Somras were, therefore, able to (re)conquer Umarkot, the city the Sodhas took from them in 1226.[25] In 1367, the new emperor of Delhi, Firuz Shah Tughluq, arrived at Thatta to reinstall the Somras. He besieged the city of Thatta, the then capital of the Sammas. Jam Juna I Samma asked for the intercession of the saint of Multan, Sayyid Jalal al-Din Bukhari, better known under the name of Makhdum Jahaniyyan Jahangasht (d. 1383). He convinced the emperor of Delhi to give up the siege.[26] The area of Umarkot was indeed at the centre of various conflicts and both local and extra-local interests. On the local level, it passed under the successive control of the Somras and the Sodhas. At the regional level, this period was one of transition between the Somras and the Sammas. Although the latter officially took power in 1351, the Somras preserved control of certain outlying areas of Sindh, in particular the area of Umarkot.

What can one historically deduce from the legend of this saint? The biographical events of the legend show contradictions. The Pir's meeting with Baha al-Din Zakariyya would place him in the thirteenth century. Nonetheless, the second event related to the *rano* Hamir Sodha would place him at the beginning of the fifteenth century. It is consequently obvious that certain events of this legend have to be understood on an allegorical level. Knowing that the meeting with Baha al-Din Zakariyya is a commonplace event in various traditions, it is tempting to make it an episode of the symbolic narrative commonly drawn on. The object of this reconstruction could be to show that Pithoro Pir is a Sufi of high calibre: he was initiated to the Sufi path by a saint who is the ultimate reference point in such matters in the Indus Valley. At the very least it shows that Pithoro Pir was affiliated to the Sufi *tariqah* of the Sohrawardiyya.

The second episode is *a priori* more convincing as regards historical references. Pithoro Pir was already a famous saint when the fight occurred between Hamir Sodha and Hamir Somra in 1439. It is recorded that after this battle Hamir Sodha would fight Pithoro Pir: should it be understood that the saint was a partisan of the Somras? Or does it reflect only the eternal confrontation between spiritual power and temporal power—a commonplace struggle between Sufism and the Nathpanth of the area which usually ends with the victory of spiritual power? Other interesting points are to be underlined: the interpolation between the account related to Pithoro Pir and that related to Muin al-Din Chishti. The narrative scene is identical: the Sufi Muin al-Din and the Sufi Pithoro Pir are both miraculously victorious over a Hindu king, but for reasons difficult to explain, the second Sufi curiously bears the name of the king overthrown by the first Sufi. It is probable that Pithora/Pithoro is a deterioration of Prithvi ('Earth' in Sanskrit) since his story gave rise to an abundant epic literature. It is difficult not to establish the link between the two characters.

To a certain extent, the legend of Pithoro Pir echoes an event of fundamental historical importance: the invasion of Muhammad Shihab al-Din of Ghor in 1192, the following creation of the Delhi sultanate in 1206, and subsequent beginning of Muslim domination on the Indian subcontinent. This date unquestionably marks a watershed in the history of South Asia. The narrative related to Pithoro Pir has a limited range: it occurs in eastern Sindh. It appears like an adaptation of a master narrative epic to a different and more modest reality and context. If it is not possible to specify the historical circumstances of the life of Pithoro Pir, one can—at least—observe that the period when he lived was disturbed.

Drawing on the pattern of confrontation between Muhammad of Ghor and Prithvi Raj, Pithoro Pir's legend narrates the confrontation between two Rajput clans: the Sodhas and the Somras. Is it an allegory of the competition between Islam and Hinduism? Knowing that the latter were Muslims, one can interpret the narrative as a duplicate of the Ghurid/Chauhan one. The balance of power between Muslims and Rajputs was about to be reversed in eastern Sindh, as had previously happened in the kingdom of Prithvi Raj centuries before. In this context, the double affiliation of Pithoro Pir with the Sohrawardiyya *tariqah* and to the Nathpanth gives evidence that a reconciliation eventually occurred through non-orthodox traditions, to paraphrase Gulraj, inside Islam and Hinduism. It is now necessary to turn to another question: how did a Sufi tradition get to be managed by Hindu Rajputs and what was the impact on local social structure.

A MASTER-DISCIPLE SYSTEM AND THE STRUCTURE OF LOCAL SOCIETY: 'COMMUNITAS' AS A TOOL OF SOCIAL CONTROL

Pithoro Pir is said to have disappeared underground in his sanctuary. The place where he disappeared has become the subject of a particular veneration: a small altar has been built and a *puja* is carried out daily. The sanctuary containing Pithoro Pir's tomb is called *mari* and it is located in the village of Pithoro, which lies between Mirpur Khas and Umarkot, on the railway line that formerly connected Hyderabad (Sindh) to Barmer and Jodhpur (Rajasthan). As with many other saints, the sanctuary's site bears the saint's name.

Like many renunciants, Pithoro Pir did not marry. Pithoro Pir transmitted his knowledge and authority to his brother Bhanwarji, whose tomb is in a small temple located below Pithoro's mausoleum. The present *pir* of Pithoro, Hathesingh, is the descendant of Bhanwarji and the twenty-second *pir* of the line. His authority as *pir* comes only from this kinship. In Weberian language, this authority is best referred to as hereditary charisma.[27]

Other descendants of Pithoro Pir's brother form a kind of sacerdotal caste within the sect. Known under the inexact name of Pithoro Pir Potas (i.e., descendants of Pithoro Pir) these kin of the Pir's brother are the sect's priests (*gurara*). It is interesting to note that Pithoro Pir Potas, although being Hindu, compare themselves with Sayyids rather than with the Brahmans. In the middle of the nineteenth century, Burton mentioned that they were a highly respected group. This reverence came certainly from their kinship with Pithoro Pir but also due to the knowledge they had in the interpretation of scriptures.

With regard to religion, Burton says without ambiguity that Pirpanthis are 'neither Hindu nor Moslem'. It is a commonplace statement in Sindh that is generally applied to a particular category of the population called *achut* in Sindh or, in Gandhian parlance, Harijans (i.e., children of God). The *achuts* are also known as Untouchables. To say that they are neither Hindus nor Muslims is often a pejorative assertion since it means that these populations practice coarse pagan worships like animism, knowing that they do not adhere to any major institutionalized religion, like Hinduism, Islam, or Christianity. Burton specifies that the disciples of Pithoro Pir 'have many ceremonies directed by their priests'.

Another socially contentious point relates to the caste to which Pithoro Pir is supposed to have belonged by birth. Hathesingh, the twenty-second *pir*, claims being a Thakur (i.e., a lord or master and an honorary title for Rajputs). Rajputs are subdivided into many clans: the *pir* belongs to the Sodha. According to Sartani, Pithoro Pir was himself a Parmar Sodha by birth as well as attested in the *bhajans*.[28] Other sources, including Burton, claimed him to have been a Menghwar (i.e., an Untouchable). Sodhas form the dominant group of Rajputs in Sindh. According to their tradition, they came from Ujjain, in Malwa in 1226.[29] Their chief, Parmar Sodha, would have been the established king or *rano* of Umarkot. The majority of Sodhas had become landowners and farmers. The *Gazetteer of Sindh*, published in 1907, describes them as worshipers of Shiva and does not mention Pithoro Pir.

Nonetheless, the cult of Pithoro Pir is managed historically by Sodha Rajputs. The Pithoro Pir Potas officiate in the villages as priests of Pithoro Pir. For instance, in the temple of Bhuj, the main priest (*pujari*) is a Pithoro Pir Pota and the singer of *bhajans* is a Sodha Rajput. In Pithoro, the *pir* himself officiates each evening after sunset. The ritual is a form of *puja pat* that is divided into three principal sequences:[30] (1) the preliminary (*arti*) during which the *pir* lights the candles, and where *bhajans* are sung without instrumental accompaniment, (2) the invocatory prayer (*dua*), and (3) the ritual of communion (*piyalo*). The *pir* performs this last rite only with its disciples (*murids*) and apart from the sanctuary. The formula of the *dua* is basic: '*Dado bhali kundo*!' (Dado will bring only good to you!).[31] It is noteworthy that the ritual of *piyalo* is common in Sindh and Gujarat. It is performed by the Sufis of Sehwan Sharif, by the Mahapanthis, and by Ismailis. It is the most widespread form of initiation to a spiritual Master. It is, however, difficult to know if this ritual has a common origin on the other side of the Indo-Pakistan border, and given the social meanings of inter-caste commensality in the context of South Asia, one can see in the *puja pat* rituals (especially in the *piyalo*) a process by which a 'communitas' is given birth.[32] The members of the different castes who are followers of Pithoro Pir share the drinking of blessed water. Through it, the caste barriers are abolished because their status is not relevant during the ceremony.

Who are the disciples of Pithoro Pir? When the question is asked, the *pir* enumerates about fifteen communities. One can divide them into three principal categories: the 'untouchable ones', Muslims, and Sodhas. Among the untouchable ones, three groups are prevalent: Menghwars, Bhils, and Kohlis. Among the Muslims of Sindh, one can quote Sindhis like the Sammas, Panhwars, and Baloch (among whom are Marris and Legharis). In Kutch, devotees are found among the Menghwars, Bhils, Kohlis, Sutars (carpenters), and Sodhas, while Muslims do not seem to venerate Pithoro Pir. Other Rajputs from the Jarejas of Kutch attend the Pir's temples but they are not strictly disciples of Pithoro Pir and do not make the *puja*. Another distinction must be mentioned: the disciples of Pithoro Pir mingle together in Sindh, whereas in Kutch, the Untouchables worship separately from Rajputs in the different temples.

Despite this complicated mix of followers, two communities dominate when speaking about the worship of Pithoro Pir: Menghwars and Sodha Rajputs. The social stratification of the caste system makes it tempting to argue that the master-disciple relationship is based on caste stratification embodied in a feudal society or, at least, on a clientele-type organization. While possible economical dependence could hardly be taken as a deciding factor, the social domination of the Rajputs cannot be contradicted. The Rajputs affiliate themselves to the *varna* of the Kshatryas. They are twice-born Hindus, and as their name states, they are from princely or royal origin.

In Thar Parkar, the Sodhas enjoyed privileges of sovereignty under the suzerainty of the raja of Jodhpur until 1813, when the Talpurs seized the city of Umarkot. Under the Talpurs, many Sodhas just refused to pay levies and the *mir* had to send a large force to reduce the people to submission: several chiefs were taken prisoner. After the British conquest, the eastern part of Thar Pakar was placed under Kutch while the west, including Umarkot, became a part of Hyderabad division. The British abolished all the fees the Sodhas used to collect such as emoluments from fields and rent free lands, as well as taxes on Hindu marriages, free food the Banias were forced to provide them and so on. Finally, the Sodhas were further forbidden to wear arms.[33] In 1846, the district was in open rebellion in which the Sodhas obviously played a leading role. The government asked them to state their grievances and a compromise was reached.[34]

What I wish to stress here is the nature of exclusive royal power enjoyed by the Sodhas in the area of Umarkot. At the other end of the social hierarchy stand the Menghwars. They are the most numerous group of Untouchables in all of Thar Parkar. Oral tradition is consistent that the majority of disciples are Menghwars (also known as Meghs or Meghvals). Burton, while not referring to any Rajput, does identify Pithoro Pir as the patron saint of the Menghwars. Sartani also stated that he is the *pir* of the Menghwars (*Menghwaran jo pir*).[35] Menghwars form a protean unit that shares activities generally related to working with skins of animals. They are, for example, tanners, leather dealers, or shoe-makers. As these activities are connected with dead animals, they are regarded as degrading within the Hindu system. Thus, Hindus classify Menghwars among the Untouchables. Robert Deliège writes that Menghwars nowadays account for 13.1 per cent of the Untouchables in Gujarat, 40 per cent of those of Jammu and Kashmir, and 14.7 per cent of those of Rajasthan.[36]

In Pakistan, one finds Menghwars in both Punjab and Sindh but no statistics are available. The Menghwars are also called Dhedhs. Burton certifies that the Menghwar term is a polished name for Dhedhs: for him, it acts as a single group. Both are nevertheless presented like distinct groups in the *Gazetteer of Sindh* published in 1907. Dhedhs are 70,678 (including 30,000 in Thar Parkar). They are specialists in the extraction of animal skins. The denomination of Menghwar is reserved for groups who specialize in working with leather, especially shoemakers but also weavers. This distinction could imply that they were two separate groups but, in any case, both activities are characterized by impurity and thus the state of being untouchable. These Menghwars were not classified under this name in the census of 1905. No explanation is given. In other provinces (like Punjab and Central Provinces) the term Dhedh is used to enumerate any person belonging to a low caste having a relationship with leather.

Although Pithoro Pir is the *Menghwaran jo pir*, the Menghwars venerate other deities too. In Sindh and Kutch, Pithoro Pir is associated with two categories of charismatic figures: the regional divinities and the pan-Indian divinities. The last category is usually limited to various representations of Devi, the wife of Shiva. The most frequent forms are Sitala Mata (the powerful goddess of smallpox) and Kali Mata. In Thar Parkar, a small part in the home is reserved for both Pithoro Pir and Sitala Mata. In the temple of Singh Bawani in Makli (near Thatta) one finds rooms dedicated to Pithoro Pir while others are devoted to pan-Indian divinities.

The most important feast in the worship of Pithoro Pir is the annual festival or *melo*. It commemorates the death of the *pir*; considered more like a mystical union with God (i.e., his absorption in God) it represents a final exit from the cycle of the reincarnations. As in other parts of Sindh (and in the neighbouring Indian and Pakistani provinces), the *melo* is both a pilgrimage and a gigantic fair. There are no recent statistics but in the 1920 *Gazetteer of Sindh*, the *melo* of Pithoro Pir was second in terms of the number of pilgrims: 30,000 devotees gathered together then, in comparison to 40,000 for Udero Lal, and only 4,000 for Ramdeo Pir in Tando Allahyar, and 8,000 for Lal Shahbaz Qalandar in Sehwan. The products most sold at the *melo* were the copperware, silk cloth, embroideries, saddles, and harnesses. Total sales amounted to three lacs of rupees.[37]

Sources are not concordant with regard to the dates on which the *melo* occurs. Smyth reports the date of first Badho. Although this month of the lunisolar calendar of Sindh lasts from mid-August to mid-September, Smyth explains that it is towards the beginning of September. September was also the given month by the *Gazetteer of Sindh* of 1876. On the other hand, Sartani mentions both Cheti Chand and the New Moon (*bij*) of the month of Badho.[38] The fair lasts seven days. In Kutch, an informant at the temple of Bhuj gave the date of 26 March for the *melo*. Finally, Jetho Lalwani confirms that the *melo* of Bhuj occurs every year for Cheti Chand. There are various explanations for this divergence of dates.

A recent event gives evidence of the entanglement between social dominance exercised by the Sodhas over the Menghwars and the cult of Pithoro Pir. For twenty years, a group of disciples who belong to the

Menghwars rejected spiritual allegiance to the *pir* of Pithoro. The head of the dissidents, one Totaram, decided to organize a separate *melo* in May. Totaram is presently involved in a lawsuit with the *pir* of Pithoro about the management of the sanctuary. Obviously, the party led by Totaram contests the communitas formed by the untouchable followers of Pithoro Pir. They denounce this communitas as being intrumentalized by the *gaddi nashin* and as reinforcing his social control as a Sodha Rajput.

This contestation is expressed through the creation of an association known as the Scheduled Castes Federation of Pakistan (SCFP), better known as 'Pakdalits'. According to its president, Sadhumal Valasai, the Dalits are not Hindus: 'In Pakistan the common Dalits know nothing about Hinduism except Manu's words that they are born to serve the caste people to improve their status in their next life'. He adds: 'They are a lot of confused people who don't know why they are Hindus and why they are still attached to "vulture-culture" Hinduism'.[39] The SCFP states that only Muslims can restore the dignity of the Dalits. The Pakdalits argue that Article 20 of the Constitution of 1956 abolished Untouchables and that Article 28 claims that the State shall endeavour to promote the special care, as well as the educational and economic interests of Untouchables. The Sodha Rajputs are the main targets of the Pakdalits but until now, the remote area of Thar Parkar is still under the control of the Sodha Rajputs.

CONCLUSION

This brief study of the tradition of Pithoro Pir provides a number of clues regarding the questions raised in its introduction. One can consider this path as a religious tradition located beyond Hinduism and Islam as normative religions. Typically, the tradition embodies a Sufi character as founded in the great Sohrawardi figure of Baha al-Din Zakariyya. Most interesting is the second phase of his religious formation in which Pithoro Pir was also initiated to spirituality by a Nath.

At the symbolical level, we saw that his legend was drawn under historical narratives, but after having rebuilt them in a new framework. The interpolation between the Hindu *raja* and the Sufi can be explained by the successive stages through which the narratives have passed since the time of Chand Bardai. We can state that this original matrix was first reinterpreted according to a key local historical episode, that of the rivalry between Hamir Sodha and Hamir Somra. The battle that occurred in the middle of the fifteenth century put a final end to the domination of Muslim Rajputs (i.e., the Somras).

Although Pithoro Pir is acknowledged by the disciples and the masters as an authentic Sufi, his belonging to the Sodha Rajputs is stressed in the *bhajans* and in *kafis*. Finally, the caste affiliation seems far more meaningful in comparison to the religious or even spiritual affiliation. Obviously, by managing the sect of Pithoro Pir, the Rajputs could reinforce the domination they already had over low castes like the Menghwars through classical networks of patron-client ties. As in many other cults practiced by untouchable communities, the core of the ritual is the *piyalo*, a kind of communion whose object is to give equal status to all participants (although only during the time of the ceremony). In fact, the ritual of *piyalo* gives birth to a communitas. For a few years now, one can observe dissension among the followers of Pithoro Pir. The episode of changing the date of the *melo* has therefore to be understood as a social claim expressed by the 'oppressed' communities against the dominant ones in the context of both the Hindu caste system and the worship of Pithoro Pir.

NOTES

1. Sara Ansari, *Sufi Saints and State Power: The Pirs of Sind, 1843–1947* (Lahore: Vanguard Books, 1992).
2. Jethmal Parsram Gulraj, *Sind and Its Sufis* (Lahore: Sang-e-Meel Publications, 1979 [1924]), 76–77.
3. Ibid., 83.
4. Mawlana Qazi Muhammad Iqbal Husayn Saheb Naimi, *Tazkirah-ye Awliya-ye Sindh* (Karachi: Ilmi Kitab Ghar: 1998).
5. Richard Burton, *Sindh and the Inhabitants of the Valley of the Indus* (Karachi: Indus Publications, 1987 [1851]); Malwa is a part of the Indian state of Rajasthan and British sources usually report that Menghwars come from this region (E.H. Aitken, *Gazetteer of the Province of Sindh* (Karachi: Indus Publications, 1986 [1907]).
6. For an overview of the similarity regarding the contents of *pothis* belonging to distinct religious communities, see Michel Boivin, 'Ginan and the Management of Religious Heritage among the Ismaili Khoja—With a Special Reference to the Sindhi-speaking Area', in Françoise Mallison and Tazim Kassam, eds., *Ginans: Texts and Contexts: Essays on Ismaili Hymns from South Asia in Honour of Zawahir Moir* (Delhi: Matrix Publishers, 2007), 41–47.
7. Raichand Chatunmal Sartani, *Pir Pithoro Saheb* (Mirpur Khas: Pakistan Edition, 1955). Hathesingh, the current 'guardian of the throne' (i.e., *gaddi nashin*) of Pithoro Pir's sanctuary, informed me in an interview that he has heard about a booklet on Pithoro Pir but that he has never seen it. Ghulam Ali Allana mentions Sartani's book in the bibliography of his book on the culture of Sindh but without specifying any bibliographical source (Ghulam Ali Allana, *Sindhi Culture: A Preliminary Survey* (Karachi: Indus Publications, 1986).

8. Raichand Harijan, *Tarikh-e Registan* (Hyderabad: Sindhi Adabi Board, 1956).
9. Ibid., 19–26.
10. Kutch is a part of the Indian state of Gujarat, with Bhuj as its capital. It is separated from Sindh by the Rann of Kutch. The language spoken, Kutchi, is nevertheless a Sindhi dialect. The Rajput dynasty who used to rule the country is Jareja, a clan of the Sammas of Sindh.
11. Sartani, 53–62.
12. Ibid., 54.
13. Ibid., 59.
14. On Rama Pir (or Ramdeo Pir), see Sohail Amir Ali Bawani, 'Beyond Hindu and Muslim: Rethinking Iconographic Models and Symbolic Expressions from Sindh/The Case of the Tradition of Rama Pir', *Nukta Art* 1–2 (2007): 64–71. For more detail on Udero Lal, see Parwani in this volume.
15. J.W. Smyth, *Gazetteer of the Province of Sind: B Volume VI, Thar and Parkar District* (Bombay: Government Central Press, 1926), 45.
16. Zawahir Moir, 'The Life and Legends of Pir Shams as Reflected in the Ismaili Ginans: A Critical Review', in Françoise Mallison, ed., *Constructions Hagiographiques dans le Monde Indien: Entre Mythe et Histoire*, (Paris: Librairie Honoré Champion, 2001), 373–375.
17. Michel Boivin, 'Reflections on Lal Shahbaz Qalandar and the Management of his Spiritual Authority in Sehwan Sharif', *Journal of the Pakistan Historical Society* 50.4 (2003): 43.
18. Sartani, 25.
19. D.N. Lorenzen, *The Kapalikas and the Kalamukhas: Two Lost Shivaite Sects* (Delhi: Motilal Banarssidas, 1991 [1972]), 37.
20. P.M. Currie, *The Shrine and Cult of Muin al-Din Chishti* (Delhi: Oxford University Press, 1992 [1989]), 29.
21. On Goga Pir, see: Margaret Mills, Peter Claus and Sarah Diamond, eds., *South Asian Folklore: An Encyclopaedia* (London: Routledge, 2003), 270. On Muin al-Din Chishti, see: Currie, 29–30.
22. Aziz Ahmad, 'Epic and Counter-Epic in Medieval India', *Journal of the American Oriental Society* 83.4 (1963): 470.
23. Ibid., 474.
24. Local tradition states that the Somras are Sodhas converted to Islam, probably under the Ismaili persuasion.
25. Umarkot is said to have been founded by the Somra Umar. His son was Pithu, but according to Mir Masum, Umar and Pithu were the same individual.
26. The Indus Valley was still to be invaded in 1397. Pir Muhammad was in Multan and the following year, his father Timur Lang (Tamerlane) put an end to the sultanate of Delhi. Jam Juna II Samma, who controlled Sindh then, sought alliances with the sultan of Gujarat.
27. Max Weber, *The Sociology of Religion*, trans. Ephraim Fischoff (London: Methuen, 1965 [1922]).
28. Sartani, 4.
29. The alleged origin of the Sodha Rajputs is Malwa. As noted, according to Burton, the Menghwars also claim to be from Malwa. While there is no formal explanation for this correlation, it hardly seems a random coincidence.
30. The *puja pat* is a ritual in which a ceremony (*puja*) is performed on a small table (*pat*) used as an altar. It is the main ritual among the different sects to which the local

Untouchable castes belong (Dominique-Sila Khan, *Conversions and Shifting Identities. Ramdev Pir and the Ismailis in Rajasthan* (Delhi: Manohar, 1997).

31. The use of the word 'Dado' addresses several issues. The devotees do not agree among themselves on its interpretation. One can summarise their points of view to three versions: (1) Dado is an honorary title of Pithoro Pir, (2) Dado is the name of his grandfather, and (3) Dado is another term to designate the *guraras* of the sect. The word Dado refers to another sect which is known under the name of Dadupanth. It draws its name from a saint (*sant*) named Dadu (1544–1604), which results in Dado in Sindhi. A native of nearby Gujarat, this disciple of Kabir was born into a Hindu family. He converted to Islam and became a renunciant. His sanctuary is in Rajasthan, close to Jaipur. Although one finds some Sindhi words in his oracles (*vani*), he does not seem to have had disciples in Sindh. On the other hand, in Sindh, a site which is less than one hundred kilometers from Pithoro is connected with a certain Pir Dadu. In the middle of the sixteenth century, this Ismaili *pir* was established in Fateh Bagh. According to his tradition, he was constrained by a bigoted *qazi* to flee Sindh and to take refuge in Kutch. His two brothers, Ara al-Din and Jamar al-Din, did not succeed in escaping with him: they were captured and beheaded. Two mausoleums were built in their memory at Fateh Bagh. Pir Dadu ended his life under the protection of the *rao* of Kutch and his mausoleum is in Bhuj.
32. Victor Turner, *The Ritual Process. Structure and Anti-Structure* (Hawthorne, NY: Aldine de Gruyter, 1997 [1969]), 96–97.
33. A.W. Hughes, *Gazetteer of the Province of Sindh* (Karachi: Indus Publications, 1995 [1876]), 863.
34. When the eastern part of Thar Parkar was reincorporated into Sindh in 1856, it gave birth to another rebellion under the leadership of the *rano* of Parkar. Colonel Evans, from Hyderabad, quickly took the city before it was attacked by the Kohlis but did so in vain. In 1860, the *rano* and his minister were tried for sedition and sentenced to fourteen and ten years in exile (Ibid., 864).
35. Sartani, 39.
36. Robert Deliège, *Les Intouchables en Inde: Des Castes d'Exclus* (Paris: Imago, 1995), 41–42.
37. Smyth, 45.
38. Sartani, 49.
39. Yoginder Sikand, 'Plights of Dalits in Pakistan,' 6 March 2004 (See the following URL: http://www.counter currents.org/dalit-sikand060304.htm).

CHAPTER 7

Getting Ahead or Keeping Your Head? The 'Sindhi' Migration of Eighteenth Century India

Matthew A. Cook

Among South Asians, Sindhis are considered businessmen of great skill, for which they are admired but also feared; a common North Indian proverb warns, 'If you meet a snake and a Sindhi, kill the Sindhi first'. South Asians also believe Sindhis live everywhere. As one Indian interviewee put it, 'You'll find a Sindhi anywhere because he'll go anywhere just to get ahead'.

Among Sindhis, however, the ubiquity of their business-oriented community is a sad consequence of being so dispersed, a fact popularly explained as resulting from their exclusion from Pakistan in 1947. Since Partition in 1947, Sindhis have travelled the world looking for opportunities. Their communities exist in metropolises throughout the world, including Hong Kong, Mumbai, London, and New York. However, despite frequent economic success in their new homes, Sindhis still experience a deep sense of loss. A Sindhi man in Mumbai once expressed this sentiment to me when, with glazed eyes, he said sadly: 'No land, no identity'.

I believe the landscape of South Asian history suggests a different reading of the Sindhi condition. In fact, the engine of Sindhi identity has always been the displacements that have challenged their existence. The realities of place and of the imagination for Sindhis have always blurred. Forced migration during Partition is only one historical example of this social fact. This chapter examines another example: the eighteenth century migration of 'Sindhis' to Sindh.

I argue that Sindhis who fled Pakistan during Partition are part of a community that has historically been mobile. I also argue that state disintegration and formation have always played a role in this mobility. To illustrate these arguments, this chapter examines how Partition-fleeing

Sindhis are the descendants of Punjabi refugees who arrived on the lower Indus during the eighteenth century. First, I address the disintegration of the Mughal imperial state in the Punjab. I show, focusing on the Punjabi city of Multan, how state disintegration brought refugees—specifically from the Khatri community—to Sindh. Second, I investigate how economic and political factors associated with Mughal successor state formation encouraged Khatri migrations. Third, I examine family history and religious practice to illustrate the Khatri characteristics of a Sindhi identity. I conclude with a discussion of the continued importance of the state to migration and suggest that a Sindhi future can be built with less anxiety about loss by understanding the community's past.

STATE AND ECONOMIC DISINTEGRATION AND THE DISLOCATION OF POPULATIONS

According to Ansar Zahid-Khan, in *History and Culture of Sind: A Study of the Socio-Economic Organization and Institutions During the Sixteenth and Seventeenth Centuries*, the 'insignificant' number of non-Muslim Sindhis made the maintenance of specific community boundaries among them difficult.[1] As a result, non-Muslim Sindhis 'merged into a composite caste, the Lohana'.[2] During the eighteenth century, the constitution of the Lohana increasingly reflected communities from areas outside Sindh. One such community were the Bhattis. Hailing from the area around Jaisalmer in Rajasthan, many Lohana families claim a Bhatti heritage (e.g., the Hindujas and Dariris). Such large numbers of Bhattis were absorbed into the Lohana during this time period that some nineteenth century British colonial officers define the Lohana as Bhattis.[3]

The names of many Sindhi *viradaris* (patrilineages) reflect migrations to Sindh from Rajasthan. Lohanas and Rajasthanis, for example, often share first-name endings with the suffix 'mull' or 'mal' (e.g., Ramomal, Parsomal, or Wahumal).[4] These suffixes—along with those of Das and Ram—specifically connect the Lohana with another community from western South Asia: the Bhatia.[5] The Bhatia are a community of Bhatti who are socially 'degraded' because they participate in the trading profession. While often endogamous, the Bhatia did not strongly follow endogamy in Sindh where marriage outside the community only entails a fine.[6] For example, the Bhagchandani Lohana *viradari*—who lived and worked in the Hyderabad area as government officers, engineers, and auditors, as well as traders—are originally Bhatias.

Religious practice also reflects the Lohana's absorption of Bhatias. Sect affiliation usually marks Bhatias off as a distinct community: they utilize Pokarna Brahmans from Rajasthan while most Lohana employ Punjabi Saraswat Brahman and/or Nanak Panthi ritual specialists. However, Lohanas also occasionally employ Pokarna Brahmans. Furthermore, some Lohana *viradaris* share with Bhatias a common Vaishnavite identity by belonging to the Vallabhacharya sect.[7] Such similarities reflect the fact that Bhatias and Lohana share ancestral histories from the Punjab.[8] The Bhatia and other migrants—most notably Khatris—came to Sindh in the eighteenth century from places like the Punjabi city of Multan and were absorbed into the folds of the Lohana community. The character of this process is illuminated by the political economy of eighteenth century Punjab.

The Punjab, in the twilight of the Mughal Empire, was *not* an area of undisturbed prosperity. Natural events, like the silting of the Indus River, had a serious long-term effect on the region: its river trade routes fell into relative disuse and goods had to be transported via road. Road transportation greatly increased the cost of merchandise in the region and Punjabi cities (e.g., Multan) were adversely affected.[9]

Dependence on road routes was further detrimental to regional trade since eighteenth century Punjab was an increasingly violent place. Nadir Shah's invasion and the subsequent Mughal defeat in 1739, effectively ended the latter's imperial control in the Punjab. Ten years later, Ahmad Shah Durrani invaded and annexed areas of the Punjab to his Afghan kingdom. Throughout the century, invasions and sieges ravaged the Punjab. The Marathas attacked and occupied the Punjab in 1758–59. In the last part of the century, the Punjab witnessed continual warfare between the Afghans and the Sikhs. The Sikhs occupied Multan in 1772, lost it in 1780, and then—in twenty-eight years of on and off warfare—mounted multiple attempts to recapture the city.[10]

With the disintegration of the Mughal imperial state, commerce in the Punjab became dislocated as local groups fought one another for regional and local control. Rural *zamindars* (i.e., landowners) and peasants from the Punjab's dominant Jat community increasingly challenged Mughal authority. While many uprisings proceeded through their own logic, as a whole, they collectively represented an attempt to gain greater local control over the Punjab's revenues.[11] For example, *zamindars* prevented Mughal *amils* (i.e., government workers) from enforcing state regulations to realize rural revenue. In the area of Sindh Sagar, Mughal *amils* failed to collect a single penny from the rural *zamindars*.[12]

Locals making their fortunes at whatever cost seriously disturbed trade through the Punjab during the eighteenth century. Major routes, like that between Lahore and Multan, increasingly became vulnerable to raids by local *zamindars*.[13] Local disruptions combined to result in a general regional decline that threatened large numbers of peasants with impoverishment. This situation developed into violent rural protest. Chetan Singh, in 'Polity, Economy and Society under the Mughals', states:

> There is sufficient reason to suggest that much of the unrest that the region witnessed toward the end of the seventeenth century and in the beginning of the eighteenth was very closely associated with a growing economic crisis that originated at least partly from the long-term decline of trade and commerce in the region. While the urban population was better placed to salvage the remnants of a failing economy, the adjacent rural, yet commercialized, areas were forced into rebellion. Towns became the prime target of assault as disorder overtook large parts of the Punjab and other adjacent territories.[14]

Pauperized rural peasants and *zamindars* during this period found a common voice of protest in Sikhism, dominated at the time by the rural Jat community.[15] According to Muzaffar Alam, in *The Crisis of Empire in Mughal North India*, the rising popularity of Sikhism was largely due to the Punjab's sour economic reality:

> The change in the nature of the Sikh movement from one of relatively strong peasantry movement for raising themselves socially in the seventeenth century and earlier eighteenth century to one of impoverished *zamindars* and peasants struggling for survival and maintenance of their existing positions in the eighteenth century can only be appreciated in the light of the history of the economy of the region.[16]

In response to Sikhism's growing momentum, the Mughal state increasingly used provincial resources to suppress rural peasant and *zamindar* rebellions.[17] The resulting violence created an atmosphere of complete uncertainty in the Punjab as rural rebels assaulted urban areas, which included the symbols and structures of Mughal authority and government worker populations. For example, peace and commercial prosperity came to a violent close in Batala when Sikhs attacked it in 1709.[18] Chetan Singh, in *Region and Empire: Punjab in the Seventeenth Century*, writes that violence during this time was best characterized as urban-rural: 'Towns were the prime targets of assault. Little distinction was made by the rebels regarding the religion of the urban residents'.[19] In the town of Karnal, 'a hundred or two hundred Hindus and Musalmans who had been made prisoners were made to sit down in one place and were slaughtered'.[20] According to Singh, 'the towns-folk in turn seem to have been almost unanimously opposed to the rebels'.[21] The area around Multan—from which many Lohana claim a heritage—witnessed particularly violent rebellions. In 1700, Prince Muhammad Muizzuddin, the *nazim* (governor) of Multan, personally led Mughal imperial forces against rebels. However, despite many military expeditions, the Multan rebellions were never ultimately suppressed.

Under the Mughals, Multan was an urban commercial centre with great regional economic influence. Located at the crossroads of the overland and river/sea routes that connected India with Afghanistan, Persia, and the Arabian Sea, the city was a major distribution and commercial centre.[22] However, the city's location on the main highway leading to Central Asia also made it vulnerable and a target of attack.[23] Consequently, Multan supported a military cantonment designed to (1) resist invaders, and (2) support Mughal frontier areas like Qandahar from foreign (i.e., Persian) attacks.[24]

Declines in trade, as much as regional violence and foreign aggression, brought hard times to eighteenth century Multan. Stephen Frederic Dale states: 'Most of the merchants from Mughal India who conducted business in Iran, Turan or Russia…migrated to those areas from Multan'.[25] Nearly all these non-Muslim Multanis were from one community: the Khatri.[26] The eighteenth century saw major economic setbacks for Multani-Khatri merchants in Persia. These setbacks, in conjunction with the disintegration of the Mughal Empire, contributed to Multan's general decline.[27] For example, in 1722 Ghilzai Afghans sacked Isfahan. This attack ended Safavid rule and produced a power vacuum that endured through the rest of the century in Persia. After the Ghilzai attack on Isfahan, security for trade—a distinguishing feature of the area during the latter part of Safavid rule—disappeared. The area became a territory where pastoral nomads contended each other for power:

> The Ghilzai sack of Isfahan badly damaged the prosperous base of what was probably the largest community of Indian businessmen outside of the South Asian subcontinent at the time, while the ensuing country-wide disorder allowed various combatants to plunder merchants throughout the country. Then in 1745/46 Nadir Shah Afshar's relentless campaigns and fiscal exactions dealt the decisive blow to the prosperity of the mercantile communities in Isfahan and the economy of the country as a whole.[28]

The fall of Isfahan also 'fatally compromised' Multani-Khatri merchants who lived in Astrakhan (i.e., the Caspian Sea region). With (1) fewer merchants arriving from India via Persia, and (2) a serious decline in Iranian textile production (the staple commodity of Indian commerce in Astrakhan), trade dropped off considerably. The fortunes of Multani-Khatri merchants in the region plummeted:

> By 1735 the number of Indians who travelled to Astrakhan each year had dropped to less than half the number that had arrived annually before 1722, and by 1758 the value of silk and cotton exports from Iran and the Caucasus to Astrakhan had declined to 40,000 roubles per year, down from the 230,000 roubles' worth of cloth that had been shipped to the city in 1744. These trends translated into a dramatic deterioration of the commercial influence of Astrakhan Indian merchants. Whereas late as the 1730s and 1740s Indians still carried on about one-third of the values of Russia's average trade with Iran and the Caucasus, by 1785 their share of this trade had fallen to between 7.3 and 5.6 per cent.[29]

With overseas fortunes decreasing and regional violence rising, Multan's revenues declined. By 1750 the Mughal revenues realized from Multan decreased by over one-third.[30] During this same period, local archives record Khatri traders moving in large numbers from Multan to the south in search of new opportunities. For example, just under sixty per cent of recorded migrations by traders in the Bikaner archive (circa 1700–1800) were from Multan and the majority of these were Khatris.[31] Violence, economic hard times, and (according to Chetan Singh) increasing corruption became so bad that it 'caused all Multan men to leave the place'.[32]

KHATRIS AND SUCCESSOR STATE FORMATION

The Khatri were particularly hard pressed by the Punjab's changing economic and political fabric. Large-scale Punjabi commercial activity was dominated by only a few communities and particularly important among them were the Khatri.[33] The Khatris' fortunes as traders were closely linked with political stability and this meant, in the Punjab, the maintenance of the Mughal imperial state.[34] Local rebellions and their subsequent economic dislocations had a major adverse effect on the fortunes of the Khatris.

To fully grasp declining Khatri prosperity requires understanding imperial policy that prevented the formation of a united Mughal successor state in the Punjab. With the death of Bahadur Shah in 1712, imperial state policy aimed to drive wedges between the Punjab's various non-Mughal communities. One goal was to alienate Khatris from the region's dominant community, the Jats. With this goal in mind, Khatris were inducted into the structures of Mughal imperial service.[35] Muzaffar Alam states:

> The Mughals tried to consolidate their power in the Punjab through the trading community. The Mughals may not have recognized the economic advantages of the absorption of the Khatris into the imperial service; they appear to have appreciated its political implications. As the crisis enveloped the region and the threat to the Mughal power increased from the peasants, its dependence grew on the Khatris and other trading communities.[36]

In government service, the Khatris were no mere agents and clerks, but workers whose job primarily was to maintain on a secure footing the economic position of *jagirdars* (Mughal nobles).[37] The *jagirdars* of the Punjab had trust in, and sole dependence upon, Khatris.[38] In conflict with rebellious agrarian groups, the *jagirdars* depended heavily on Khatris (rather than *zamindars*) as provincial *ijaradars* (revenue farmers). As *ijaradars*, Khatris came into conflict with rural landowners in order to realize their *jagirdars*' revenue expectations: to collect revenue Khatris began to arrogate the 'customary perquisites of the *zamindars*'.[39] The appropriation of *zamindar* status greatly enriched the Khatris. This new wealth—even in the face of decreased trade—helped establish Khatris as highly placed aristocrats in the hierarchy of Mughal officials. For example, substantial numbers of Khatris acquired eminent urban positions as *diwans* (ministers), *umaras* (nobles), and *a'yans* (notables).[40] The Khatri's dominance of Mughal imperial service was so overwhelming that Muzaffar Alam concludes: 'The Mughals seem to have ruled the Punjab…through eminent Khatris'.[41]

The Khatris' appropriation of *zamindari* perquisites and dominance in government service worked to drive a sharp wedge between urban Khatris and rural Jats. Two phenomena revealed this increasing gap in solidarity: (1) the Khatris' alienation from, and (2) increased Jat support for Sikhism. For example, when asked for support in Sikhism's fight against the Mughals the Khatris 'submitted, in reply, that they were extremely weak and could not afford to incur the enmity of their rulers', and 'requested to be left alone'.[42] The abolition of the *mansad* (i.e., regional collection agent of the Guru)—an institution largely in Khatri control—also drove Khatris from the Sikh movement. Relations between Khatris and Jats soured to such a degree that the latter debated 'excommunicating' the former:

> The meek submission of the Khatris to the imperial order to shave off their beards might have created a breach between them and their associates on the one hand and the Sikhs of Banda on the other. This would have led to debate as to whether without the five 'Ks' a Sikh could remain a true Sikh.[43]

In response to rural Jat hostility, Khatris strongly supported eighteenth century Mughal military campaigns against Sikhs. With their fortunes closely linked to Mughal political stability, the rural uprisings by Jat Sikhs caused the Khatri considerable financial losses. These losses further widened the gaps between the Khatris, the Sikh movement, and agrarian communities. Ultimately, these gaps became unbridgeable. The decline in Mughal and the rise in Sikh political power in eighteenth century Punjab produced social, economic, and political hardship for the Khatri. The region's changing social, economic, and political fabric dislocated populations. During this period, Alam states that 'a large number of the traders seem to have migrated from their hometowns in northern and western Punjab to the east and to the south of Multan in Sindh'.[44]

With the breakdown of the Mughal Empire, local rajas, nawabs, raos, and amirs became practically independent in their regions. As they ceased to be financially tied to the empire, many searched for new avenues of revenue. Many promoted commerce as a long-term mechanism to help balance budgets (e.g., with income from customs and excise duties).[45] Duties remittances, free land for homes and shops, and government help to realize loans were all offered to attract relocating traders.[46] The movement of relocating traders involved in banking played a key role in the establishment of Mughal successor regimes. They offered credit and liquid cash and 'were recognized as a critical prop by all the regional powers concerned'.[47] Sindh, with its newly established successor state in the eighteenth century under the Kalhora family, fell into this regional pattern. Sindh, particularly in comparison to the Punjab of this era, presented opportunities for the Khatris.

At the close of the seventeenth century, the Kalhoras rose to power in Sindh. *Fakirs* (religious mendicants) by profession, they gathered a following and engaged the Mughals in guerrilla warfare. In 1701, Yar Muhammad Kalhoro secured a *sanad* (grant) from the Mughal emperor with a title under the imperial system. His rule lasted for eighteen years. The first nine were spent in warfare that increased his territory and power.[48] The following nine years were devoted to consolidating power. Contemporary English accounts portray Sindh as prosperous. Alexander Hamilton in 1699 describes Sindh's port city of Thatta as 'the emporium of the province, a very large and rich city'.[49] Alexander Burnes later calls the area 'flourishing'.[50] Robert Erskine (of the East India Company's factory in Sindh), reflecting on pre-1757 Sindh in 1761, states: 'under so good and quiet a Government…it must prove an advantageous settlement to the Hon'ble company'.[51] S.P. Chablani, in *Economic Conditions in Sind, 1592–1843* states: 'Sind at this time [i.e., until 1750], as we have seen, was a prosperous land, with large and populous towns, a thriving agriculture, and a flourishing industry, fortified by far-flung trade'.[52]

Sindh's trade routes made the area attractive to both Khatris and other traders (like the Bhatia) from the Punjab. It had trade connections with Afghanistan, Khorasan, Arabia, Persia, Turkey, Mesopotamia, Asia Minor, China, and West Europe, as well as with coastal ports in the Persian Gulf, Diu, Cambay, Goa, Surat, and other areas along the Malabar coast.[53] Sindh's land routes connected it to the West: goods passed through Johi in the Larkana district, crossed over to Balochistan through the Mulla Pass in the Kirthar mountain range, and through Persia on the way to the Mediterranean. Alternatively, goods reached Persia via Tando Rahim Khan, Pandhi Wahi, Lak Rohel, Lak Phusiand, and Lak Gare near Kathrach before going on to Turkey. Finally, although less common, there was a route to Persia via Las Bela, and Makran.[54] Trade with Afghanistan and other territories to the north went by 'highway' from Bukkur (later Shikarpur) through the Bolan Pass in the Suleiman-Hala mountains to Qandahar, Hari Rud, Merv, and, finally, Turkistan.[55] Talking of the period when the Punjab was experiencing unrest and turmoil, Chablani concludes that Sindh was prosperous:

> Sind in the seventeenth and first part of the eighteenth centuries, which coincided with the rule of the Moghals and the early Kalhoras, occupied an important place in the commercial world. It supported a well developed agriculture as also a dozen flourishing industries, and it was well known not only for the abundance of grain and dairy products, but also for the excellence of its textiles, indigo and saltpetre, leather goods and curios. Its industrious and enterprising population carried on a thriving trade not only with the more important emporiums of India—Multan and Lahor, Agra and Ahmedabad, but also with Arabia, Afghanistan and Khorasan, Persia, and Turkey, Mesopotamia and Asia Minor, West Europe and China. Its coastal trade with the ports in the Persian Gulf and on the Malabar coast was considerable; and it was at this time that the European nations—the Portuguese, the British and the Dutch, established their 'factories' in the province.[56]

Great opportunities were made even more available to Punjabi migrants in the eighteenth century. Plague and famine in the late seventeenth century greatly depopulated Sindh and created economic niches that needed to be filled. British accounts from 1659–60 state famine 'swept away most part of the people…never famine raged worse in any place the living being hardly able to burye [*sic*] the dead'.[57] Hamilton observed in 1696 that there was a 'severe plague to the affect the town [Thatta] and the circumadjacent country, to such a degree that, in the city only, above 80,000 died of it'.[58]

The opportunities of Sindh were attractive not only due to the socio-political and economic unrest of the Punjab, but by the simultaneous decline of Surat as a major trade centre (Surat is located to Sindh's south). The disintegrating Mughal state in Surat—like that in the Punjab—had serious regional repercussions. With the local aristocracy no longer under Mughal state control, aristocrats freely practiced self-aggrandizement. The outcome of such actions was a total collapse of security for trade.[59] While local figures freely fought for contracting revenues, forced loans and extortion became increasingly common. For example, Sohrab Khan in 1725 (in a bid to maintain his position as governor) resorted to large-scale extortion of Surat's merchant communities.[60]

Eighteenth century attacks on Surat by the Maratha successor state made it even more inhospitable to trade. Raids organized by the Peshwa and the Gaekwad were particularly harsh on local traders as neither 'had any qualms about attacking and looting mercantile centres and property.'[61] Maratha ill-treatment and oppression forced many traders to leave regions south of Sindh. When the Marathas sacked Bir Nagar, its bankers and traders fled as far away as Agra and Benaras.[62] In response to Maratha attacks, local authorities adopted repressive mercantile taxation policies to redirect resources toward defence.[63] Violence, taxation, and extortion combined to turn the Surat area into 'such a state of wretchedness that merchants and traders left their native land, abandoned their hereditary dwelling places and dispersed over distance countries'.[64] Surat's cash shortages and common bankruptcies contrasts with Sindh, which had a favourable balance of trade and a steady inflow of gold and silver.[65] With the disintegration of the Mughal imperial state to its north (Punjab) and to its south (Surat), Sindh was a land of trade and economic opportunity. The combination of trade opportunities, with the Kalhora state's need for experienced government workers, drew the Khatris and other migrants to Sindh during the eighteenth century.

THE HOMOLOGIES OF KHATRI AND LOHANA CULTURAL PRACTICE

A variety of Khatri families, such as the Chatpar and Pagrani, fled the Punjab for a better life in Sindh during the eighteenth century. However, in contrast to the Chatpar and Pagrani, many Khatris left behind pre-migration identities. For example, one of the largest Khatri migrant families, the Advanis, were absorbed into the Lohana after they came from Multan in 1701.[66] The forefather that this clan, from whom its patrinym derives, was Adumal, a soldier and councillor who found opportunities working for the Kalhora leader Yar Mohammad Kalhoro. The Advani's Lohana *nukh* (or faction) name, Maghu Khatri, reveals their Punjabi heritage (some members of this *nukh* still live in and around Multan).

The most noted Khatri to leave Multan for Sindh was Gidumal. Gidumal—famous in Sindhi literature for his faithfulness, learning, wisdom, and attainments—was employed as the *diwan* to the Kalhora leader Noor Mohammed. As *diwan*, Gidumal played a pivotal role in Kalhora inter-state relations (particularly with Persia and Kutch), the accessions of Noor Mohammed's sons Mohammed Murad Yar Khan and Ghulam Shah to the Kalhora leadership, and the 1768 establishment of Hyderabad.[67]

In *Sindhi Culture*, U.T. Thakur argues that migrants, once in Sindh, were 'assumed to be a Lohana'.[68] Thakur maintains:

> Matrimonial relations demand only a different totem and by lapse of a generation or two, the new totem comes to be included in this caste [the Lohana] and it loses the memory of its previous descent. The Lohana origin is claimed for the new totem which is merged in the general body of the Sind Hindus. By this process the people with different totems who migrated from Rajasthan and the Punjab and professed Lohana occupations [i.e., trade/business and government service] have acquired membership of the Lohana caste.[69]

Because of this process, homologies exist between Khatri and Lohana nukhs.[70] The Khatri sub-category of Rohra is a Lohana *nukh* name.[71] The Lohana *nukhs* of Suchdeo, Bajaj, Lund, Chutani, Kukreja, Chawla, Lumaria, Machcharia, Makaria, Kasturia, are also Rohra sub-communities.[72]

Khatri mythology also reflects Lohana socio-structural categories. For example, the Advani family occupies a social position entitled *bhardwaj*, that is the product of a 'mixed' *varna* (i.e., caste) union. The origin of this term is explained by Khatri mythology:

> The tradition most generally believed is that when Parashuram, the Brahman warrior, subdued the Kshatris, he persecuted them to such an extent, and was so determined to annihilate their race, that he violently caused the miscarriage of every pregnant woman he could find. Through fear some of the women in the family-way took protection with certain Brahmans, and when detected, the protector saved them by giving the persecutor to understand that they were Brahmanis [female Brahmans]. The Brahmans ate food from the hands of the women, and thus satisfied the persecutors that they were actually Brahmanis. The children of these women were the ancestors of the present Kshatris [i.e., Khatris]. In proof of the truth of the tradition, they point to the fact that Sarasvat Brahmans still partake of food cooked by Kshatris.[73]

This story is parallel to those found among the Lohana who also utilize the services of Saraswat Brahmans: in Sindh, Saraswats partake in food cooked by the Lohana. Other common conventions, with regard to religious practice, point toward the incorporation of Khatri migrants by the Lohana in the eighteenth century. For example, there are socio-structural continuities in the roles that Sikhism plays in these two communities.[74]

In *Sindh Story*, K.R. Malkani writes: 'Almost every Sindhi Hindu is a follower of Guru Nanak'.[75] According to the 1911 census, the majority of Sindhi Guru Nanak followers were, in fact, Lohanas. It is also important to recognize the historical fluidity of religious identity in Sindh. Many Lohana simultaneously revere Darya Pir—the 'spirit' of the Indus who is said to have saved them when they fled from Multan—while adhering to the faith of Nanak. In the sixteenth century, the Lohanas are said to have exclusively worshipped Darya Pir.[76] However, throughout the seventeenth and eighteenth centuries, religious adherence to Guru Nanak worship spread through Sindh. According to Thakur, the bulk of the Lohanas 'call themselves Nanikshahi though many of them are Darya-panthis still'.[77] Moreover:

> With the growth of Sikhism in the Punjab, the people who migrated to Sind oppressed by wars, introduced Sikhism which like any other religion was received, in a form modified to a great degree as part of the religion, by the Lohanas. It became a blended faith, known as Nanak Panth. [78]

The Lohana characterize Nanak Panth as 'an easy blend of Sikhism and Hinduism'.[79] The influence of Sikhism from the Punjab in this 'easy blend' is reflected in Lohana educational practices. Gurmukhi (Punjabi script), in addition to Arabic/Sindhi script, was learnt as 'the books of the Nanakpanthis who form a large portion of the Hindu population in Sindh are written in that character'.[80] Richard Burton, in 1847, emphasizes the influence of Sikhism from the Punjab in Sindh when he observes that Lohana prayers 'are usually in the Punjaubee, rarely in the Sanscrit or Persian languages'.[81]

Nanak Panth's ritual structures resemble those of eighteenth century Punjabi Sikhism in a number of ways. Ritual terminology in Nanak Panth evokes Sikhism. Its sects, the *Udasi* and the *Jagiasi* are described as descended from the two sons of Guru Nanak: Baba Srichand and Bahi Lakshmichand.[82] Though small, the Udasi sect was distributed throughout Sindh and historically occupied high positions in the region's major temples.[83] Udasis, like their Punjabi counterparts, did not marry and their temple positions, upon their death, are passed on by selection from within their sect.[84] In contrast, members of the Jagiasi sect (also called *Bhais*) were householders. While Saraswat Brahmans officiated deaths, births and marriages, the majority of the Lohanas had these and other rituals performed with the help of Bhais either in the home or in temples (i.e., 'gurudwaras').[85] Bhais formed the backbone of Lohana ritual practice in pre-colonial Sindh:

> They [Bhais] were distributed throughout Sind almost everywhere, even in the smallest villages, where no Brahmins were available. Every village had a temple of this faith as the number of Brahmins in Sind was very small; and as this caste is not limited to hereditary members, any member of the Lohana caste could set up a temple called Tikano or Darbar. He attends the temple wherein is kept the Adi Grant, the sacred book of this panth, sometimes together with Shrimad Bhagwat and other Hindu shastras. He prepares the sacred cake called the 'Kanah Saheb' which must be revered by Nanikshahis, who will pay, to have it made for them, in times of trouble or difficulty. It is not an endogamous caste and being flexible in nature the number of its member varies from time to time.[86]

An important sub-sect of Jagiasis are the *Masands*. Originally ministers to Sikh gurus, they collected religious offerings. A hereditary category, *Masands* claim descent from the ten original Sikh gurus and are particularly relevant as they were exclusively from the Khatri community. Khatris controlled this position within Sikhism until the eighteenth century when 'their extractions led to their extermination',[87] and to the general abolition of the *masand* system in the Punjab. The abolition of this system, in conjunction with their increased involvement in the Mughal state, produced tensions between the Khatri and communities that supported Sikhism. Such tension, as discussed earlier, decreased Khatri prosperity and, ultimately, drove many of them to migrate from the Punjab to Sindh.

Conclusion: Recognizing the State and a Future's Dependence on the Past

With interest in globalization growing, the relationship between culture and migration is increasingly under examination. Much of this work remains grounded in the twentieth and early twenty-first centuries. In contrast, the Lohanas of Sindh represent—as early as the eighteenth century—a community transformed by the cultural dynamics of migration. While their post- and pre-Partition realities of place and of the imagination have always blurred, they have also always carried the state's 'trace'. It is tempting to (1) consider the hyphen that links particular communities or nations to the state as a site of dis-juncture, and (2) argue that states are increasingly unlikely arbiters of people's long-term relationships. However, the state's historical transformation continues—whether in pre- and post-Partition Sindh, the Balkans during the 1990s or contemporary Darfur—to impact migration around the world: migrants' 'deterritorialized' solidarities are often forged from within the violence of state formation and/or disintegration.

Sindhis' responses to past experience provide positive insights in the current cultural dynamics of their deterritorialization, as well as the Sindhi 'state' and its possible future. Such stories of the past not only illustrate displacement as an engine of Sindhi identity but also elucidate the realities of migrants more generally as they are caught in the webs of multiple relationships. By adding historical depth, the Sindhi case helps illuminate encounters with modern transnational border crossings in which migration is undertaken not only to 'get ahead' economically, but to 'save one's head' in politically and socially unstable situations.

NOTES

1. Ansar Zahi-Khan, *History and Culture of Sind: A Study of the Socio-Economic Organization and Institutions During the Sixteenth and Seventeenth Centuries* (Karachi: Royal Book Company, 1980), 308–309.
2. Ibid.
3. James Tod in James Campbell, *Hindu Castes and Tribes of Gujarat* (Haryana, India: Vintage Book, 1988 [1901]), 121.
4. Motilal Jotwani, *Sindhi Literature and Society* (New Delhi: Rajesh Publications, 1979), 117.
5. Azimusshan Haider, *History of Karachi* (Karachi: Ferozsons, Ltd., 1974), 15.
6. U.T. Thakur, *Sindhi Culture* (Bombay: Bombay University, 1959), 91; C.J. Daswani and S. Parchani, *Sociolinguistic Survey of Indian Sindhi* (Mysore: Central Institute of Indian Languages, 1978), 22.
7. R.E. Enthoven, *The Castes and Tribes of Bombay* (Delhi: Asian Educational Services,

1990 [1922]), 383; Thakur, 71. For example, Kaka Bhagavandas (1842–1922), the father of the famous Sindhi freedom fighter J.B. Kripalani was a member of the Vaishnavite sect Shri Nath Dwara located in Mewar, Rajasthan (K.R. Malkani, *Sindh Story* [New Delhi: Allied Publications, 1984], 78).

8. Thakur, 89.
9. Tavernier in Chetan Singh, 'Polity, Economy and Society under the Mughals', in Indu Banga, ed., *Five Punjabi Centuries: Polity, Economy, Society and Culture, c. 1500–1990* (Delhi: Manohar, 1997), 54.
10. Stephen Frederic Dale, *Indian Merchants and Eurasian Trade, 1600–1750* (Cambridge: Cambridge University Press, 1994), 131.
11. Muzaffar Alam, *The Crisis of Empire in Mughal North India: Awadh and the Punjab, 1707–48* (Delhi: Oxford University Press, 1986), 13.
12. Ibid., 184.
13. Muzaffar Alam, 'Politics Under the Later Mughals', in Indu Banga, ed., *Five Punjabi Centuries: Polity, Economy, Society and Culture, c. 1500–1990* (Delhi: Manohar, 1997), 71.
14. Chetan Singh, 'Polity, Economy and Society under the Mughals', 58.
15. Alam, 'Politics Under the Later Mughals', 70.
16. Alam, *The Crisis of Empire in Mughal North India*, 181.
17. Ibid., 189.
18. John F. Richards, *The Mughal Empire* (Delhi: Cambridge University Press, 1993), 195–196.
19. Chetan Singh, *Region and Empire* (Delhi: Oxford University Prwss, 1991), 281.
20. Ibid.
21. Ibid.
22. Willem Floor, 'The Dutch East India Company's Trade with Sind in the 17th and 18th Centuries', *Moyen Orient and Ocean Indien XVIe–XIXes.* III (1986): 112.
23. Humaira Faiz Dasti, *Multan: A Province of the Mughal Empire, 1525–1751* (Karachi: Royal Book Company, 1998), 202.
24. Ibid., 311.
25. Dale, *Indian Merchants and Eurasian Trade*, 55.
26. Ibid., 58. For a discussion of trading communities of these areas see the comments of Eugene Schuyler in Geoffrey Wheeler, *Turkistan: Notes of a Journey in Russian Turkistan, Kokand, Bukhara and Khuldja* (London: Routledge & Kegan Paul, 1966), 107, 134, 204, and 255. Also see Alexander Burnes, *Travels into Bokhara* (London: John Murray, 1835).
27. Ahmad Nabi Khan, *Multan, History and Architecture* (Islamabad: Islamic University, 1983), 85–140.
28. Dale, *Indian Merchants and Eurasian Trade*, 129.
29. Ibid.
30. Noman Ahmed Siddiqi, *Land Revenue Administration Under the Mughals, 1700–1750* (Bombay: Asia House Publishers, 1979), 164–171.
31. B.L. Gupta, 'The Migration of Traders to Rajasthan in the Eighteenth Century', *Proceedings of the Forty-Eighth Session of the Indian History Congress* (1988): 313–316.
32. Singh, *Region and Empire*, 227–228.
33. Singh, 'Polity, Economy and Society under the Mughals', 56.
34. Alam, 'Politics Under the Later Mughals', 74.
35. Alam, *Crisis of Empire in Mughal North India*, 169–170.
36. Ibid., 203.
37. Alam, 'Politics Under the Later Mughals', 74–75.

38. Alam, *Crisis of Empire in Mughal North India*, 174.
39. Ibid., 152.
40. Ibid., 171.
41. Ibid., 184.
42. Ganesh Das Vadera, *Char bagh-i-Panjab*, trans. J.S. Grewal and Indu Banga (Amritsar, India: Guru Nanak University, 1975), 124. For a discussion of Jat dominance within Sikhism see W.H. McLeod, *The Evolution of the Sikh Community* (Delhi: Oxford University Press, 1975), 1–19.
43. Alam, *Crisis of Empire in Mughal North India*, 150.
44. Ibid., 184.
45. Ghan Shyam Lal Devra, 'A Study of the Trade-Relations Between Rajasthan and Sindh/Multan (1650–1800)', *Proceedings of the Thirty-Ninth Session of the Indian History Congress* (1978): 583–584.
46. B.L. Gupta, 'The Migration of Traders to Rajasthan in the Eighteenth Century', *Proceedings of the Forty-Eighth Session of the Indian History Congress* (1988): 312–313; Devra, 583–584.
47. Lakshmi Subramanian, *Indigenous Capital and Imperial Expansion: Bombay, Surat and the West Coast* (Delhi: Oxford University Press, 1996), 10.
48. Haig in S.P. Chablani, *Economic Conditions in Sind, 1592 to 1843* (Bombay: Orient Longmans, Ltd., 1951), 17.
49. Hamilton in Chablani, 54.
50. Burnes in Chablani, 75.
51. Erskine in Chablani, 75.
52. Chablani, 131.
53. Ibid., 99.
54. Ibid.
55. Pithawalla in Chablani, 99.
56. Chablani, 164.
57. Ibid., 13.
58. Ibid. English accounts sometime attribute the 'sickly' state of Sindh to the Indus. The river apparently occupies higher ground than the surrounding country. So when the river floods, damage to the lands around it can be extensive. Such flooding could produce conditions for a variety of water borne diseases and sicknesses.
59. Subramanian, 23.
60. Ibid., 33.
61. Ibid., 57.
62. Ibid.
63. Ibid., 15.
64. Ibid., 57.
65. Chablani, 164.
66. I am grateful to the now defunct World-Wide Centre of Sindhi Studies in Bombay for access to Lohana genealogical records from the *pindas* of Hardiwar, Kashi, Prayag, and Nasik.
67. B.D. Mirchandani, *Glimpses of Ancient Sindh* (Bombay: Saraswati Gulrajani, n.d.), 35; Maneck Pithawala, *Historical Geography of Sindh* (Jamshoro: Institute of Sindhology), 139.
68. Thakur, 68–69.
69. Ibid.
70. Ibid., 60.
71. Ibid., 58. This classification of the Rohra is not without debate among Punjabi Khatris.

However, the internal dynamics of the Khatris is not the topic at hand. Rohras in the Punjab were called *bhais* or *seth* (Lohana name suffixes) and worked as bankers and traders for the rural sector. As bankers and traders, they were particularly open to the rural revolts of the eighteenth century. A fact reflected in the high number of totemic clans that the Rohra and Lohana have in common.

72. Ibid.
73. Campbell, *Hindu Castes and Tribes*, 55–56. Enthoven, twenty-one years later, duplicates Campell's story in *The Castes and Tribes of Bombay* (page 208). Also see Pierre Lachaier, 'The Merchant Lineage Firm and the Non-Invisible Hand: Pune, Maharastra', in Philippe Candene and Denis Vidal, ed., *Webs of Trade: Dynamics of Business Communities in Western India* (Delhi: Manohar, 1997), 35.
74. Motilal Jotwani, *Sindhi Literature and Society* (New Delhi: Rajesh Publications), 64–65; Zahi-Khan, 316; Daswani and Parchani, 21. For an example of this correlation on Lohana education see Sarla J. Narsian, 'Historical Development of Education in Sindh', in Mubarak Ali, ed., *Sindh Observed: Selection from the Journal of the Sindh Historical Society* (Lahore: Gautum Publishers, 1993), 266.
75. Ram Jethmalani in Malkani, xv.
76. Zahi-Khan, 312.
77. Thakur, 71.
78. Ibid., 21.
79. Daswani and Parchani, 21.
80. Narsian, 'Historical Development of Education', 266.
81. Richard Burton in R. Hugh Thomas, ed., *Memoirs on Sind: Selections From the Records of the Bombay Government, Vol. 2* (Karachi: Karimsons, 1979 [1847]), 650.
82. Jotwani, 64.
83. Thakur, 65.
84. Ibid.
85. Daswani and Parchani, 21.
86. Thakur, 64–65.
87. Ibid., 65.

CHAPTER 8

Richard Burton's Sindh: Folklore, Syncretism, and Empire

PAULO LEMOS HORTA

Richard Burton became a writer, a translator, and commentator on Islam during the five formative years in Sindh (1844–1849). During this time, he produced his first efforts at literary translation,[1] plans to translate the *1001 Nights*,[2] and three monographs: *Scinde or the Unhappy Valley* (1851); *Sindh, and the races that inhabit the valley of the Indus* (1851); and *Falconry in the valley of the Indus* (1852).[3] In contrast to other British travelogues of Sindh that viewed the region chiefly in terms of its strategic value to other colonial interests in the subcontinent,[4] Burton's writings present Sindh as pivotal to the dissemination of religion and folklore from the Middle East to India and vice-versa and as possessing a distinct and syncretic culture. Burton arrived in Sindh in his early twenties as an officer in the British East India Company and his quick mastery of Indian vernacular languages would earn him the post of translator for the company and intelligence gatherer for the region's conqueror and governor, Sir Charles Napier. It is in Sindh that Burton developed and articulated his ideas of culture, syncretism, translation, and empire that imprinted a corpus that would grow to nearly a hundred works of ethnography, travelogues, and literary translations. This early body of writing reflects key concerns that would shape his later efforts, such as the conviction that a national literature is most vibrant and most expressive of a people in a culture's formative stages when the tendency toward supernaturalism and superstition prevails. Sindh also provided Burton with a cultural laboratory to test his early theories about the advantages and disadvantages of certain forms of cultural and religious syncretism. The early sketches of cross-cultural parallels with Celtic and Anglo-Saxon culture would be brought to fruition in his mature literary translations, notably the version of the *1001 Nights* he completed in the 1880s while acting as British Consul in Trieste.

Current English-language scholarship presents Burton as a representative Victorian. Scholars such as Edward Said and Dane Kennedy exaggerate the extent to which Burton, as a child in Italy and France, and youth on the subcontinent, inhabited bubbles of Englishness—'close-knit communities' where locals were shunned and 'English identity' stressed more than in England.[5] The differing assessments of Burton offered by Said and Kennedy—who present him as a categorical imperialist and a cultural relativist respectively—reflect different intellectual histories of Victorian England. They mostly ignore how Burton was influenced by the different contexts and intellectual communities he inhabited throughout his life. French-language scholarship has been more attentive to the possibility of rebellion that travellers saw in the 'Orient'. Roger Célestin has noted the tendency toward experimentation in which the individual Western subject explores the exotic 'as a means of severing ties with Home, thus discovering or recovering material that confirms and strengthens individuality rather than serving, illustrating, or reinforcing systems'.[6] Burton is present in Sindh not just as an agent of imperialism, but also as an agent of the self: there he finds a syncretic substance that gives him the means to rebel against Britain and John Bull's stereotypical notions of culture and belonging. Jean-François Gournay has accurately observed that Burton was 'a stranger to his times, a stranger to himself, who in a perpetual quest for an identity that eluded him tried on a multitude of characters, [as evident] in his frequent recourse to pseudonyms and the frenzy of his activity as a translator'.[7] To pay attention to the genesis of Burton's ideas from his experience in the Sindh of the 1840s is less to damn Burton as a typical imperialist or tacitly rehabilitate him as a cultural relativist (the goals of Said and Kennedy) than to produce a more nuanced understanding of the aesthetic and political case for empire that he did espouse.

One benefit of this approach is the illumination of Burton's ethnological method in his literary translations. Burton's translation of the *Nights* can be traced to his experience of Sindh through his approach to philology and folklore and interest in syncretism and sexuality. Burton's *Nights* translation was first conceived as a collaboration that resulted from a friendship forged in Sindh with John Steinhauser. This collaboration would never materialize, but the imprint of the Sindh experience is apparent in both the form of Burton's 1885 translation of the *Nights* and the matter of its commentary. Burton's Sindh writings claimed that a delight in literatures of supernaturalism was universal, anticipated his later preference for translations from Eastern folklore, and exposed cross-cultural affinities between old English ballads and 'Old World Oriental songs' that would shape the distinctive aesthetic choices of his *Nights*. Burton's time in Sindh also provided him with a syncretic understanding of Islam specific to that part of the Muslim world, one that would influence his conception of Islam in the *Nights*. Burton was not principally concerned with the normative Islam of jurisprudence that defined Edward William Lane's version of the *Nights* (1839–1841).[8] Burton's translation would reflect an inclusive understanding of Islam that absorbed the folklore, syncretism, and sexual practices he observed in Sindh. While Lane interpreted the *Nights* as illustrative of a Middle Eastern Islam (rooted in his belief that the tales originated in medieval Cairo), Burton enlarged the scope of his ethnological commentary about the *Nights* to encompass all dominions of Britain, the 'greatest Mohammedan empire',[9] in accordance with his belief that the *Nights* was a multi-authored product of cultural syncretism. Accordingly, the *Nights* inherited comparative notes on Islam, Hinduism, Sufism, the writing of love letters, *bhang*, sexual practices, and funereal rites all born of Burton's Sindh experience.[10]

AN EYE FOR SYNCRETISM IN THE SINDHI OBSERVANCE OF ISLAM: BELIEF IN THE MIRROR OF INK AND THE JINN

Burton introduces his sympathetic treatment of the cultural syncretism of Islam in Sindh by affirming the syncretic quality of all faiths and asking rhetorically if, as each new religion borrows from its predecessor, 'the spirit of the latter ever departs'.[11] He compares the debt that Sindhi Islam owes Hinduism to that owed by Northern Protestantism to 'the stern and rugged animus of Druidism' and by Mediterranean Catholicism to the pantheistic faith that 'peopled earth, air and sea with forms of ideal beauty' and 'gave rise to the arts and sciences which humanized that portion of mankind'.[12] Sindh is a place where the adoption of Hindu sites of worship and devotion to Hindu saints are 'acceptable acts of religion' rather than 'abominations' as seen by the Arab Muslim.[13] Burton delights in chronicling notable traces of 'paganism' evident in the adopted faith of Sindhi Muslims: belief in alchemy, animal shrines, the coexistence of jinn and Rakas, witches who act the part of 'Mercurys of illicit love', mermen and mermaids, and talismans to ward off the evil eye and to procure romantic love. He details various Sindhi forms of divination, among them oneiromancy, palmistry, divination by knotted strings, and clairvoyance with the aid of a mirror of ink.[14] In each case, Burton is attentive to the social role performed by inherited superstitious beliefs in Sindhi Islam. Amatory talismans, for instance, bind faithful couples together and excuse adultery: 'It is to the advantage of all parties to support the idea. The magician gains money by teaching his craft, the fair sex have a valid excuse when detected in grave delinquency, and the husbands are consoled by the reflection that the chastity of their spouses could yield to none but preternatural influence'.[15] Superstitions pertaining to thievery and the recovery of lost property can be self-fulfilling, for the thief's belief in them can often betray his guilt.[16] This attentiveness to the syncretism of Sindhi Islam anticipates Burton's later commentary on religion in the *Nights* and the *Pilgrimage to Meccah and al-Medinah*.[17]

The distinctiveness of Burton's attraction to the cultural syncretism of Sindhi Islam is evident in his handling of two aspects of popular Muslim belief, defined for a generation of British readers by Edward William Lane's work on Egyptian Islam in the 1830s: divination with the mirror of ink and the belief in the jinn. In his *Account of the Manners and Customs of the Modern Egyptians*, Lane stresses the Islamic and Egyptian cultural specificity of the experiments he witnesses, in which a famous Cairo magician, Abd el Kadir, enables a young boy to achieve clairvoyance with the aid of a mirror of ink poured onto the boy's hand.[18] Lane cites in Arabic and English the charm containing a verse from the fiftieth chapter of the Quran that the magician writes 'to open the boy's eyes in a supernatural manner; to make his sight pierce into what is to us the invisible world'.[19] Here, as in his other ethnographic writing, Lane meticulously relates observations of Islam that he can personally attest to through his experiences in Cairo and collaborations with local informants (in this case, Abd el Kadir). Burton in contrast intuits that the presence in Sindh of 'the Egyptian practice of seeing figures shifting over the ink poured into a boy's hand' must point to a pre-Islamic genesis for this mode of divination. Clairvoyance with the aid of the mirror of ink is practiced in Sindh—by Muslims and Hindus alike—and he interprets this fact as evidence for his conjecture that it likely originated in India: 'That poisonous source of three parts of the superstitions which have inundated Europe and Asia; thence it might have travelled westward to Egypt and the Maghrib'.[20] A quick study, Burton affirms that he need not observe the operation in person, 'having heard of it sufficiently often to be assured that my informants were not deceiving me as regards the practice of it'.[21] As in the notes to the *Nights*, the slightest thread of etymological, historical, or social evidence inclines Burton toward cross-cultural conjecture in his writing on Sindh.

Lane's ethnographic commentary stressed the distinctly Arab and Muslim genealogy and cosmography of the jinn, in accordance with his belief that the *Nights* reflected Cairo's medieval culture. Lane's eight-page note on the jinn aims to correct 'the erroneous accounts that have been given of these fabulous beings by various European writers' with reference to Arabic works, and to refute Schlegel's contention that the frequent mention of jinn in the *Nights* was 'more consistent with Indian than with Arab notions'.[22] Lane carefully situates the jinn in the Quran, *hadith* literature and the accounts of local informants in Cairo and sketches out the complex hierarchies of distinct tribes of the jinn including the ifrits, ghouls, and *marids*. Burton, in his 1851 note on the Sindhi belief in jinn, would in effect reverse Lane's emphasis by pointing out the correspondences observed in Sindh between Muslim belief in the jinn, ghouls and marids, on the one hand, and Hindu and pre-Islamic belief in fairies, ghosts, and 'powerful fiends' (such as, 'Dew, Rakas, and Pap' on the other).[23] Consistent with his eye for the manner in which all religions borrow from each other, Burton's 1851 note on Sindhi belief in jinn and *Peri* (or fairies) further speculates that, since the word fairy is of Persian origin, 'it is not uninteresting to trace the gradations through which the beautiful sylphs of [Persian] Guebrism dwindled down into the pigmy green folk of Northern Europe'.[24] Burton's note on the jinn in his 1885 *Nights* would echo the insights and the language of his earlier writing on the syncretism of Sindhi belief in jinn and fairies by tracing the derivation of this belief to 'the Div and Rakshah of old [Persian] Guebre-land and the 'Rakshasa', or 'Yaksha', of Hinduism'. 'It would be interesting', the note to the *Nights* speculates further, 'to trace the evident connection, by no means "accidental", of "Jinn" with the "Genius" who came to the Romans through the Asiatic Etruscans'.[25]

Above all, it is the practice of Sufism, as observed in Sindh, that persuades Burton of a deeper syncretism between Islam and Hinduism in the region, a combination of the two belief systems that forms a new system.[26] Burton objects to the dismissive manner in which Orthodox Islam interprets the imprint of Hinduism upon Sufism, deriding the latter as a strategic deployment by heretical caliphs 'of some new and enticing doctrine, borrowed from a polytheistic people' to undermine the orthodox tenets of their Imams.[27] He counters that the resemblance between Sufism and the Vedantic system is 'wonderful' and admires the equivalence between modern Sindhi and Indian notions of penance and the Sufi

Riyazat, for in both 'the divinae particula aurae in man' is emancipated from the 'tyranny of impure matter' and acquires 'supernatural powers of metamorphosing the body'. In both systems of thought, he stresses, this emancipation has similar effects:

> [T]ransferring the mind to men and beasts, forcibly producing love, causing the death of foes, knowing what is concealed from humanity, seeing spirits, fairies, devils and angels, flying in the air, counteracting magical arts, prevention of pain, curing the venom or wounds of animals, alchemy, healing the sick, subjugating the planets, visiting the heavens, and obtaining by prayer all that one desires.[28]

In contrast to the Orthodox theologian of Islam, who might regard a resemblance between Hinduism and Sufism as cause for dismissing the latter's worth, Burton praises the 'prudent archaeologist' who recognizes similar developments 'among similar races, in similar climates, and under similar circumstances,' and understands that 'human nature always presents a general resemblance'.[29] From this perspective, Sufi assertions such as 'universal charity and love' flow 'from the source of all goodness' correspond not only with those of Vedantic thought but prove 'so consistent with man's reason, so useful to his interests, so agreeable to his passions and desires, that their origin must belong to the dark beginning of human society'.[30] The Sufis responsible for the syncretic practices observed in Sindh are not to be dismissed as heretics, but rather commended for blending polytheism with monotheism, religion's 'poetry' with its 'prose'.[31]

Burton favourably contrasts his eye for cross-cultural parallels and syncretism with the myopia of the professional class of European Orientalists that visited Sindh during his residence there.[32] In his 1847 manuscript translation of *Bidpai's Fables*, for instance, Burton notes the discrepancy between the predestination of Sindhi and Indian folklore and the free will of Quranic Islam. Glossing the line, 'Vain are regrets, whate'er the pen of destiny/Assigns to mortals, that, and only that can be', Burton protests that it was wrong for British and French Orientalists to 'suppose that Islam is a religion of predestination' as 'the Arabian Prophet was most severe in his declamations against predestinarians and called them "the Magians" (or Infidels) of his faith'.[33] Burton recognized the difficulty of reconciling the tenets of the 'Arabian prophet' with the practice of Islam in Sindh and India and with the morals of subcontinental folklore.[34] In the various notes on predestination sprinkled throughout his *Nights*, Burton would wrestle with the tension he observed between folklore's stress on fate (indebted to pagan belief-systems) and the emphasis of

Islamic theology on free will. He notes that predestination is present in Muslim observance not only in the 'Night of Power' and 'skull-lectures of the vulgar' (the belief that fate is written in the sutures of the skull) but also in the 'Guarded Tablet of the learned'.[35] The pervasiveness in the *Nights* of this 'still popular Moslem feeling', Burton confessed, caused a friend to complain that in reading the work she was made to feel 'as if the world were a jail'.[36] The last note to the *Nights* on this subject explains the failure of its authors to reconcile freewill and fate within the broader history of the inability of all other authors, 'Moslems and Christians', to make the 'two contraries agree'.[37]

Burton would opt for inclusiveness in his notes on Islam, addressing popular and learned superstition alongside traditions of commentary on the Quran. As a result, his work on Sindh encompasses a notion of Islam that absorbs folklore, superstition, syncretism, and sexuality. This writing contains the first cryptic allusions to the sexual practices that would often dominate Burton's notes to the *Nights* and were greatly responsible for the work's controversial quality. Sindhi Islam often appropriated Hindu sites of pilgrimage and, at some of these sites, Burton observes: 'certain upright stones stained with vermilion and decked with huge garlands of withered flowers'. However, imagining John Bull's demand for an explanation of 'these upright stones, daubed with red', Burton does no more than hint at the practice of women visiting the stones in the hope of bearing a boy.[38] He is more forthcoming in sketching his theory of the geographical determination of sexuality, noting that Sindhi women felt a greater 'amativeness' than Sindhi men 'as is often the case in warm and damp countries, lying close to mountains'.[39] Burton's more systematic discussion of the formative influence of climate and geography on sexuality would appear in his discussion of the Sotadic Zone in the 'Terminal Essay' to the *Nights*. In this respect, as in the observations on religious syncretism and Sufism, the writing on Sindh anticipates the scope and method of Burton's later commentary on Islam and the 'Orient' in the *Nights*. He reports on practices of folklore and sexuality in the context of a notion of Islam open to cultural syncretism of the sort first observed in Sindh.

Burton stresses the usefulness for the cause of empire of his work as a translator and ethnographer, and in particular of the more inclusive notion of Islam of his Sindhi writing. The intended preface to the unpublished *Bidpai's Fables* bemoans the British colonial administrators' ignorance of the people they lord over in the subcontinent. In the conclusion to *Sindh* Burton justifies the inclusion of a section considering Sindhi language and folklore in terms of its use in the task of colonial administration. The 'Translator's Preface' to the *Nights* in 1885 would take this argument a step further by arguing that the study of Persian and Arabic should replace that of Greek and Latin for the colonial administrators of England as the 'greatest Mohammedan empire in the World', and that these officials should govern with sympathy for Muslim customs and beliefs.[40] Governing with sympathy for local customs and beliefs would entail a different sort of empire, decoupled from a mission to impose Christian and English values. This advocacy of sympathy—being 'familiar with and favourably inclined to [Muslim] manners and customs if not to their law and religion'—need not amount to the cultural relativism attributed to Burton by Dane Kennedy.[41] Burton operated from his own set of universal assumptions about culture, including his belief in a common genesis for supernaturalism in beliefs and literature around the world. He can be said to have articulated a proto-social Darwinian theory of cultural and religious evolution even before he encountered the work of Darwin. In his work on Sindh, Burton proves less a cultural relativist than a champion of Islam and a critic of Hinduism. He faults visiting Orientalists for being inattentive to the virtues of Muslims and the flaws of Hindus.[42] An asymmetry characterizes the cultural tolerance he advocates in his writing on Sindh and subsequent work. On the one hand, he defends Muslim manners, customs, and laws from the threat of the imposition of English and Christian manners and laws. On the other hand, he does not oppose other forms of cultural assimilation and imperialism, and praises the benefits of the spread of Islam not only in the subcontinent but also in Africa. Indeed, in viewing Islam as a reformation of Christianity, Burton's 'Terminal Essay' to the *Nights* presents Islam as a more fully evolved form of the Christian faith.

POETRY AS THE EXPOSITOR OF A PEOPLE: SINDHI LANGUAGE AND LITERATURE

New to Burton's writing on Sindhi language and literature is the claim that the region possesses a distinct linguistic and literary tradition with its own original rhythms, meters, and peculiar poetic devices, which Burton claimed was second to no other vernacular tradition on the Indian subcontinent. Burton does not, in the manner of other English authors on Sindh, regard Sindhi as a mere corruption of another language.[43] Nor does he hold all Sindhi cultural expressions to be derivative reflections of foreign cultural influences. Rather, he is curious about the cultural achievements of Sindhi literature, in particular about the achievements of

Abd el Latif in the culturally syncretic poetic forms made available by his engagement with Sufism. Sindhi linguistic syncretism interests him as strongly as the religious syncretism of Muslim practice and ritual in Sindh, and he is curious about the incorporation of a high number of Sanskrit and Arabic words in Sindhi.[44] Burton's belief in the greater vibrancy and ethnological value of a people's earliest poetry leads him to speculate why certain traditions—the Sindhi and the Irish—have been able to preserve a measure of their early poetry's expressiveness and openness to the supernatural while others have not. The general trend he identifies in most modern national literatures in East and West is a decline from the formative stage in which literature was inextricably linked to the quotidian rhythms and acts of the individual and the collectivity—such as love and war—with an accompanying loss of aesthetic and ethnological expressiveness. For Burton, the act of translating Eastern folklore generates a new awareness of the need to recuperate the vitality of early literary traditions in English language and literature. Indeed, he will claim that the vigour of the 'Old World Oriental Song' can only be translated via the form of the Old English Ballad.

Burton's interest in how a 'pagan' faith shapes Muslim devotion in Sindh finds an analogue in his writing on Sindhi language and culture in an attentiveness to how pre-Islamic linguistic and literary conventions determine Sindhi literature, even when it deals with expressly Muslim genres and themes. From his belief that literature is most expressive in a culture's formative stages follows the conviction that the distinguishing traits of a pre-existing national language and literature can be excavated from underneath the mediating influence of Islam. This belief is articulated most systematically in the 'Terminal Essay' to the *Nights*, where Burton extrapolates backwards from the decadent sophistication of the oldest Arabic poetry (refined over centuries) to establish the character of pre-Islamic Arabs. Bedouin culture would have been unrivalled in its vitality and expressiveness due to its freedom from modern notions of belonging and possession. Burton paints an idyllic portrait of the typical day in the life of the Bedouin, encompassing weapons practice, racing, hunting, drinking, gambling, and music, and sings the praises of pre-Islamic high festivals in which blood feuds and wars were suspended and poets challenged each other in songs of love and war. The nomad's movement would have enabled life to be vigorous, noble, independent and free. In this portrait, early Arabic poetry expressed the Bedouin's bond with nature, and its meters and rhymes captured the sounds and rhythms of the everyday life of the Bedouin. Burton stresses the vitality of the primitive measure of the song of camel-drivers, lovers and warriors, and traces the imprint of the first original meter in Arabic poetry's subsequent elaborate metrical systems.

Burton's writing on Sindhi literature already accentuates the extent to which poetry was interwoven with elemental patterns of everyday life in Sindh before the arrival of Islam and the influence of Arabic and Persian. He stresses the copiousness of available terms to describe the sounds of nature and animals and notes the onomatopoeia that governs the derivation in Sindhi of different words to distinguish the cry of a child (the buzzing of bees or flies), a cry of pain (the trumpeting of an elephant) and an unpleasant cry (the cry of a camel).[45] Sindhi poetry's chief distinction for Burton is its possession of an original meter or 'description of verse', while 'all its neighbours, even the Pushtu, are obliged to content themselves with borrowed meters'.[46] The development of a meter original to the Sindhi language and region allows for great flexibility in modifying word endings to suit rhyme schemes, and hence a superiority 'in various minor points of refinement and cultivation' to 'most dialects of Western India'.[47] Consequently, no vernacular Indian language 'possessed more, and few so much, original composition', and Burton ventures that Sindhi poetry is no less accomplished than Hindi or Marathi poetry. He praises Sindhi poetry for a 'great variety of expression', idiomatic 'terseness' and 'freshness', and a predilection for alliteration that gives it 'a very distinct and peculiar rhythm'. Above all, he emphasizes how its rhythms are inextricable from those of everyday life in Sindh: war songs were performed in battle by a bard who accompanied the chief during combat; brief love songs were set to music and were a staple of popular poets; musical 'couplets' (the *baita*), compositions of two or three verses with a meter peculiar to Sindh, were 'a great favourite with all classes'. Further, the 'message' (*sanyaro*) of love accompanied by a pipe (*nai*) was second to no other music in popularity among the 'wilder clans'.[48]

Extrapolating from the first principle that the tendency toward supernaturalism is universal at the formative stage of literature, Burton's work on Sindh articulates the underlying conviction that the prophecies of Sindhi folklore and literature possessed counterparts at once more familiar and credible to the English reader. In his sympathetic account of *The Seven Prophecies of the Samoi*, Burton evokes the counterpoint of British credulity in the prophecies attributed to Ercildoune: 'the lines are undoubtedly ancient, for they are generally known throughout the country. Like "The Prophecies of Rymer, Bede and Merlin", they are implicitly believed by the people'.[49] He admires the calculated opacity of the writing in Sindhi prophecies, which allow a great flexibility in suiting historical fact to prophetic allusion, remarking 'in vagueness, ambiguity, and other tricks of areolation, they very much resemble the productions ascribed to the bard of Ercildoune, and our other seers in olden time'.[50] This cross-cultural counterpoint provides the basis for Burton to assert the reasonableness of universal belief in prophecy: 'such prophecies being in fact mere efforts of memory, causality, and comparison, or as the metaphysician expresses it "the operation of a sound and combining judgment"'.[51] From this contrapuntal perspective, Burton sympathetically considers the widespread Sindhi belief that the British conquest of Sindh helped fulfil *The Seven Prophecies of the Samoi*. He acknowledges the uncanny accuracy of certain predictions pertaining to the conquest: the British preference for 'thin grey steeds', the reversal of fortune of the Balochis under the new rule, and the welcome the women offered the invaders. 'Peculiarly happy', he observes, 'is the allusion to the way in which these ladies behaved when we first took the country'.[52] A surprising empiricism—a willingness to test the hypothesis of prophecy or superstition against the record of history and his own experience—informs Burton's occasional retort to John Bull's presumed scepticism on these matters, 'though you may not attach much importance to such coincidence, I do'.[53]

Burton spies an affinity of matter and at times of meter between early Eastern and Old English literatures that allows him to be optimistic with regard to the possibility of rendering Eastern poetry in vibrant English verse. This affinity would make possible cross-cultural translations that preserve the originals' preferred subject matter and poetic devices, such as supernaturalism, assonance, and alliteration. In this respect, Burton's writing on Sindhi poetry and folklore anticipates the method of his *Nights* translation. In *Sindh and the Races that Inhabit the Valley of the Indus*, Burton asks his reader to sympathetically assess the 'peculiar' reliance of Sindhi poetry on the poetic device of alliteration through the prism of the conventions of the Old English poem. He reasons that alliteration is a 'poetical ornament' particularly well suited to the sensibility of a more formative developmental stage of civilizations East and West, when poets were 'willing to sacrifice sense to sound'.[54] To clinch this point Burton proclaims the alliteration of Abd el Latif's poetry 'quite as artfully and successfully managed as in any of the productions of our Anglo-Saxon ancestors'.[55] Taking this statement of affinity between Eastern and Anglo-Saxon verse one step further, Burton boldly asserts in the 'Terminal Essay' that the old Oriental song of the poetry preserved in the *Nights* can be conveyed in poetic form in English only by the verse of the old English ballad. In this manner Burton's belief in cross-cultural affinities between Old English verse and the formative poetry of the Sindhis and Arabs informed his confidence that the latter could be rendered in English without sacrifice of sense or meter.

Suspicious of many forms of cultural syncretism, Burton found a positive model for the creative possibilities of cultural mixture and syncretism in Abd el Latif's poetic articulations of Sufism. For Burton, the potential for a culturally syncretic work to transcend the limitations of regional or national literature are well demonstrated by the presence of the work of Abd el Latif within the canon of Sufi literature alongside 'Ibn Fariz among the Arabs, Hafiz in Persia…and Abd el Rahman among the Affghans'.[56] As he considers the 'remarkable' imprint of each writer's nationality on his articulation of Sufism, Burton is taken by the ability of Abd el Latif and Abd el Rahman to transcend the limitations of their local vernacular linguistic and poetic conventions and traditions.[57] Having to borrow its more abstract terms from Persian and Arabic, Sindhi was a more 'primitive' language that did not allow the scope or vocabulary for Abd el Latif to rival the metaphysical speculations of Hafiz. Yet for Burton, Latif's work possessed the virtue of being more 'homely', 'common-place' and 'practical' than the work of the Persian poet.[58] Thus, despite the apparent disadvantage of 'contending against a barbarous dialect', and armed only with the stock devices of 'alliteration, puns, and the jingling of words', Abd el Latif succeeds in composing beautiful and delightful verse.

Burton's writing on Sindhi poetry anticipates the most distinctive and controversial formal choices of his translation of the *Nights*, including the preservation of over 10,000 lines of poetry (which other translators omit or abridge) and the adoption of rhyming and alliterative poetry and prose in English (which no other *Nights* translator has attempted). A key impetus for Burton, glimpsed in his writing on Sindhi poetry, is that of educating the English ear in the melody of foreign meters and poetic devices such as alliteration and assonance. Popular Sindhi love songs set to music were 'not unpleasant to the European ear' Burton insisted in his earlier writing, but first one had to overcome the unfamiliarity of the 'the strange meter'.[59] Burton's stubborn insistence on preserving foreign rhyme schemes and poetic devices in his translation of the verse and prose of the *Nights*, when he had faced criticism for doing so in his previous literary translations, has puzzled scholars.[60] Yet arguably it was not merely an idiosyncrasy of style (attributable, say, to his affinity to Pre-Raphaelite and

Decadent aesthetics) but rather was anchored in his first experiences of the Indian subcontinent. This insistence on preserving the rhyming prose, alliteration and assonance of his Eastern original would be key to both the perceived aesthetic failure of Burton's *Nights* translation—in the view of some reviewers who claimed it was not written in the English of his age or any other—and its perceived genius for authors like James Joyce, who admired precisely the infusion of a foreign idiom.[61]

Burton's writing on Sindhi folklore anticipates his writing on the *Nights* in claiming that English poetry is in need of a cultural transfusion from translations of non-Western folktales to rediscover the early vitality and expressiveness of its own language and poetic forms. Burton's observation that Sindhi and Arabic literatures possessed pristine beginnings and have deteriorated slowly over time is familiar from Orientalist scholarship, yet in his writing it is coupled with the startling observation that English letters have similarly devolved into mediocrity. The trajectory of English poetry was already an unlikely subject of criticism in *Scinde, or the Unhappy Valley,* which takes the literary form of a dramatic monologue directed at the stereotypical Englishman John Bull. For Burton, British poetry is no longer vibrant and interwoven with life's elemental rhythms of love and war as in Sindh poetry but stale and drilled at school with the aid of corporal punishment—as he notes sarcastically with reference to 'dear Old Oliver [Goldsmith]'s rod-taught lines upon the subject of deserted-villages.' To the presumed anchoring of English identity and poetry in romantic evocations of rural belonging, Burton retorts: 'I regret to say, that the Scindians…having no word to explain your "home", attach none of those pretty ideas to the place in question, which supply Mr John Bull, Mrs B. and the children, with matter for eternal maudlin'.[62] The 'old world Oriental song' was intoxicating and 'spirit-stirring', the 'Terminal Essay' to the *Nights* would proclaim in a comparable vein, 'to the tongue water and brandy to the brain—the clean contrary of our nineteenth century effusions'. Burton's dismissive estimation of nineteenth-century English poetry and of romantic notions of belonging reinforces, by contrast, the regenerative effects he ascribes to the study of Eastern folklore and its translation in the tongue of the Old English ballad.

Burton's writing on Sindh makes evident that he was dissatisfied with the forms of 'Anglo-Indian' identity he encountered in Sindh, be it in terms of the British failure to adapt to the region or of the Sindhi attempt to emulate British mores. Burton's 1843 satiric manuscript *Anglo-Indian Glossary* demonstrates his rapid disenchantment with the British officer's identity in India and with the broader function of the British East India

Company in the imperial enterprise. While Burton's career in the Company was dependent on his mastery of local languages, this manuscript reveals he held no illusions as to the possibility of cultural mediation afforded by his official role as interpreter. The *Anglo-Indian Glossary* defines interpreters like himself as officers periodically called upon to make themselves 'ridiculous by screaming out' in dialect before ten thousand natives and Burton suggests that the only respite comes from sick leaves or arrests which afford 'the most graceful hours' of literary labour.[63] Service under Charles Napier in Sindh as a local informant or spy may have encouraged Burton to question the purpose of the British East India Company. Sir Charles Napier did not believe that the cause of empire could be entrusted to a business concern, confiding in his diary in 1846: 'The whole system of Indian government is constructed for robbery and spoliation, not for conquest, not for good to the multitude, not for justice!'[64] Even in his published work on Sindh, Burton could not hide his sarcasm with regard to the British presence in the subcontinent. When breaking the eighth commandment, he suggests that, 'good Madam Britannia' displays 'a lot of piety, much rhapsodizing about the bright dawn of Christianity, the finger of Providence, the spread of civilization, and the infinite benefit conferred upon barbarians by her permitting them to become her subjects, and pay their rents to her.'[65] During his tenure in Sindh Napier did not prioritize anglicizing the natives and Burton would go further—in some cases advocating the reversal of British policy and the restoration of native custom. Burton's idiosyncratic imperialism—not to be confused with anti-imperialism or cultural relativism—ventured that a more efficient and powerful imperial rule would be produced by the education of colonial administrators in Eastern rather than classical languages and literatures.

This dissatisfaction with the 'Anglo-Indian' identities available to him in Sindh would find an analogue in his attitude towards cultural syncretism in the region. He was pessimistic about the forms which cultural borrowing most often took in Sindh—a servile assimilation to the culture of the conquerors—while he would find praise only for the forms of cultural syncretism that 'semi-Orientals' like himself could either forge or recognize with their privileged cross-cultural insight, for example in the case of Sufism. His writing on Sindh sometimes presents cultural borrowings in terms of the 'corruption' of one language by another,[66] religious adaptations in terms of the 'contamination' of the faith and ritual of the conquered people,[67] and racial mixture in unflattering terms of physical description.[68] For him local assimilation to English manners proved no exception to this rule: he holds a particular disregard for 'grotesque' imitations of 'Ultra-European dress' and 'the English salon'.[69] Burton craves neither the 'Indian' life of the English in Sindh, nor the 'English' life some Sindhis adopted. The few positive glimpses Burton offers of a 'third variety' of culture involving the English in Sindh—'neither European nor oriental but an artful though mongrel mixture of the two'[70]—pertain to instances of English accommodation to local manners and he, therefore, entreats John Bull: 'Can you not, O stiff-necked gentleman, accommodate yourself a little more readily to these habits and customs of "foreign parts"?'[71] Not content with the mixed forms of cultural identity available to him, Burton experimented with creating other forms of cultural immersion by establishing a pattern of disguises he would continue in later life—notably in his pilgrimage to Makkah.

Accordingly, the task of arbitrating between incompatible and promising forms of cultural mixture falls for Burton not to the 'England-English' (who refuse to adapt) or the 'Anglo-Indians' (assimilated locals) but to 'semi-orientals' like himself, who hover between the two cultural spheres.[72] Burton is not averse to speculating on forms of racial and cultural syncretism he himself might envision as helpful, advocating in one instance an infusion of the 'manly races' of the mountainous region that could improve the races of the valley.[73] Above all, he proves optimistic about the forms of syncretism that he could identify and emulate, recognizing in Abd el Latif's Sufism an expression of cultural syncretism that transcends the mere assimilation of a conquered people to the culture of their conquerors. The example of Sufism demonstrates to Burton that the frontier zone of Sindh, between Islam and Hinduism, could generate a true syncretism that combines two belief systems to form a new system that re-evolves and becomes self-referential.[74] By preserving a harmonious blend of Hinduism and Islam, just as the Sindhi language was able to absorb a certain proportion of words from Sanskrit and Arabic, Sufism in Sindh would transcend the fixed imbalances of power that appeared to define other forms of cultural borrowing in the region. Sufism would be the form of faith Burton would return to in his own life and the Sufi mystical poem was the genre in which he would create his own most personal poetic work, *The Kasidah*, which combines Sufism with agnostic freethinking and social Darwinism.

Burton would deem himself even less constrained than el Latif by either Eastern and Western traditions in his literary translations from Eastern languages, feeling himself to be a 'semi-oriental' privileged with the ability to make East-West cross-cultural connections that enabled the translation of Eastern texts into English without the loss of idiomatic poetic devices or ethnological significance. In Burton, Dane Kennedy recognizes well the riddle 'of an agent of imperialism wielding what are widely regarded as the weapons of the weak [mimicry and hybridity]'.[75] Kennedy's solution is to reclaim Burton as a cultural relativist. This would appear to be an attempt at the tacit rehabilitation of a figure Edward Said had singled out as exemplary of the affiliation of Orientalist knowledge with imperialist power despite an apparent empathy for cultural difference. To frame Burton's articulation of literature and empire within his experience of Sindh is to understand that his critique of an assimilationist model of Empire does not prevent his espousal of another model of imperialism and that his empathy with a foreign culture need not signal cultural relativism. Burton believed his Sindhi travelogues and literary translations would prove useful to the administrators of Empire precisely due to the inclusiveness of his notion of Islam, encompassing folklore and sexuality, and his expansive mode of Orientalism, which allowed for cross-cultural analogies within Eastern cultures and between East and West.

NOTES

1. Richard Burton, *Ahlák I Hindi, or, a translation of the Hindustáni version of Pilpay's fables, by R.F. Burton. Lt. 18th Regt. Bombay, N.I. with explanatory notes, and appendix by the translator* (Bombay, 1847). Fifty handwritten leaves and seventy-eight typescript leaves, respectively 104a and 104b in B.J. Kirkpatrick's *A Catalogue of the Library of Sir Richard Burton, K.C.M.G. held by the Royal Anthropological Institute*. Burton Collection, Huntington Library, San Marino, California. My citations refer to the typescript manuscript.
2. Richard Burton, *The Book of the Thousand Nights and a Night, with Introduction, Explanatory Notes on the Manners and Customs of Moslem Men and a Terminal Essay upon the History of the Nights, Vol. I–X* (Benares: Kamashastra Society for Private Subscribers Only, 1885–1887). Following Burton's practice, hitherto *Nights*.
3. Richard Burton, *Scinde Or the Unhappy Valley, Vol. I and II* (New Delhi: AES, 1998 [1851]); Richard Burton, *Sindh and the Races that Inhabit the Valley of the Indus; with Notices of the Topography and History of the Province* (Karachi: Oxford University Press, 1973 [1851]); Richard Burton, *Falconry in the Valley of the Indus* (London: John van Voorst, 1852).
4. Alexander Burns, *A Voyage on the Indus, Being the Third Volume of Travels into Bokhara* (Karachi: Oxford University Press, 1973 [1834]); James Burns, *A Visit to the Court of Sinde* (Karachi: Oxford University Press, 1974 [1829]); E.B. Eastwick, *A Glance at Sind Before Napier, or Dry Leaves from Young Egypt* (Karachi: Oxford University Press, 1973 [1849]); Thomas Postans, *Personal Observations on Sindh; The Manners and Customs of Its Inhabitants, And Its Productive Capabilities: With a Sketch of Its Recent History, A*

Narrative of Recent Events, and an Account of the Connection with that Country to the Present Period (Karachi: Indus, 1973 [1843]).

5. Dane Kennedy, *The Highly Civilized Man: Richard Burton and the Victorian World* (Cambridge, MA: Harvard University Press, 2005), 17 and 19.
6. Roger Célestin, *From Cannibals to Radicals: Figures and Limits of Exoticism* (Minneapolis: University of Minnesota Press, 1996), 6.
7. Jean-François Gournay, *Richard F. Burton: Ambre et Lumiere de l'Orient* (Paris: Desclee De Brouwer, 1991), 124.
8. Edward William Lane, *The Thousand and One Nights, Commonly Called, in England, the Arabian Nights' Entertainments: a New Translation from the Arabic, with Copious Notes, Volumes 1–3* (London: Charles Knight, 1839–1841).
9. Burton, 'The Translator's Foreword', in *Nights*, I: xx.
10. For instance, Burton's observation that, 'It is meritorious to accompany the funeral cortege of a Moslem even for a few paces' (Burton, *Nights*, II: n83) echoes the mention that it is prestigious to accompany a funeral procession in Hinduism and Islam (*Sindh* and the Races, 349–358 and 273–282). The *Nights* comparisons of the Muslim jinn to the Hindu Rakshasa (I: n12, III: n259) echo the earlier discussion of demons in Sindh (*Sindh and the Races*, 174–177, 146, 147, 175, 181). The *Nights* note on letter-writing (III: 24) cites *Scinde* (chapter IV).
11. Burton, *Sindh and the Races*, 172.
12. Ibid.
13. Ibid.
14. Ibid., 174–194 (quotes 173 and 175).
15. Ibid., 179. See also page 180 for the use of amatory talismans in the service of fidelity.
16. Ibid., 183.
17. The 'Terminal Essay' would spy traces of polytheistic faiths in Islam and Christianity as evidence of a common source for the world's major religions. Burton reclaims for instance the archangel Gabriel common to Islam and Christianity 'as a manifestation of the first intelligence that enabled Zarathrusta' in the *Nights* 'Terminal Essay' (Burton, *Nights* X: 129) and articulates a theory of the unity of the world's religions in this essay and in his *Kasidah*.
18. Edward William Lane, *An Account of the Manners and Customs of the Modern Egyptians* (New York: Dover, 1973 [1836]), chapter 7.
19. Ibid., 276.
20. Burton, *Sindh and the Races*, 181–182.
21. Ibid., 181.
22. Edward Lane, 'Notes to the Introduction', in Burton *Nights*, I: 26, 33.
23. Burton, *Sindh and the Races*, 174.
24. Ibid., n403.
25. Burton, *Nights*, I: 10. This connection is reinforced in the index entry on this note included in the appendix to the *Nights*, 'Jinn = the French génie, the Hindu Rakshasa or Yaksha' (Burton, *Nights*, X: 306).
26. To borrow the definition of syncretism articulated in Derryl MacLean's *Religion and Society in Arab Sind* (Leiden: E.J. Brill, 1989), 151–153.
27. Burton, *Sindh and the Races*, 199.
28. Ibid., 199–200.
29. Ibid., 200.
30. Ibid.
31. Ibid.

32. Burton, *Scinde*, II: 7.
33. Burton, *Pilpay's Fables*, 22 of the typescript mss.
34. Ibid., 33 of the typescript mss.
35. Burton, *Nights*, VII: 135 and III: 123.
36. Ibid., VI: 202.
37. Ibid., IX: 80.
38. Burton, *Scinde*, I: 119–120.
39. Burton, *Sindh and the Races*, 295 and n416.
40. Burton, 'The Translator's Foreword', in Burton, *Nights*, I: xx.
41. Ibid.
42. Burton, *Scinde*, II: 7.
43. Burton protests that Sindhi is 'not, as has been asserted, a mere corruption of Hindustani' (Burton, *Sindh and the Races*, 69).
44. Burton, *Sindh and the Races*, 71.
45. Ibid., 367–368.
46. Ibid., 386.
47. Ibid., 75.
48. Ibid., 79.
49. Ibid., 87.
50. Ibid., 88.
51. Ibid., 388.
52. Ibid., 89 and 91.
53. Burton, *Scinde*, I: 64.
54. Burton, *Sindh and the Races*, 386.
55. Ibid., 383.
56. Ibid., 202.
57. Ibid., 202–203.
58. Ibid., 203.
59. Ibid., 386.
60. The exasperation of Burton scholars with this insistence is perhaps most strongly stated in a private page of notes 'On Burton's Character' by biographer Fawn Brodie preserved at the Huntington Library.
61. In this spirit Joyce would adapt Burton's alliterative version of the formulaic ending of all *Nights* tales—'And they led the most pleasurable of lives and the most delectable, till there came to them the Destroyer of delights and the Severer of societies and they became as though they had never been'—to his own purpose in *Finnegans Wake*: 'And they leaved the most leavely of leaftimes and the most folliagenous till there came the marrer of mirth and the jangtherapper of all jocolarinas and they were as were they never ere.' Quoted in Aida Yared, 'Joyce's Sources: Sir Richard Burton's *Terminal Essay* in *Finnegans Wake*', *Joyce Studies Annual* 11 (Summer 2000): 124.
62. Burton, *Scinde*, I: 182.
63. Quentin Keynes Collection of Burton manuscripts.
64. Entry dated 2 April 1846 quoted in Fawn Brodie, *The Devil Drives: A Life of Sir Richard Burton* (New York: W.W. Norton, 1967), 58.
65. Burton, *Scinde*, I: 182.
66. A typical example: 'The language of these mountaineers is the Belochki, either a barbarous corruption, or more probably an unpolished cognate dialect of that venerable and most beautiful tongue, the Persian' (Burton, *Scinde*, II: 199). Burton complains of the corruption of 'Beebee', a lady, into 'Booboo', of 'Seedy' as a corruption of the Arabic word for 'my lord', of the 'corrupt dialect of "the Moors",' of corrupted Portuguese

words, and of locals 'Salaaming to the river, and mangling an Arabic sentence' (respectively, Burton, *Scinde*, I: 39, 52, 55, 272 and II: 300).

67. Burton notes that, 'the Hindoo's religion has, like the Moslem's, been contaminated by contact with strangers', and generalizes 'when the Polytheist and the Monotheist meet on at all equal terms, the former either ruins, or subjects himself to the latter' (Burton, *Scinde*, I: 246 and 230).
68. Burton remarks of the 'mass of the population' in Sindh that 'the connexion with the superior sub-family has, however, failed to produce a strictly speaking improved development', and typically comments on a mixed group: '[t]he people are partly Scindian, partly Beloch: both are equally savage and ferocious' (Burton, *Scinde*, I: 251 and II: 188).
69. Burton, *Scinde*, I: 42 and II: 143.
70. Burton, *Scinde*, II: 278. The passage refers to the adoption of attire neither English nor local. Elsewhere he writes: 'I have learned how largely we gain…by widening the pantaloons, and by exchanging the beaver for a turban' (Burton, *Scinde*, II: 33).
71. Burton, *Scinde*, II: 156.
72. Burton habitually uses the formulation in passages such as 'We semi-orientals understood….' (Burton, *Scinde*, I: 195). In contrast he admonishes '[y]ou England-English' for deserving the label 'Britons fierce to strangers' due to a 'fashionable superciliousness and a *guindé* attempt at exclusivity' which compares unfavourably with the hospitality of both the English and locals of the subcontinent (Burton, *Scinde* II, 28–30).
73. Burton states: 'The latter experiment might easily and profitably be tried' (Burton, *Scinde*, II: 125).
74. Here again I am indebted to Derryl MacLean's *Religion and Society in Arab Sind* (particularly 126–158).
75. Kennedy, 68.

CHAPTER 9

1947: Recovering Displaced Histories of Karachi[1]

VAZIRA FAZILA-YACOOBALI ZAMINDAR

Let me begin with a map from the pages of the 1951 Census of Pakistan, for it places Karachi at the heart of a subcontinent on the move. As the fact of Partition transformed the provincial port on the peripheries of British India into an administrative capital of a new state—the Pakistan Census Area—the map captures the dramatic flow of people into the city. People left their birthplaces in unprecedented numbers and came, as graphically represented, from all the different 'zones' of the subcontinent.

The numerical majority clearly came from north India, although the 1951 Census categorized all the displaced people as *muhajirs*. *Muhajirs* figured prominently in tables and charts which demonstrated their economic and cultural dominance in the city post-1947, and Urdu was recorded as the language of the new majority in the city. Those who claimed Karachi as their birthplace were now a minority.

Most studies of the city tend to focus on *muhajirs*, the Muslim refugees that flowed into the city and have shaped its politics since 1947. On the other hand, the census map renders invisible the flow of people out of the city, the Hindu refugees that once formed 47.6 per cent of the city. Historical accounts of the city have noted the religious diversity of pre-Partition Karachi's population, the contribution of Parsi, Hindu, Muslim, British, and Goan Christian individuals to the growth of the city and unremarkably mention that as a result of Partition '[t]he most significant change was demographic'.[2] But the silence around this dramatic exodus renders this loss of a multi-religious city as a natural process rather than a problem of history in need of enquiry—they naturalize Pakistan as a pre-dominantly Muslim nation-state.

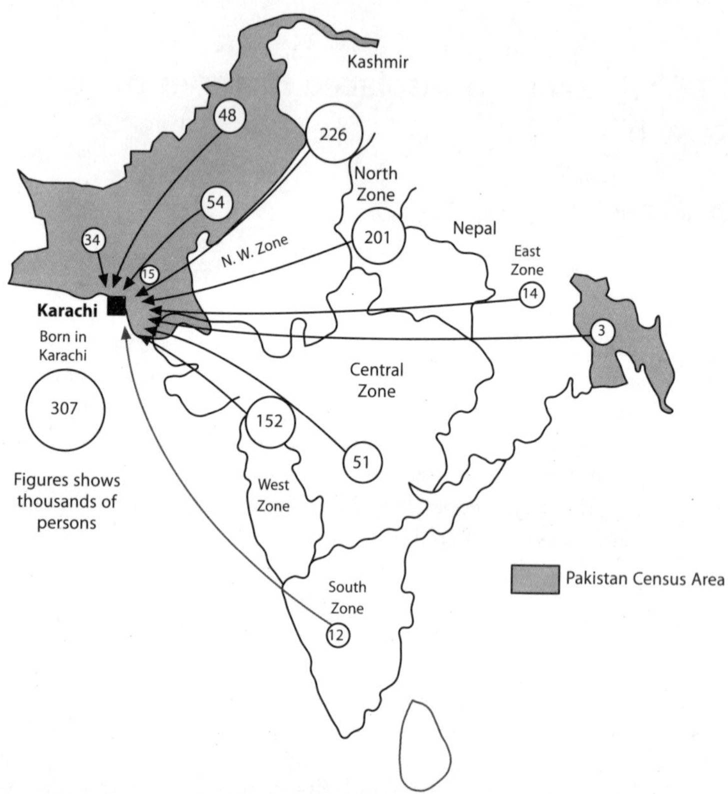

Sindh was a region that was particularly characterized for its 'communal harmony' and, in the days leading up to Partition, Sindh's Governor, Francis Mudie, described it as a place which '[c]haractistically…carries on almost as if nothing had happened or was going to happen', and that he '[didn't] expect many real Sindhi [Hindus] to leave the Province'.[3] In keeping with Mudie's view, Karachi did not experience the scale of violence that ensued in Punjab and Delhi. However, by the time 'the most notable communal incident' took place on 6 January 1948, Hindus and Sikhs were already leaving the city and the province in large numbers. In fact, the 'incident' took place as Sikhs from various parts of Sindh arrived in Karachi to leave by ship for India and were taken in open horse carriages to a *gurdwara* in the city. Reportedly, Muslim refugees surrounded the *gurdwara* and attacked it and this led to rioting in the city which was brought 'under control' when the army was deployed.[4] But what led to the exodus in a region well-known for 'communal harmony'? Did the flows of Muslim refugees—outsiders without a Sindhi ethos—have something to do with it, as Ghulam Husain Hidayatullah, the governor to follow Mudie believed?[5]

In this chapter, I examine the specific conditions that shaped this exodus from Karachi to show the role of both the emerging states of India and Pakistan in its unfolding, as well as its effects on anguished debates on the contours of an imagined 'Muslim nation'. In my book, *The Long Partition*, I argue that an inter-state agreement on the transfer of population along religious lines in murder-cleaved Punjab opened up the question of where religious minorities belonged for the rest of the subcontinent. Sindh, with its history of 'communal harmony', then became crucial in the equation. For some, 'Pakistan' had been imagined as providing protection to all the Muslims of the subcontinent (including Muslims that remained in India) by the 'hostage' presence of significant Hindu minorities within the territorial limits of Pakistan and, thus, this exodus unravelled more than Sindh's multi-religious identity. Recovering this history of displacement bears a special burden, for it reveals the contingent, contested, and fraught process that followed the Partition of 1947 to produce a nationalized geography of South Asia.

The Push and Pull of Displacement

'Mahatama Gandhi and the Congress leaders should be informed that Hindus of Sindh cannot live in honour there and therefore the Indian Dominion Government should take up the task of evacuating, relief and rehabilitation', Choithram P. Gidwani, the President of the Sindh Provincial Congress Committee, proclaimed to Rajendra Prasad, the first President of India, after a meeting of Sindhi Congressmen. Gidwani and other Congress leaders of Sindh campaigned vociferously for the Indian government to arrange a planned evacuation of Sindh's minorities, along the lines carried out by the Military Evacuation Organization (MEO) in West Punjab, but the problem they faced was that, 'Due to peace [in the province], the Government of India [wa]s not assisting them'.[6]

Because of the campaign by Sindh's Congressmen for the planned evacuation of Sindh's minorities, many of Pakistan's leaders and bureaucrats believed that the exodus of the economically significant Hindus of Sindh was being orchestrated by Congress leaders to sabotage the very existence of Pakistan. For instance, it was believed that 'harijans' were being encouraged to leave so that the sanitation of Karachi, Hyderabad, and Sukkur would be impaired, resulting in 'epidemic and pestilence'. More seriously, the departure of Hindu merchants, bankers, and other businesses would disrupt the economic life of Karachi and Sindh and this would destabilize the nascent state.[7] In keeping with such a view, Syed Hashim Reza, the first post-independence administrator of Karachi, wrote in his autobiography that, soon after Partition, Acharya Kripalani, the President of the All India Congress Committee (AICC) who was from Sindh, visited the province and advised Hindus and Sikhs to leave Sindh as quickly as possible. Arguing that as no 'communal disturbances' had taken place in Sindh for centuries, Reza suggested that Kripalani was not so concerned for the safety of the minorities but wanted to destroy the economic structure of the Province.[8] Sindh Police records also claim 'on good authority that though Kripalani openly advised Hindus not to migrate, he secretly favoured migration and asked Hindus to leave Sindh as early as possible'.[9] Later, in a Constituent Assembly debate, Hashim Gazder of Sindh also took this view when he claimed that Sindhi Hindus 'were quite happy here in Sindh; there were no murders, no dacoities; there were no loots of any kind'. Instead, he held that Sindh's minorities were not 'pushed out' but rather 'they were pulled out according to a planned programme by the Congress leaders' and Kripalani, who came 'with the ostensible purpose of telling people not to go from Sind...wherever he went he told them to get out of Sind'.[10]

Despite this view held by Pakistani officials, large numbers of Hindus and Sikhs had already begun to leave Sindh even prior to Kripalani's visit in late September 1947. Ansari, for instance, notes that by mid-September some fifty thousand 'non-Muslims' had registered with local Congress organizations for aid in leaving Sindh.[11] Although the first departures were largely of Gujaratis, Marathis, and other non-Sindhi Hindus, as anticipated by Mudie,[12] the advice of Kripalani, Gidwani, and other leaders cannot alone account for the mass exodus.

Despite the celebration of Sindh's pre-Partition 'communal harmony', Mudie's *Forthnightly Reports* suggest that there had been a growing political rift between the provincial Muslim League and the Congress. On a number of provincial issues the Sindh Muslim League's stance was seen as a foreboding of Muslim dominance, whereby economically significant Hindus of the province would be marginalized.

For one, when the Sindh Assembly opened on 17 February 1947 with a Muslim League majority, the house broke with the region's tradition by adopting both the Speaker and the Deputy Speaker from the League when the practice had been to select a Deputy Speaker from the opposition.[13] Further, by March 1947, at least two divisive issues faced the house—the Sindh University Bill and the Sindh Landholders Mortgage Bill. Even after the administrative separation of Sindh from the Bombay Presidency students in the region had to go to Bombay University to give their matriculation exams and, therefore, there had been a long-standing political consensus that Sindh needed its own university. However, a Sind University Bill which provided for a Muslim majority on the various university bodies was passed by the Muslim League-dominated assembly, even though the Congress members vehemently opposed it. The Education Ministry justified this legislation on the basis that Muslims were severely under-represented in education and government in Sindh.[14] But with Partition imminent, the 'controversy', which was widely covered by the press, did little to reassure the province's Hindus for—even after lengthy negotiations—only token conciliatory resolutions were passed to set up a Board of Studies for Hindu culture, as well as an advisory panel to represent minority interests. Similarly, the Sind Landholders Mortgage Bill was seen as giving Muslim *zamindars* leverage over Hindu *banias* by allowing a *zamindar* to give oral evidence at variance with a sale deed. The Congress opposition to the passing of this bill was such that an appeal was made to the Viceroy in Delhi to withhold his assent to the Bill.[15]

Both these Bills were included in a polemical brochure produced by the Sindh Congress, 'Why the exodus from Sind?'[16] It argued that Hindus were leaving Sindh 'because in actual fact, the Muslim League government of Sind were *even before Pakistan was established*, deliberately and more or less systematically pursuing with neck-break speed a policy of ruthless suppression of the Hindus of Sind' (emphasis added). The brochure foregrounds the seeds of distrust in regional politics which were now being rehearsed amidst the anxieties of Partition. At its core was the very uncertainty of what was to be the nature of the Pakistani state, whether claimed on behalf of Muslims, it could eschew the question of religious identity in the making of its citizens.

Jinnah's often-quoted speech of 11 August 1947—'in course of time, Hindus would cease to be Hindus and Muslims would cease to be Muslim…in the political sense as citizens of the State'—is usually offered as evidence of a promise of equal citizenship for all in the Pakistani state. Reza recalls, in his autobiography, accompanying Jinnah to the Swami Narayan temple in the heart of Karachi where 'non-Muslim refugees' from different parts of Sindh were awaiting their departure by ship to India.

Jinnah, according to Reza, made every effort to reassure the province's Hindus but that they said 'that while they had full trust in him, it could not be said about the petty officials who had communal bias'.[17] In addition, Ayub Khuhro (the Premier of Sindh) and other Sindhi leaders attempted to retain Sindh's minorities for they also feared a loss of cultural identity with the Hindu exodus. However, after the riots of 6 January 1948, when Khuhro toured Sindh with Sri Prakasa, the Indian High Commissioner, to urge the Sindhi Hindus to not leave their homes, a *Hindustan Times* reporter observed that 'Hindus stopped their car every few miles and urged for arrangements for early evacuation'.[18]

Further, the Sindh government attempted to use force to stem this exodus by passing the Sindh Maintenance of Public Safety Ordinance on 21 September 1947. Given that the majority of Sindh government servants were Hindu, their departure meant in the initial stage that many offices could function for only part of their working hours; half the civil and criminal courts were closed, and some banks and businesses were able to operate for only a few hours a day. In addition, it was feared that the departure of Hindu *banias* would lead to a breakdown in the rural credit system. Thus, the ordinance, in addition to giving the government wide powers for policing the province, also allowed for the 'control of essential services' so that those services deemed 'essential to the life of the community' were prohibited from leaving.[19] The coercive ordinance only exacerbated fears of mistreatment by the new state and led to an increase in exodus.

The Indian state's official position on displacements outside of Punjab was broadly that minorities should remain where they were and, in the case of Sindh, it was 'not to encourage the evacuation of non-Muslims from Sind', although the Indian High Commission in Karachi would give all assistance of travel to those who wished to depart.[20] It has been argued that, in the case of Sindh, the Indian High Commissioner gave free ship tickets to those who wanted to leave and thus encouraged migration, although at the time the High Commission denied this.[21]

However, when the High Commissioner protested against the Public Safety Ordinance, he not only argued 'that persons who desire permanently to go to India and to seek a home there should be afforded every facility to do so'. Importantly, he also stated that although 'who is to be deemed a citizen of Pakistan and who is a citizen of India' was still indeterminate at this stage, yet, 'those who wish to go away permanently from Pakistan and to live in India, have chosen to be the citizens of India'.[22] Sardar Patel had given an assurance prior to Partition that 'whatever the definition [of

Indian citizenship] may be, you can be rest assured that the Hindus and Sikhs of Pakistan cannot be considered as aliens in India'.[23] According to Patel's view, all Hindus and Sikhs who resided in Pakistan were a natural part of an Indian nation and this underpinned the Indian state's position on non-Muslim refugees.

When 'serious communal rioting' broke out in Karachi on 6 January 1948, Bhaskar H. Rao, the official recorder of the Indian government's *Story of Rehabilitation*, described it as an 'orgy of looting and arson' in which the Congress office in Karachi was also attacked.[24] It marked the formal change of the Indian government policy on Sindh, as a Director General of Evacuation was appointed on 14 January 1948 to formally assist the evacuation of 'non-Muslims who wished to migrate from Sindh to India'.[25] It was at this point that Sindh's 'non-Muslim refugees' became officially incorporated as 'displaced persons' under the rubric of rehabilitation in Indian legislations to follow.

The Indian government's response to Sindh's Hindus in particular, and Hindus and Sikhs in Pakistan more generally, resolved the question of where this religious minority belonged. They could migrate to the territory of India and become Indian citizens and this remained the case even as restrictions on movement and citizenship laws began to be formulated over the following years.

STATE OF EMERGENCY

Although 'peaceful' conditions in Karachi were widely remarked upon, it was a relative and contingent 'peace', for a state of emergency encompassed most of the subcontinent as stories of violence in Punjab and Delhi circulated through newspapers and by word of mouth. Its discursive effect can be read in two words that appear in all the official reports in Sindh—'panic' and 'fear'. It was thus 'a state of uncertainty, bordering on panic' and 'the fear complex' that was used to explain in part the departure of the province's Hindus. 'Rumours' that Hindus would be slaughtered in place of goats and sheep on Id-ul-Zuha day, or that their drinking water would be poisoned or that their properties would be confiscated entered police records as outrageous and therefore imaginary or fictive fears that were spreading unnecessary panic.[26] But as writings on rumours in moments of social crisis suggest, their 'contagion' and meaning were constituted by the wider context.[27]

Wild rumours operated alongside extremely partisan accounts of the Punjab violence, the growing visible presence of Muslim refugees on the streets, and a reported increase in stabbings and robberies. Police reports string a list of crimes—a Sikh bookbinders shop set on fire in Saddar, or a crockery shop in Jodia Bazar robbed, a temple desecrated, and so on.[28] These facts at another time may not have been as alarming to the city's Hindus, but in this context served to heighten extant anxieties. The Pakistani state attempted to respond with alacrity and Jinnah was particularly keen that 'law and order' in Karachi be given the highest priority. Thus, in early September, curfew was imposed in the city as a preventive measure, and then whenever there appeared to be 'trouble'.

However, curfew alone could not provide the necessary reassurance to the city's Hindu residents. The 'trespass of Hindu houses by Moslem refugees' became one of the most common crimes and probably contributed the most significantly to a sense of a changing social order in which the place of long-standing Hindu residents of the city was uncertain.[29] A Sindhi Muslim newspaper described how the arrival of Muslim refugees had resulted in Hindus feeling like 'a stranger or a foreigner in his own land of birth'. The author noted that 'unauthorized forcible occupation of houses and seizures of property' were taking place. He gave an instance when a government servant in Karachi had gone for a walk with his wife after locking the house but, on his return, found that it was occupied by 'Muslim refugees' who would not vacate the premises. He also noted that, in Ramswami quarters, houses of poor people were broken into and quietly occupied in the absence of the occupants.[30]

Gidwani similarly complained to Liaquat about this 'lawlessness', as he noted that when 'the inmates [of houses] go out on work and duty, the locks are broken open, the belongings pilfered or thrown out and the flats occupied with impunity. When the occupants return and ask for their belongings only they are violently threatened and made to run away.'[31] Thus, in letters to Kripalani and other Congress leaders, Sindhi Hindus noted with trepidation that 'Punjabis', referring to Muslim refugees, had moved into Hindu buildings, making it 'very difficult to live'.[32]

As police reports began to classify 'trouble from the refugee', another letter requested Congress help in leaving because 'ladies cannot move out on the roads being always under the fear of too many Punjabi Muslims moving on the roads'.[33] Although an apparently trivial concern, it articulated the uncertainty and fear that was generated by the arrival of 'Muslim refugees'. Thus, many Hindu men, who were employed in Karachi or had ancestral homes and businesses here, began to send their wives and children, and other members of their families to India while they remained in the city.

However, 'Muslim refugees' were not the only source of anxiety. Another account highlighted the role of the Pakistani state in requisitioning and allotting houses which still had people living in it. It noted that, 'although in several cases stay orders have been issued, considerable excitement has been created among Hindus at the notices served on them. It may be noted that only Hindus have been served with such notices'. I discuss in the next section the measures taken by the Pakistani state to house the new government in the city. The account argued that the government 'interprets that any house or bungalow with two or three persons constitutes an abandoned property'. It stated that it was 'true that several persons have sent part of their family outside but on that ground to drive out the remaining members of the family in the streets looks extremely unreasonable'. In addition, it noted that representatives of the Hindu Cooperative Housing Societies had been called by the Minister Pir Ilahi Bux, who asked them to give the government four or five bungalows from each society by making 'certain adjustments' by 'voluntarily housing two families in one house'.[34] This process of 'making room' for the new state, albeit a piece-meal process, led to the expression that 'Sindhis [were] squeezed out of Sind'.[35]

Other letters to the AICC and Kripalani also record similar fears of discrimination in the new state in urging the Indian state for help to leave. One writer argued that 'violence in Punjab' coupled with 'new Ordinances from the Government [for housing], their Communal Policy in service, education, business', were some of the reasons for leaving Sindh. The Piece Goods Merchants Association wrote to Kripalani for assistance in relocating to Bombay for they felt that 'Muslim outsiders' were receiving facilities from the state over the 'legitimate rights and interests of the Hindu merchants'.[36]

However, not everyone wrote for help to leave. Some wrote seeking reassurances to stay and their letters suggest that the decision to leave for many was a contingent one. One Shamdas wrote movingly from Sehwan, 'well known from Kalander Lal Shabaz whose shrine and fair is famous throughout the world'. He worried that if 'at any time situation at Karachi and Hyderabad go worse and my relations might migrate...what will be the fate of mine and of my valuable property on which my large family of 12 members is depending'. A Mr Malkani wrote to Nehru that 'Sind is today in the grip of a tidal wave of panic and migration which none but you or Bapu [Gandhi] can stop. You alone can allay this panic and reduce the resulting emigration'.[37]

A large number of letters were from the employees of Karachi Port Trust, for they had initially believed that they would have the possibility of 'opting' to work for India or Pakistan.[38] When they found out that they were not included in this scheme, they wrote individual letters of appeal for help. One Mr Thadani of the Port Trust made his case to Kripalani as follows:

> I find that many Hindus are leaving Sind. It may be taken for granted that nothing untoward incident may happen in Sind as both Pakistan and Sind governments have taken strong measures to protect minorities but as many have left and many more are thinking of leaving it may appear awkward for the remaining Hindus to remain in Sind....I think all who remain will be without their kith and kins. It will therefore be advisable if one leaves early 'sooner the better'.[39]

However, the president of the Sarva Hindu Sindh Panchayat wrote to Kripalani to ask for the Sindh Congress to be dissolved so that his party could instead represent Hindu interests in the Sindh legislature, and provide leadership to those who were considering staying but were uncertain. He optimistically 'calculated that 70 per cent of Sind Hindus will not leave and if things grow better—as it is hoped—a large number of evacuees will return back'.[40]

The Panchayat president's analysis particularly foregrounds the contingent nature of many people's decisions to leave their homes, as well as hopes to return if conditions allowed it. It is with this ambivalence that displacements began but became more decisively shaped with the shift in the Indian government's official policy towards Sindh's Hindus, and as Hindu houses and lands became a contested part of the calculus of housing Muslim refugees.

Karachi's Housing Crisis

One letter to the Urdu newspaper, *Jang*, argued that there were three groups of displaced that the term *muhajir* encompassed that had arrived in Karachi and were in need of housing. Firstly, there were Muslim government employees from all over India who had 'opted' to work for the Pakistan government and were looking for housing for their families. Secondly, there were *sarmayadar muhajir*s, those migrants with *sarmaya* or capital, who could afford to buy houses for themselves. And finally, there were the *tabah-o-barbad muhajir*s who had lost everything and were destitute.[41]

Prior to Partition, Karachi had been a small provincial centre, albeit Jinnah's birthplace, and was declared the new capital when it was offered by the Sindh Muslim League.[42] Given that the city had to house a federal government and all its personnel, largely coming in from the 'outside' in Karachi, unlike Delhi, a housing crisis was already anticipated, albeit not of the proportions that ensued. Even though government employees were asked not to bring their families with them, Mudie anticipated having to find accommodation for about 20,000 people in one month, an extravagant number given Karachi's size.[43]

The Sindh government vacated a number of its premises for the federal government and several military barracks were converted to house government employees. Despite these measures, for the first years the government of Pakistan operated 'out of packing crates, hutments, tents', and many government employees remained without housing.[44] Reza recalled with sentiment in his memoir that the 'Central Government had to start from scratch with all sorts of make-shift arrangements. Assistant Secretaries and Superintendents had to work in open verandas. Thorns were used instead of pins, stools and benches were used instead of chairs and no one complained, such was the joy of working for one's own Government and people'.[45] Such felicitous recollections of Karachi's beginnings as Pakistan's capital are common in recent writings on Karachi.[46] Amina Apa, who initially lived in a room in Martin Quarters, a converted barracks, recalled how seven of her adult brothers and sisters had to live with their elder brother, a government employee, and his wife and children: '*Ek hi nalka tha, aur subha men lambi line lagti thi...magar there were no complaints, woh mahol hi esa tha* [there was only one tap, and in the morning a long line would form...but there were no complaints, those conditions were such]'.

However, these conditions were not felicitous for everyone or borne with such forbearance by everyone in the city. In order to house the government, legislations were passed to control building materials and requisition housing, which affected the Hindu residents of the city differentially. For instance, Mudie saw his housing task as that of displacing the city's Hindu population when he remarked that, '[t]he Pakistan Government want to bring 4000 clerks, in addition to officers. To turn 4000 clerks, mostly Hindu, with their wives and 'family members' out of their houses in Karachi and to put in their places 4000 Muslims, mostly from the Punjab and the UP, in one month, is administratively impossible except under war conditions'.[47]

However, when government servants began arriving from the terrible conditions of Purana Qila and other Muslim camps, they arrived in Karachi with all their family. Thus, there was not even sufficient housing for officers and the Estates Office in charge of housing government servants in general was inundated with more requests than it could fulfil. One 'grief-stricken and poor' government clerk wrote his story of suffering after arriving at Karachi's train station to the newspaper:

> I spend the night on the platform there only, and then the next morning reported to work. At the same time I put in a request for a quarter, and then returned to my family on the platform, to find that my family had been removed from the station and put on the street. This was the harshness of the railway officials. Then we remained at the station as my wife had fever and we were worried. I wrote clearly in my request that my wife and children are sick because they have spent the last three months in extreme hardship.[48]

He went on to narrate the ill treatment he received at the Estates Office, and concluded that '*itna tabah-o-barbad ho-ne ke ba'd abhi kuch kami reh gai thi jo yahan puri ho rahi hai* [after being devastated so much if there was anything left it is being completed here]'.

There were Muslim League supporters and educated and wealthier Muslims, the *sarmayadars*, who had chosen to move to Pakistan or establish second homes here and, in anticipation of Partition, had bought houses in the city. Mudie noted that, '[t]he leading Muslim Advocate in Lucknow told me recently that he was to retire in a year and settle down in Karachi, and one of the largest Muslim *taluqdars* in Oudh bought a house here about two months ago. Even the Nawab of Bhopal is trying to buy land near Karachi on which to build a house'.[49] These *muhajirs* were able to buy properties from departing Hindu families and this set them apart.

But by early September, Hidayatullah noted that 'destitute refugees' were arriving in Karachi at the rate of 400 daily.[50] By mid September 27,000 refugees were reported to have come to Sindh and a week later their numbers had doubled.[51] It was these Muslim refugees that were considered as the 'refugee problem' as the increase in incidents of violence in the city was associated with them and they were received with some hostility by the Sindh government.[52] Initially, there were no arrangements for organizing them into camps and they quickly became a visible presence in the city as footpaths filled up.[53] By the time some camps were set up many more refugees had arrived and housing refugees became a critical issue.

The housing crisis placed the Pakistani state in a predicament, for on the one hand it was attempting to reassure Sindh's Hindus to remain in their homes and, on the other hand, there were thousands of Muslim refugees without shelter. However, in response to the housing crisis, the government passed the Sindh Economic Rehabilitation Bill for taking over 'abandoned' properties and allotting them to Muslim refugees. This task of taking over and allotting 'abandoned' houses to *muhajirs* fell to the Rent Controller's Office. A Custodian of Evacuee Property was not set up in Karachi until 1948, for unlike the Punjab and Delhi there had been no instant 'mass abandonment' due to violence. This also made the Rent Controller's task an extremely difficult one for, although Hindus were leaving, it was unclear if a house was 'abandoned' or not if the owner left without declaring his intentions. As I mentioned earlier, most people were uncertain of the future and their decisions to leave were largely contingent. So, many had locked their homes and gone, with the hope of returning once conditions improved. Further, in many cases part of a family remained in Karachi while a part left for India. Thus, although Hindus were leaving, their houses were not 'empty'. At the same time 'abandoned houses' were being demanded by angry 'Muslim refugees', who claimed an entitlement to the new nation-state.

The first largest group of 'Muslim refugees' arrived from Delhi. The Urdu newspaper, *Jang*, which had also migrated from Delhi to Karachi, initially catered to Delhi's Muslim refugees by carrying announcements of those who had arrived and were looking for their relatives, lists of missing people, as well as detailed stories of what was going on in Delhi. *Hakims*, tailors, restaurants and a number of other businesses used *Jang* to announce their new addresses in Karachi, as well as invited job applications from cooks and tailors who were specifically from Delhi. This was also where *muhajir* grievances were registered and it is here that the struggles over housing are most evident.

Muhajir anger was two-fold—on the one hand it was directed against the Pakistani state and in particular the Sindh government and, on the other hand it was directed against the Hindus of the city. The ambiguous reception of the Sindh government towards them led to complaints of ill treatment and 'unislamic behaviour' for not receiving them with the hospitality that they had expected of *ansars*.[54] Writers in *Jang* expressed a sense of being duped or deceived into believing that they would be welcomed in Pakistan, which would be a haven for them. As one *Jang* editorial remarked, 'the heaven that [they] had imagined and come to, it is completely different from that'.[55]

The perception that the government did not care about their well-being was most pronounced when a Muhajir Committee, set up by the government of Sindh, resigned on the grounds that they were unable to do their job of housing *muhajirs*. *Jang* argued that although the committee had presented its problems to the chief minister of Sindh, they were met with indifference. Further, the Rent Controller's Office became the focus of a great deal of dissatisfaction for it was felt that the institution had become corrupt in the face of a greater demand for houses than that which was available. Thus, there were charges that only 'those who bribe get a house', and that in return for remuneration several allotment orders were being issued for a single house. Thus, *Jang* argued that, 'poor *muhajirs* who get an allotment order do not get a house because several allotment notices are issued because of the high amount of corruption'.[56]

Given that the Rent Controller's office was the only means to officially obtain houses for those who could not afford to buy them, *muhajirs* gathered here every day in large numbers and it is not surprising that this became the site of many altercations and fights. On one occasion, *Jang* reported that a refugee entered the Rent Controller's office to tell him his complaints and the Rent Controller slapped and pushed him out of his office. This immediately fed into a general perception of insult and ill-treatment of *muhajirs* in the new state and a threatening crowd gathered and started chanting anti-Rent Controller slogans. A frightened Rent Controller, it was reported, sneaked out through a back door and the office was closed. *Jang* sympathized with the *muhajir* predicament when it remarked that, 'On the one hand non-Muslims are asking twice thrice the price for their houses and goods, and on the other hand people who have to go to the Rent Controller's Office have to face so much harassment'.[57]

Thus, government attempts to convince Sindhi Hindus to stay in the province was criticised by *muhajirs* as 'the Hindu appeasing policy' of the government and Hindus became the focus of both anger and suspicion. While many *muhajirs*, including those from Delhi, were survivors of considerable violence, resentment of ill-treatment elsewhere became directed against Hindus in Sindh. There was indignation that Hindus were evacuating safely to India while Muslim refugees were being 'plundered' in India. 'Sind's Hindus are so lucky', one article remarked that, 'although the rest of the country is on fire Sindh is safe...and they are able to sell their ten year old and small houses for double, triple the price'.[58] In addition, Hindu loyalty to Pakistan was questioned by declaring that their hearts were still in India. Sinister intentions were attributed to the city's Hindus. Claims were made by *Jang* that, 'For the third time attempts have been made to poison the water tank of government quarters at Jacob Lines and Jat Lines'. It remarked with bitterness that, 'Yet the Sindh government is dreaming of their return'.[59]

By questioning their belonging and rendering them suspicious, an equation emerged in *muhajir* opinion whereby Hindus were believed to be leaving (sooner or later) and therefore their houses necessarily theirs for the taking. If there were still people living in the houses this was only because they were trying to sell or rent their properties to the *sarmayadar muhajirs*. 'Karachi's rich Hindus' were seen as making profit out of their plight, in particular through the customary *pagri* system. A *pagri* was a form of 'illegal payment' that had developed as a way to circumvent colonial rent restrictions. Landlords demanded a large lump-sum payment in lieu of the low monthly rent and this also made it very difficult for refugees without means to rent houses in the city.[60]

It was argued that this situation, combined with the corruption and inefficiencies of the Rent Controller, was leaving poor *muhajirs* on the streets with no choice but to 'break in and occupy houses'. Breaking in was still not a resolution to their housing problem, for after forcible occupation 'they go and submit a request for allotment for that house. But if someone has already submitted an application for that house before him, then the house is allotted to the first person, who comes with the police to take possession, and the second *muhajir* is once again on the street'. Thus, the poor refugees were 'roaming with their families from place to place'.[61]

Jang editorials were largely sympathetic to these seizures, and explained:

> In this regard, Hindus have also left, but leaving behind one or two persons in the house. Often *muhajirs* find such people's closed houses and they think that they are empty, and therefore they try to occupy/seize it. Hindus complain, make a noise and run away from Sindh. Then the government tries to stop them and for this it comes up with such harsh policies.[62]

The 'harsh policies' that the government adopted was to reverse these occupations through police intervention. These attempts to reverse occupations were represented in *Jang* as denying *muhajirs* their rightful housing. One letter to *Jang* complained of a 'Hindu policeman' in Artillery Maidan who, despite 'hundreds of empty houses' in the area, prevented those even with permits from the Rent Controller from occupying the houses there. The writer complained that 'without finding out the occupying Muslim's position he speaks in a crude and rough manner and this is unacceptable'.[63]

Further, several proposals were put forward for identifying houses which were truly 'empty', none of which involved the Rent Controller's

Office. One of them was that the Government of Sindh should announce that any Hindu leaving Karachi should inform the Refugee Committee that his room will be 'empty' and be allowed to leave only on approval from them. This way the Refugee Committee could make a list and provide housing to the Muslim refugees.[64] Another article in *Jang* argued that 'stopping the fleeing Hindus and finding housing for the *muhajirs*' were connected problems because Hindus were leaving because '*muhajir*een threaten them' in order to get housing. Therefore, identifying 'empty houses' was imperative. It called for a Muhajir Committee to be given extended powers to find houses and issue orders for occupation. In order to find 'empty houses' the ration card should be taken of any Hindu leaving Karachi and from that their home address could be found out and added to 'the list of vacated houses'. Further, only fifteen days should be given to Hindus who make 'the excuse of temporary departure' and then the house should be considered vacated. Further, the Muhajir Committee should enforce allotments and not allow transfers in order to end competing occupations and *pagri-bazi*.[65]

The Sindh government was unlikely to give such powers to a Muhajir Committee and continued to attempt reversing occupations that were increasing with growing numbers of *muhajirs*. In December, a crowd of reportedly over 500 refugees gathered and attempted to forcefully occupy a building that still had people living in it. The residents fought back the attackers and the police arrived and removed the *muhajir* intruders. *Jang* focused on the plight of the homeless refugees and described them as screaming and yelling in desperation when they were brutally pulled out by the police.[66] But such occupations, despite their reversals, could only have been terrifying for the residents as they became threatened on an every day basis.

The riots of 6 January 1948 were a continuation in some sense of this on-going violence, and massive looting and seizures of houses were an important part of the riots. The scale and visible nature of the violence dispelled the notional 'peace' in Karachi and sharpened contending political discourses. On the one hand, it became an occasion for local Hindu leaders as well as Sindhi Congressmen in India to emphasize that, 'Hindus no longer feel safe in Sind'. On the other hand, it allowed the Sindh government to announce that there was no more place for *muhajirs*.[67]

Jang made conciliatory statements that Sindh's Hindus should not leave. As refugees were targets of policing and refugee camps were searched for arms, *Jang* complained that it was unfair to blame *muhajirs* for the violence for, as one article argued, that, 'Muslim *muhajirs* saved not just one, but hundreds of Hindu lives', and that the present restrictions against them were unwarranted, and that the searches were particularly harsh. Khuhro was particularly targeted for his statements blaming *muhajirs* for the violence and led one editorial to state that 'the Premier of Sind is a friend of the Hindus and does not want to see Hindustan's Muslim *muhajirs* in Sind'.[68]

Surplus and Quotas

As Sara Ansari has argued, Sindhi Muslim leaders tried to limit the flow of 'Muslim refugees' into the province because they began to fear that refugees would benefit more than Sindh's Muslims from Partition and that Sindh's economic and cultural life would be impaired by the Hindu exodus.[69] As a result, tensions arose between the Sindh government and the Pakistan government as to how many 'Muslim refugees' Sindh could accommodate as part of rehabilitation efforts. A file on the discussion between the provincial and central government is quite revealing of the science of planning and rehabilitation in the making of a national economy of a modern state.

The Ministry of Refugees and Rehabilitation argued, on the basis of figures provided by the MEO, that West Punjab had received a 'surplus' of 12 lakh refugees. The notion of 'surplus' was based on numbers of 'Muslim refugees' that had arrived 'over and above the non-Muslim population that ha[d] left the province' of West Punjab. It was stated that this 'excess' was composed entirely of 'agriculturalists' as the 'exchange' of 'urban non-agriculturalist' had been almost equal.[70] In order to 'distribute' this 'surplus', a conference of District Officers was held on 22 and 23 November 1947 at Lahore to discuss how many refugees each district could 'absorb'. 'Quotas' were set for each province and it was agreed by the bureaucrats present that Sindh should 'absorb' 5 lakhs of this 'excess'. Their planning was informed by 'A Note on Statistics of the Refugees and Evacuees' Problem', a set of tables and charts prepared by Professor M. Hasan, Secretary of the Board of Economic Inquiry of West Punjab.

This quantifying of people into classifiable populations that could be neatly represented in calculations of planning is not of itself remarkable. James C. Scott has argued how aspirations of 'legibility' have been central to a bureaucratic and scientific control of 'reality' and this is borne out here.[71] It shows how a statistical notion of 'surplus' and 'quotas' was extracted from the terror and confusion of people's lives to make 'refugees' manageable in a national economy. However, these calculations had far-reaching power in constructing a political commonsense about how many Muslim refugees the Pakistani state could accommodate. In this equation, the Pakistani state was a finite territorial entity that could only accommodate as many as those 'non-Muslim refugees' who were leaving. The notion of 'surplus' or 'excess' was predicated on assumptions about how many people a piece of land could support, assumptions which more contemporary debates on 'overpopulation' and 'population control' have since brought to question.[72]

Furthermore, Professor Hasan based his 'absorption figures' for Sindh on the numbers of 'non-Muslim evacuees *who must have left the Province of Sind by now*'. According to Hasan, Sindh had 7.81 lakh non-Muslim 'agriculturalists or rural non-agriculturalists', and 'as *most of these must have left Sind* (both emphases added)', he argued that the Province could accept 5 lakh Muslim refugees in their place. However, he himself noted that his calculations faced the 'limitation that all non-Muslims will not be evacuating from Sind'. Here the term 'evacuee' no longer meant a person leaving to take temporary refuge but rather presumed a permanent departure, and an entire religious community was being regarded as 'evacuee' to make 'space' in a new nation regarded as both territorially and corporally contained.

When Sindh's political leaders refused to accept their 'quotas' of refugees and contended that Sindh could instead accept only 1.5 lakh refugees, the quibble over numbers was not, as Scott argues, merely planning-gone-wrong because on the ground realities had not been sufficiently accounted for. 'Planning' by the new state had to grapple with an emerging politics of entitlement to the nation. It is important to note here that in the discussions that ensued there was no argument over the calculated numbers of departing 'non-Muslims' or over a question of their possible return to their homes.

Ayub Khuhro, in a letter to Jinnah, argued that Hasan's figures were incorrect on a number of accounts. Khuhro stated that there were 14 lakh Hindus in Sindh but most of these were living in urban areas with 2.5 lakh in Karachi alone. However, he argued that 4 lakh Muslims had already 'replaced the outgoing urban Hindus since the 15th of August 1947', and in other towns of Sindh the population had also doubled. Further, people were still coming in by rail from Rajputana and by ship to Karachi and there was 'no means of stopping or controlling this influx'. Thus, Khuhro pointed out that Muslim refugees coming in from outside divided Punjab were not being included in the official resettlement calculus, but were a reality in Sindh.

Importantly, in rural areas, the centre of contention, he argued that 'the Hindus were no doubt owners of land but it was the Muslim who actually tilled the soil' and that the Sindhi Muslim peasants should have first rights to the land. Thus, according to Khuhro, this left only lands abandoned by Sikhs in Sindh, an area that could support 10,000 families (i.e., a total of 50,000 people). In addition, Sindh's [Muslim] *zamindars* might perhaps be persuaded to employ another 10,000 families. By this means he considered it possible to resettle not more than one lakh refugees.[73]

Khuhro's resistance to the central government's rehabilitation figures were based on claims of entitlement for Sindh's Muslims to the new economy of the nation. But his calculations of how many Muslim refugees could be accommodated on Sindh's lands drew upon the same assumptions as that of the central government—that the land could support only the number of 'evacuees' that were leaving. This conception of people on land in an economy of the modern state, filtered into political debates on how many Muslim refugees from India a territory could accommodate and thus the legitimate need to draft limits to its proclaimed nation.

UNMAKING THE 'MUSLIM NATION'

If Professor Hasan's statistics provided a numeric clarity to shape bureaucratic policy, there were numerous political imaginaries of the Muslim nation that now had to contend with these calculations of the modern state. These ideas of the Muslim nation were centrally concerned about the ambiguous status of Muslims that remained in India and the on-going Hindu exodus from the city was extremely important to it.

As Muslim refugees in Karachi confronted substantial ambivalence from the Sindh government that wanted to restrict their numbers, an important narrative of '*muhajir qurban*' or 'sacrifice' began to take shape as a trope to claim inclusion in the emerging nation-state. This trope made claims to extraordinary entitlement to Pakistan by arguing that *muhajirs*, or north Indian Muslims, had been at the forefront of the Pakistan movement and had made the greatest *qurbani* for it by leaving their homes in India. For instance, one *Jang* editorial argued:

> *Pak sarzameen Karachi men ek taraf Hind se muhajireen arahe hain. In men ziyada tar log hain jo Pakistan ka 'alam baland karne aur Pakistan hasil karne*

> *men sab se ziyada qurbanian di hain* [*Muhajirs* are coming from India to the pure land of Karachi. Most of these people made the most sacrifices for raising the flag of Pakistan and for obtaining Pakistan].

This trope would gain increasing prominence in the ensuing years to argue against growing restrictions by the Pakistani state on the coming of Muslim refugees from India. It was also fundamentally tied to the argument that Muslims in India could not be legitimately excluded from a Pakistani nation-state, for they were a part of a Muslim nation that the very idea of Pakistan was meant to 'safeguard'.

H.S. Suharwardy, in an extraordinary address to the first Constituent Assembly of Pakistan, argued that Pakistan had a responsibility towards Muslims that remained in India:

> At the time when we were divided, it was not said as I have heard it said by the Satraps of Pakistan that Muslims of the Indian Union were warned that you will be in the hopeless minority, that you may be exterminated, that you may have to suffer all kinds of difficulties, that you may be enchained, enslaved and that the Muslims of the Indian Union then said that it did not matter if that was going to be their lot so long as a large number of their brethren living in the majority Provinces were able to have an administration of their own.... Sir, that is only one side of the story. The other side of the story was that you told the Muslims of the Indian Union at the same time that the division of India would solve the communal problem; that that would be the greatest safeguard for the minorities within Pakistan and the greatest safeguard for the minorities within the Indian Union. You have forgotten that aspect of it.... Your corners are closed to the Muslim of the Indian Union. You have said that they may not come here and perhaps, Sir, from the point of view of Pakistan that is the best policy, because if the Muslims of the Indian Union have to leave those shores and decimated on the way, say, out of three crores even one and a half crores find their way struggling into Pakistan, Pakistan will be overwhelmed. It is perhaps true that you have no other alternative but to say that. I do not want you, Sir, to fight for me...I want you to give a fair deal to the minorities in Pakistan.

His address grappled with the claim of the Pakistan movement that 'the division of India would solve the communal problem'. But how was the reality of a Pakistani state to serve as a 'safeguard' for the Muslim minorities in India? Although critical of attempts to keep out Muslim refugees, he believed that the state would be 'overwhelmed' if large numbers of Muslim refugees came to Pakistan and argued that there was 'no other alternative' but to give 'a fair deal to minorities in Pakistan' as a way to protect Muslim minorities in India.

This idea that good treatment of religious minorities on one side would ensure the good treatment of religious minorities on the other side was called the 'hostage theory' and had been in circulation prior to Partition. It now found repeated expression in the public debates on the 'Muslim nation' that followed Partition. After the riots of 6 January 1948, a *Jang* editorial appealed to its *muhajir* readers to maintain peace in the city for riots in Karachi would adversely affect Muslim minorities in India. It argued that:

> *Hindustani musalman Pakistan ke musalmanon se kuch nahin chahta. Woh sirf us se tadabur aur sabr ki bheek mangta raha hai. Hame chahye ke hum un apne bhaion ko jin ki qurbanion se hame dolat-e-azadi naseeb hui hai un ki zindagiyon ko khatre men nahin dale* [Hindustan's Muslims don't ask anything of Pakistan's Muslims. They only beg of them forbearance and patience. We should not put the lives of our brothers, whose sacrifices have given us this treasure of freedom, in danger].[74]

According to the logic of the 'hostage theory', Muslim refugees in Karachi had to be 'patient' with Hindus in the city for aggression on their part could put their 'brothers' that remained in India in jeopardy. This formulation made Muslims in Pakistan responsible for the well-being of Hindustan's Muslims. For Muslim refugees/*muhajirs*, this link had meaning not only through an abstract imaginary of a Muslim nation but through real ties of family and friends. However, to make an argument for Pakistan's duty towards Muslims in India, the diversity of Muslims that remained in India were harnessed to the cause of Pakistan. For instance, one *Jang* editorial wrote that, 'Those poor [Muslims in India] their only fault is that they are Muslims and have spent their whole life at the forefront in the support of Muslim League'.[75]

It is striking then that in Delhi's *Al-Jamiat*, an Urdu newspaper of the pro-Congress Jamiat-e-Ulema-e-Hind, Pakistan was also held responsible for collective Muslim well being through the treatment of its 'hostage' religious minorities:

> In Pakistan, extreme concern is being shown for 4 crore Indian Muslims, but Pakistan better open its ears and listen that by upsetting their non-Muslim people they are doing no service to us. All roads to our aid are closed, except one—the [good] treatment of their non-Muslims.[76]

This is one of the reasons why the Hindu exodus from Karachi became so significant, for the near-total departure of non-Muslims from West Pakistan unsettled the workability of this tenuous hostage theory. Thus, it became important in opinions in *Al-Jamiat* that conditions be created in Pakistan for Hindus who had left *to return* to their homes. It was argued that this refugee return was the 'human and religious duty' of the Pakistan government. *Al-Jamiat* campaigned vociferously for reversing displacements and the return of refugees to their homes. For instance, it promoted the 'Phir Basa'o Conference' led by Lala Bhim Singh for the return of Hindus and Sikhs to their ancestral homes in West Punjab.

An announcement in *Al-Jamiat* is particularly poignant in making this point. It appealed to Delhi's Muslims to write letters to Liaquat Ali Khan, who was to visit Delhi, to not only bring back Sindh's Hindus but also cancel the agreement on the 'transfer of populations' in divided Punjab. It argued that this, the return of a substantial religious minority in West Pakistan, was the only possibility for Muslims in India to 'live in peace'.[77]

But in the face of ongoing displacements, there was also a completely opposite point of view calling for a total 'exchange of populations' along religious lines. This total 'exchange of populations' had been clamoured for by a range of different groups, including by those who saw it as a logical outcome of Partition and essential for the making of a Hindu nation.[78] Here these ideas were a response to specifically resolving the perceived dilemma of how Muslims in India were to be safeguarded. An article on *tabadala-e-abadil* (exchange of populations) noted that, '[D]ue to Pakistan and Partition crores of Muslims are now slaves of the Indian government, and crores of Hindu have been freed of the Pakistan government'. Therefore, given the departure of minority religious communities from West Pakistan, the 'Pakistan government should announce that all the Muslims in India should be brought over here'. However, this exchange was proposed only across the western border as it was perceived that religious minorities in East and West Bengal were 'balanced'.

Importantly, this notion that the chief constraint against all Muslims coming from India to Pakistan lay in its territorial limits (an equation of how many people a land's resources could support) was resolved by making such an exchange conditional upon an expansion of those territorial limits through mutual negotiation with India. This idea of a total exchange of populations on the basis of religious community conditioned on more land reappeared again with greater force in the following years.[79] At the heart of the problem was the difficulty of transforming a non-territorial concept of nation into a territorially bounded one.

However, the sentiment that Muslims who remained in India were brothers who needed to be saved (i.e., '*apne bichare hue bhaion ko bachane ke liye*') was so strong in the *muhajir* press that the predicament that the state could not shoulder 'the burden' of unlimited Muslim refugees, but which it was obligated to protect, found repeated expression:

> Now the biggest problem facing both governments is how to protect the minorities in both places. We cannot accept that Pakistan rejoin the Indian Union and are opposed to it...at the same time we cannot leave the [Muslim] minorities unprotected...at the present time Pakistan cannot take the burden of India's Muslims, if they should migrate and come to Pakistan...so how should these innocent Muslims be saved, who because they fought and struggled so hard for Pakistan, are now in this unenviable predicament.[80]

Other suggestions included making the inter-governmental mechanism, like the Minority Board, more effective. However, it was believed that such a Board could only be effective if a significant number of Hindus remained in Pakistan. Therefore the refrain— 'We must try and keep as many Hindus as possible in Pakistan to protect the Muslim minorities on the other side'—found repeated articulation. One of the recommendations of the Minority Board had been that both the All India Muslim League and the All India Congress should cease to function as unified organizations operating in two states and be separated in command and direction. One of the reasons for their recommendation was that because the Muslim League was being blamed for the Partition, Muslims in India were being persecuted. But there was opposition to this idea on the grounds that the Muslim League was deemed responsible for all Muslims of the subcontinent and north Indian Muslims 'who were in the forefront of the League's struggle for Pakistan' needed to be strengthened, not abandoned, by Pakistan's Muslim League.[81] Thus, the Minority Board was perceived as suggesting a severing of ties between Pakistan's Muslims and India's Muslims which was considered unacceptable at this time.

This process of ideological severing took many years and became part of a 'long' process of partitioning, of making two sovereign nation-states. But the despair and fabulous proposals that ordinary people put forth in trying to make sense of the relationship of nations to religious minorities, of regional cultures to changing demographies, should not be forgotten. For it is through ordinary struggles over homes and belonging that Karachi became another city by the 1951 Census—and Sindh another region—the contingent exodus as important as the flows of those who arrived and remade the city.

NOTES

1. This essay is based on chapter two of my book *The Long Partition and the Making of Modern South Asia: Refugees, Boundaries, Histories* (New York: Columbia University Press, 2007), 44–77.
2. Arif Hasan, 'The Growth of a Metropolis', in Hamida Khuhro and Anwer Mooraj, eds., *Karachi: Megacity of Our Times* (Karachi: Oxford University Press, 1997), 174.
3. *Forthnightly Reports*, Francis Mudie to Lord Wavell, 7 March 1947 and 7 June 1947 India Office Records (IOR) MSS E/164/42/75 and 101.
4. *Jang*, 10 January 1948.
5. Ghulam Husain Hidayatullah to Jinnah, 11 September 1947, National Documentation Centre (NDC) D.O.No. C-611/117.
6. Dr Choithram P. Gidwani to Rajendra Prasad, 3 December 1947, National Archives of India (NAI) Rajendra Prasad Papers 11-P/49/1; Gidwani to Nehru, 4 October 1947, AICC G-16 1947–8/228. See also Constitution Assembly of India (CAI) 27 November 1947/790 and 'What is Happening In Sind—Weekly Diary', n.d., NAI Rajendra Prasad Papers 11-P/49/5.
7. For 'Harijan' departures, see Sind Police Abstracts of Intelligence (SPAI), 1 November 1947/496. For Hindu businesses, see SPAI, 27 September 1947, No. 39/445, and 11 October 1947/467.
8. Syed Hashim Reza, *Hamari Manzil: An Autobiography of Syed Hashim Reza* (Karachi: Mustafain and Murtazain Limited, 1991), 80.
9. SPAI, 27 September 1947, No. 39/461.
10. Constitution Assembly of Pakistan (CAP), 6 April 1951/907.
11. Sara Ansari, 'Partition, Migration and Refugees: Responses to the Arrival of Muhajirs in Sind During 1947–8', in D.A. Low and Howard Brasted, eds., *Freedom, Trauma, Continuities North India and Independence* (Walnut Creek, California: AltaMira, 1998), 100.
12. *Forthnightly Reports*, Mudie to Mountbatten, 7 June 1947, India Office Records (IOR) MSS E/164/42/101. Also in Sind Police Abstracts of Intelligence (SPAI), 6 September 1947.
13. *Forthnightly Reports*, Mudie to Wavell, 24 February 1947, IOR MSS E/164/42/72.
14. Ibid., 76
15. On Sind University Bill, *Forthnightly Reports,* Mudie to Mountbatten, 25 March 1947 and 26 June 1947, IOR MSS E/164/42; Sind Landholders Mortgage Bill, ibid., 7 April 1947/85–6.
16. The pamphlet was written by Parsam V. Tahilrami, the Secretary of the Sindh Assembly Congress Party and published in November 1947 to persuade the Indian state to intervene in Sindh.
17. Reza, 95–6.
18. 'Unrealities', *Hindustan Times*, 27 March 1948. In India there were debates on 'whether the fears of Sind Hindus are real or wholly imaginary'.
19. Liaquat Ali Khan's speech in the Constituent Assembly of Pakistan (CAP) on 16 December 1948/4–5. Ansari also outlines similar problems through other sources. Sind Maintenance of Public Safety Ordinance, in the National Documentation Centre (NDC) File 87/CF/47.
20. Constituent Assembly of India (CAI), 3 February 1948/Q55. Nehru's statement of policy was a reply to Giani Gurmukh Singh Musafar. The 'Sind question' on whether the Indian government should do more for the Hindus who wanted to leave Sindh

came up several times for discussion in the CAI. See 3 February 1948, 11 February 1948, and 6 April 1948.

21. It was argued in a note to the Pakistani Cabinet that the Indian High Commission was distributing money to *haris*, *dhobis*, and sweepers, to pay their fare by ship to Bombay. However, the Indian High Commission denied this as a matter of practice. In Ahmad Ali, 'Summary to Cabinet Ministers', 18 December 1947 (NDC 217/CF/47). Also the issue of free passage is mentioned by Ansari, and in my interviews in Bombay with a few former residents of Karachi, one of them recalled the availability of such free passages, although none of them had travelled on one.
22. High Commissioner of India in Pakistan to Ministry of Foreign Affairs and Commonwealth Relations, 3 December 1947, NDC 217/CF/47.
23. Patel to Parmanand Trehan, 16 July 1947, in Durga Das *Sardar Patel's Correspondence 1945–50* (Ahmedabad: Navajivan Publishing House, 1973), 289. As quoted in Pandey, *Remembering Partition*, 626.
24. H. Bhaskar Rao, *The Story of Rehabilitation* (Delhi: Department of Rehabilitation, 1967), 22–26.
25. *Annual Report on Evacuation, Relief and Rehabilitation of Refugees: September 1947–August 1948*, M/o R&R. GOI, New Delhi 1949, 5. It needs to be noted that, unlike the Punjab, this 'planned' evacuation was not based on inter-governmental agreement, and did not include an 'exchange' of people.
26. SPAI, 23 August 1947; 4 October 1947; 11 October 1947; 27 September 1947; 20 September 1947.
27. Homi K. Bhabha, 'By Bread Alone: Signs of Violence in the Mid-Nineteenth Century', in Homi K. Bhabha, *The Location of Culture* (London: Routledge, 1994), 286.
28. SPAI, 8 September 1947; 8 November 1947; 27 December 1947.
29. SPAI, 13 September 1947.
30. M.U. Abbasi, *New Sind*, All India Congress Committee (AICC) G-16 1947–8/208.
31. Choithram P. Gidwani to Liaquat Ali Khan, 13 September 1947, AICC G-16 1947–8/129.
32. Letter to Kripalani, 10 October 1947, AICC G-16 1947–8/144.
33. Letter to Kripalani, n.d., AICC G-16 1947–8.
34. 'What is happening in Sind', *Weekly Diary*, 2 December 1947, NAI RP Papers 11-P/49/5, and AICC G-16 1947–8/29.
35. CAP, 6 April 1951/897.
36. Puj Hindu General Panchayat Shikarpur to Kripalani, 4 November 1947 and Piece Goods Merchants Association Ltd. to Kripalani, 20 September 1947, AICC G-16 1947–8/77.
37. Shamdas s/oDewan Dewandas Ajbani to Kripalani, n.d., AICC G-16 1947–8/82; N.R. Malkani to Nehru, 6 October 1947, AICC G-16, 1947–8/198–9.
38. The fate of Karachi Port Trust employees is discussed in CAI, 27 November 1947/790.
39. Tuljaram Valammal Thadhani to Kripalani, Karachi, 20 October 1947, AICC G-16 1947–8/113.
40. President Sarva Hindu Sind Panchayat to Kripalani, 11 November 1947, AICC G-16 1947–8/85.
41. '*Makanaat aur panaghir*', *Jang*, 18 October 1947, 2.
42. Tai Yong Tan and Gyanesh Kudaisya, *Aftermath of Partition in South Asia* (London: Routledge, 2000), 179. Tan and Kudaisya argue that although a number of cities were suggested as a possible capital for the new country, including Dhaka and Multan,

Karachi was chosen because it was offered by the Sindh Muslim League, and that the fact that it was Jinnah's birthplace was incidental.

43. *Fortnightly Reports*, Mudie to Mountbatten, 29 July 1947, and 9 July 1947, IOR MSS E 164/42.
44. Tan and Kudaisya, 179.
45. Reza, 84.
46. Hamida Khuhro, 'The Capital of Pakistan', in Hamida Khuhro and Anwar Mooraj, eds., *Karachi: Megacity of Our Times* (Karachi: Oxford University Press, 1997), 95–112; Anwar Mooraj, 'Being Young in the Fifties', Hamida Khuhro and Anwar Mooraj, eds., *Karachi: Megacity of Our Times* (Karachi: Oxford University Press, 1997), 357–368; Zeenat Hisam, '*Guzare din, guzarte din*', in *Karachi ki Kahani 2*, 151–8.
47. *Forthnightly Reports*, Mudie to Mountbatten, 26 June 1947, IOR MSS E/164/42.
48. '*Ghamzadah gharib clerk ki kahani Pakistan mein*', *Jang*, 6 December 1947.
49. *Forthnightly Reports*, Mudie to Wavell, 19 March 1947, IOR MSS E/164/42.
50. PECC, 10 September 1947, NDC File no. 69/CF/47.
51. SPAI, 20 September 1947 and 27 September 1947.
52. Ghulam Husain Hidayatullah to Jinnah, 11 September 1947, NDC File no. 69/CF/47/117.
53. This image of footpaths of the city filled with people came up again and again in interviews. In 1954 it was estimated that 250,000 people were still living on the streets.
54. For instance, in '*Nadaan dost*', *Jang*, 28 December 1947 and *Jang*, 15 February 1948.
55. Editorial, *Jang*, 21 December 1947.
56. *Jang*, 26 October 1947, 2.
57. 'Rent controller Karachi *ke daftar mein hungama*', *Jang*, 5 November 1947.
58. *Jang*, 24 October 1947, 2.
59. '*Pakistan mein gadaron ki hosala afzai, kiya hukumat-e-Sind sun rahi hai*', *Jang*, 24 November 1947
60. '*Chand tajaweez*', *Jang*, 13 November 1947, 2; Letter to editor, *Jang*, 26 October 1947, 2.
61. '*Nadan dost*', *Jang*, 28 December 1947; '*Makanat aur panaghir*', *Jang*, 18 October 1947, 2.
62. '*Makanat aur panaghir*', *Jang*, 18 October 1947, 2.
63. Letter to editor, *Jang*, 17 November 1947, 2.
64. '*Makanat aur panaghir*', *Jang*, 18 October 1947, 2.
65. '*Makan*', *Jang*, 29 October 1947.
66. *Jang*, 12 December 1947, 1.
67. *Jang*, 10 January 1948; *Jang*, 13 January 1948. In CAI 3 February 1948, Q54, Nehru, reporting on the violence in Karachi, noted that although only 70 'non-Muslims' were killed, 70 per cent of their homes had been completely looted. Khuhro's speech was reported in *Jang*, 23 January 1948.
68. See *Jang*, 13 January 1948; *Jang*, 15 January 1948, 1; '*Aman*' and 'Mister Khuhro *ka qabil-e-tehseen rawaiya*', *Jang*, 15 January 1948; '*Hinduon ka inkhila*', *Jang*, 16 January 1948.
69. Ansari, 'Partition, Migration and Refugees', 100–101.
70. E de V. Moss, 'Note for Cabinet on the transfer of surplus refugees from West Punjab to Sind', Ministry of Refugees, 31 December 1947, NDC File No 80/CF/47/6-A-D.
71. James C. Scott, *Seeing Like a State: How Certain Schemes to Improve the Human Condition Have Failed* (New Haven: Yale University Press, 1998), 3.

72. There are wide-ranging criticisms of 'overpopulation' and 'population control' in the literature on 'development'. However, for an engaging critique of concepts of 'population' in the making of 'national economy', see Timothy Mitchell, *Rule of Experts* (Berkeley: University of California Press, 2002), 212–213.
73. Meeting of the Cabinet, 27 January 1948, NDC File No 80/CF/47/9-A; and M.A. Khuhro to Jinnah, 28 January 1948, NDC File 80/CF/47/10–10A. This politics of entitlement can be located broadly in a history of Sindhi nationalism. Mudie noted that 'Sind for the Sindhis' sentiment had already begun to emerge before Partition when Bihari refugees arrived in February 1947. On 22 May 1948, when Karachi was made a centrally administered area, Sindhi politicians complained that Sindh was being beheaded, and embittered provincial relations with the centre. See Ansari, 'Partition, Migration and Refugees', 103; Tan and Kudaisya, 182; Ayesha Jalal, *The State of Martial Rule* (Lahore: Vanguard, 1991), 89; H.M. Kagi, *Administrative Responses to Urban Growth: Karachi, Pakistan* (Syracuse: Syracuse University, 1964).
74. '*Karachi ke fasadat Hindustan ki Muslim aqliyat ki dushman hein*', *Jang*, 11 January 1948.
75. '*Hindustan mein Musalman qaidi*', *Jang*, 9 February 1948.
76. '*Mashriqi Pakistan*', *Al-Jamiat*, 24 October 1948.
77. *Al-Jamiat*, 11 November 1948, 2; *Al-Jamiat*, 3 March 1949; *Al-Jamiat*, 14 June 1948.
78. The exchange of populations was an idea that was circulated in many imaginaries of Partition, and not only Muslim imaginaries of Partition. That many clamoured for such an exchange of people can be seen in enraged letters and schemes sent to AICC. See AICC CL–10(1946–7). An example is Jwala Prasad Singhal's 'Prepare for Logical Consequences'. Also see: Gyanendra Pandey, 'Can a Muslim be an Indian?', *Comparative Studies in Society and History* 41.4 (1999): 613–614.
79. '*Tabadala-e-abadi ki zarorat*', *Jang*, 14 November 1947.
80. '*Aqliyaton ki hifazat*', *Jang*, 19 November 1947.
81. 'Muslim League *ki taqseem ka asar*', *Jang*, 23 December 1947.

CHAPTER 10

The Sufi Saints of Sindhi Nationalism

Oskar Verkaaik

In 1981, Oxford University Press published a volume that to some extent can be seen as the predecessor of this book. Entitled *Sind Through the Centuries* and edited by Hamida Khuhro, it was the result of an international seminar held in Karachi in 1975. The seminar was not solely an academic matter: the Government of Sindh's Department of Culture organized it. The seminar reflected not only the latest findings of the historiography of Sindh but a particular political environment that enabled—if not stimulated—a new orientation, both on the region's past and its place within Pakistan. The seminar's subsequent book implicitly argued for an undisruptive perspective on Sindh's history: a *longue durée* orientation in which Partition was a significant but not deciding moment. The book was divided into four sections. Three of the sections were historically organized: 'Sind before the Muslim conquest', 'Sind in the Early Muslim Period', and 'Sind since the Moghuls'. The latter section also included two chapters on postcolonial and/or post-Partition developments. The final section, called 'Sindhi Culture', contained chapters on issues like cultural relations between Arabia and Sindh, music, Sindhi language, and Shah Abdul Latif's poetry. The implicit message of the last session was that Sindhi culture was much older than twentieth century political events (and, to a considerable extent, untouched by these events). In her introduction, Hamida Khuhro stated that this culture was the outcome of an ancient civilization dating back to the Indus Valley Civilization but that it had also been formed by Sindh being the oldest Muslim region within South Asia (i.e., the Gateway of Islam in the subcontinent), its role in Indian history under the Mughals, and its location halfway between the Middle East and South Asia. 'This rich and varied historical background helped to produce a unique civilization in Sind,' wrote Khuhro, who also noted how the region was characterized by 'a religious eclecticism and the strong Sufi tradition of mysticism and tolerance'.[1]

In the six years between the seminar and the publication of Khuhro's book, much changed in Pakistan and the province of Sindh. In 1975, the Pakistan People's Party led by Zulfikar Ali Bhutto was at the height of its power but in 1981 a military regime under General Ziaul Haq had taken over power and a military court had sentenced Bhutto to death. This political watershed had serious ramifications for Sindh and phenomena associated with it: Sindhi nationalism, Sufism, and even Sindhi historiography and folklore. The academic production of Sindh's history and culture as unique (in both the world as well as in Pakistan) did not automatically stop with the change of power, but it certainly was no longer sponsored by state funds the way it was in 1975. The seminar itself had been somewhat of a state ritual and the publication of its findings was an act of academic resistance.

The seminar and the subsequently published volume can be seen as important moments in the production of a political Sindhi culture dating back to the 1920s and 1930s when Sindhi politicians and intellectuals began to argue for the creation of a Sindhi province separate from the Bombay Presidency. Initially, the focus was on Sindh's geographical separateness as the heir to the Indus Valley Civilization. In the 1950s and 1960s, more and more cultural and religious aspects were added to argue for Sindh's distinct position within Pakistan. *Sind Through the Centuries* gave academic weight to an imagined Sindhi ethnic culture revolving around key-themes like the Sindhi language, the poetry of Shah Abdul Latif, the Indus, the peasant or *hari,* and above all, Sufism and mysticism. In today's Pakistan, it is commonplace to call Sindh both the land of mysticism and tolerance and an ancient region of Sufis and saints (although some may add that it is also a place of feudalism and exploitation).

What is striking is that this relatively new imaginary has gained durability. It easily survives short-term political changes like military takeovers. What is more, Sindhi nationalists (as well as its opponents) seem to agree on the notion of Sindhis as essentially 'Sufi' people inclined to mysticism and religious tolerance. This chapter looks at the genealogy of this particular type of religious nationalism and places it within the larger framework of Pakistan's struggle with Islam, nationalism, and ethnicity.

SUFFERINGS OF SINDH

Although my deconstructivist perspective of ethnicity is critical of primordialist notions of cultural identity, there is no denying that ethnic culture in Pakistan can be hereditary. That is to say that there is a direct family connection between the origin of Sindhi nationalism and its academic canonization by Hamida Khuhro. In pamphlets and books but—above all—in my personal communication and formal interviews with leaders of various Sindhi nationalist organizations, it is agreed that the founding father of Sindhi nationalism (and the person responsible for the awakening of the Sindhi nation) was Hamida Khuhro's father Muhammad Ayub Khuhro. Most defenders of Sindhi culture and language view his short 1930 treatise on Sindh's unique character, entitled *A Story of the Sufferings of Sind: A Case for the Separation of Sind from the Bombay Presidency*, as the discursive alarm clock that signified the dawn of Sindhi separatism. Even G.M. Syed, the man who, without doubt, has been the main ideologue of Sindhi nationalism, mentions Khuhro's booklet as the starting point of Sindhi awareness.[2] The context of the pamphlet shows how much the formulation of the Sindhi culture was intrinsically connected to political emancipation, even though Khuhro argued the opposite by maintaining that Sindh's unique character was beyond politics.

After annexation by the British, the Bombay Presidency governed Sindh from 1847. For more than half a century there was no systematic and organized protest against this. Sindh, for instance, remained calm during the war of 'independence' in 1857. Popular uprisings did occur later on. The Hur brotherhood in Upper Sindh rebelled twice in the first half of the twentieth century under the leadership of Pir Pagaro but these events hardly mobilized the whole of Sindh's population.[3] Sindhi intellectuals were subsequently interested in establishing new forms of modern education to replace traditional education by the *syed* community and on ways to create institutions for modern higher learning where they did not yet exist in Sindh.[4] The defence of the Sindhi language was not yet an issue. However, in the early twentieth century the first forms of Sindhi political mobilization began to appear under the leadership of Ghulam Muhammad Bhurgri.[5] Bhurgri and his political friends, initially both Muslims and Hindus, were the first to voice dissatisfaction with Sindh's status within the Bombay Presidency in the 1920s. Their protests were voiced in pragmatic, bureaucratic, and financial rather than in cultural terms. Muhammad Ayub Khuhro's *Sufferings of Sind* was the first to introduce the idiom of Sindhi culture.

However, he made this introduction reluctantly. Although Khuhro, in his introduction, talks about the Sindhi 'motherland' and the 'paramount duty of all true sons of the soil of Sind to make every sacrifice to liberate their motherland from the bondage to which it has been forcibly subjected', culture—let alone religion—did not initially play a crucial role in his claims for Sindhi distinctiveness.[6] Khuhro starts by quoting medieval Arabian travel writers, historians, and geographers who distinguished between India (or Hind) and Sindh. Other quoted sources argue that Sindh was always a separate political unit, even when part of a greater civilization or empire. After a discussion of history comes geography and climate—both reported to be much more extreme and rough than in Bombay. It is only then that 'ethnological and culture difference' is mentioned in a short one page paragraph. He states that the 'mode of life, dress, and habits' are completely different than in Bombay. He also states 'life and civilization' in Sindh is 'most closely allied to Iraq or Arabia than to India'. Finally, Khuhro asserts that, although Sindhis and 'Presidency people' both wear European clothes (since today 'the Western cap fits every-one'), there is a vast difference between 'the genuine dress of Sindhis and the Presidency wallahs'.[7] Two pages on language follow that mention the region's different alphabets and Sindhi poetry, in particular he addresses the work of Shah Abdul Latif. The pamphlet then proceeds with a long exposé on political issues, which addresses whether or not Sindh is politically viable as a self-sustaining province. Khuhro asks: 'Will there be enough work for a governor and a cabinet?'[8] Making the vast and sparsely populated lands of Balochistan part of Sindh, Khuhro maintains, easily solves this question. Such a solution would also solve yet another problem. Bombay usually gets rid of 'undesirable and incorrigible Government servants' by sending them to far away Sindh where they are free to 'indulge in corruption and carry on regular exploitation....I think Balochistan would be the best place to accommodate and even improve such public servants, and hence its amalgamation is highly desirable'. Khuhro concludes this section by stating: 'whether Baluchistan is amalgamated or not, Sind, as it is, is bound to keep the new Sind Government busy'.[9] The pamphlet ends with a long discussion on why the separation of Sindh from the Bombay Presidency will not cost more than the status quo.

As a text widely believed to be the founding—or awakening—moment of Sindhi culture, the pamphlet is somewhat of a disappointment. I found it difficult to assess what the impact of its publication had been in the 1930s. With the possible exception of the geographical arguments (borrowed from ancient Arabian sources) and the brief remarks on 'culture' and language, the text contained little that was not already known or had not already been argued. Today's status of the text is perhaps better explained by the fact that Khuhro would become an important political figure—he even became the chief minister of Sindh after Pakistan's independence. As a member of a leading landowning family from Larkana in Upper Sindh, his name mattered as much, if not more, than his words. The support the separatists received from the Muslim League and the Congress Party was in any case more important than Khuhro's appeal to gain provincial independence in 1935. Nonetheless, the text introduced some themes that other writers and politicians would later take up, such as Sindh's geographical separateness from India and its unique language as expressed in Shah Abdul Latif's poems.

MARXISM, ISLAM, AND SOCIAL REFORM

According to many Sindhi nationalists (who usually preferred the term 'patriots'), the next discursive milestone of Sindhi nationalism was in 1947 by Ibrahim Joyo: Save *Sind, Save the Continent (From Feudal Lords, Capitalists, and their Communalisms)*. Unlike Khuhro, Joyo was not from a wealthy landowning family. He was born in 1915 near the village of Sann on the west bank of the Indus. His father was a peasant but also acted as a middleman between the landlord and the other peasants. Unlike most other village boys, Joyo got the opportunity to study. During his student years he became an ardent follower of G.M. Syed, who later in life become the living symbol of Sindhi nationalism. However, in the early 1940s, G.M. Syed was still a member of the Muslim League while his student Joyo was a more radical nationalist who combined Sindhi patriotism with a modern Marxist critique on feudalism and capitalism.

The booklet, approximately 140 pages long and with a foreword by G.M. Syed, was written prior to Partition when Independence had already become inevitable. It starts with a sense of urgency and warning that a crucial moment in history is about to take place. To miss it, Joyo warns in his preface, will have tragic consequences for years to come:

> We, the people of Sind, today, stand literally on the cross-roads of our History. Either we wake up from the century-old dark night of slavery, and go forward to welcome the glorious dawn of freedom, or we prefer, afresh and for ages to

> come, political subjugation and economic enslavement at the hands of our alien neighbours.[10]

On the threshold of independence and yet uncertain whether Sindh will become part of Pakistan or 'Hindustan', the fate of the Sindhi people will be decided soon. Joyo makes it clear from the start that he prefers neither Pakistan nor Hindustan since both will be 'totalitarian':[11]

> Whether in the proposed set-up for Pakistan or in that for Hindustan, we, more than four and a half millions in all, are promised to be treated merely as so many individuals with our collective homogeneity and corporate existence as a people absolutely unrecognized.[12]

He admits that both 'Pakistan' and 'Hindustan' are terms that stir up expectations in many people's minds. Nonetheless, Sindhis should not be fooled:

> No doubt, Pakistan and Hindustan are both very fine words; and when the question of having either of them is posed—well, who would like to have something, even if it be only a word! But here the question is not that of having something, but that of losing everything![13]

Joyo argues that both in Pakistan and Hindustan, Sindhis will only be a tiny minority in danger of becoming marginalized. He further asserts that Sindh's sovereignty, lost only a hundred years ago to the British, should be restored. However, Joyo does not go so far as to demand full independence for Sindh. He still leaves room for a place for Sindh in either Pakistan or India:

> [W]e, the people of Sind, must have our sovereign status and independent existence now restored to us…in either of the proposed combinations of Pakistan and Hindustan, if our presence is needed, we must be given a status of absolute equality with every other constituent Unit.[14]

Having made his demands clear, Joyo proceeds to discuss the validity of the concept of nationalism as opposed to communalism. It was a difficult task for him: not only had communalism (i.e., the Two Nations Theory that states Muslims and Hindus constitute two distinct nations) prevailed in South Asia since the early 1940s but the Second World War had given nationalism a 'bad name'. Nationalism, he claims, has two faces: fascism and patriotism. The difference between the two is that the latter combines the love for one's homeland and one's people with 'humanism' (or the 'love for the world and its humanity at large') whereas the former is a nationalism of the 'privileged classes' which seeks to enslave others (be it other nations or its own people). In its 'true' form nationalism is not jealous: loyalty for one's nation can go hand in hand with other loyalties without contradiction. This is, in fact, a law of nature.

> It is the plan of Nature that man should arrange his relationship with others on a gradually widening basis. Starting as an individual, he should organize himself into a family, a clan, a tribe, a nation or a people, and finally create a common brotherhood, community or fraternity of all.[15]

He proceeds by stating nationalism's true natural form is: 'by far, better than and superior to the irreligious communalisms of the current brand in India, which have made brutes of us all'.[16]

The difference between nationalism and communalism continues to be a key and repetitious theme in Joyo's text. At first sight, it appears as if his distinction between nationalism and communalism is one between 'history' and 'nature' on the one hand and religious politics on the other. It would appear as if Joyo advocates a modernism that writes Science (i.e., the laws of history and nature) with a capital 'S' and depoliticizes religion by turning it into a private and personal matter of life and death. However, that would be too simplistic. It is true that Joyo claims communalism 'is neither sound politics nor sound religion'.[17] To follow its logic would have disastrous and unnatural effects, such as the mass migration of people—an event that would (as we all know now) indeed take place soon after independence but that seemed absurd in early 1947 when Joyo wrote his pamphlet:

> Let us suppose that the Hindus of Sind are herded en-bloc to Madras, and the Madrasi Musalmans are transported en-bloc to Sind. It will, of course, be too cruel and too revolting to sort these peoples out and scatter them one by one in different places. That will be literally scattering them to the winds. Their language, their kinships, their affinities and associations and all the rest of it would be liquidated. So, the transfer of these peoples has, after all, to be made en-bloc. In which case, how would they be faring in their newly-found lands? What naughty problems would they not be creating for their new Governments? Just imagine one such problem—that of language; and let the rest of them lie where they are! Sind, in that case, would not be simply a Sind but Sind-cum-Madras, and Madras would at once turn into Madras-cum-Sind.[18]

Communalism is, in sum, represented as a ridiculous idea with absurd consequences. True nationalism in India is not based on religion but history, culture, and geography. Take for instance, the Sindhi nation. Joyo writes: 'That we, the people of Sind, are a distinct people, nobody can dare dispute'.[19] He points out why this is so:

> We have a distinct habit of life; we have a distinct language of our own; our customs, our manners, our tastes, our dress, even our names and various such other things concerning our day-to-day existence, together with our general outlook on life, bear a distinct imprint of the peculiar environs under which we, for centuries after centuries, have been born and have lived. Geographically, Sind, with its distinct and well-defined boundaries, with its distinct climate conditions, and with its distinct flora and fauna, occupies a singularly unique position in this vast subcontinent conveniently called India.[20]

The forces of history, culture, and geography have not only created the Sindhi nation but many other nations within India:

> India is not one country—it is a vast subcontinent containing many countries...it is not inhabited by one people, not even by two or three peoples, but by many more, all having as many and as impressive distinct features, exclusively of their own, as those that distinguish any two peoples anywhere in the world.[21]

In this multi-group representation, religion seems to play a very small part. Joyo goes as far as saying that 'religion is or should be a private affair of every individual'.[22] However, the way this phrase is framed and legitimized directly undermines this very statement. He writes the following about the private character of religion:

> In respect of personal aspect of life, the religion of Islam, while allowing fullest freedom and absolute liberty to an individual, steps in and interferes only when similar rights of another individual are threatened. Islam protects individuality, and never suppresses it. Islam is never a totalitarian religion. This fundamental principle of Islam has been universally accepted today when the whole world says, 'Religion is or should be a private affair of every individual'. What is more reassuring is that this noble principle of Islam is even practised, consciously or unconsciously, by everybody throughout the world.[23]

This passage does not ascribe the doctrine of individualism and secularism to the Enlightenment or Protestantism. Rather these modern virtues are rooted in Islam, a religion that is, in its 'truest' form, the most modern of all religions. In other words, Joyo defends his radical secularism with the help of Islam. He maintains that to oppose individualism and secularism is un-Islamic. In a similar vein, he criticizes communalism, not for wrongly mixing up religion with politics but for being un-Islamic:

> The religion of Islam...never admits of a Muslim Nationalism. To talk of Muslim Nationalism would be as meaningless and self-contradictory as to talk of world-Nationalism, for Islam represents Universalism, and can be embraced

> by any one of the hundred and one Nations of the world....A German by accepting Islam remains a German, and a Turk remains a Turk.[24]

Similarly, advocates for Pakistan are themselves far from good Muslims:

> It may...be that the present official protagonists of Islam themselves may be the least Islamic in their attitude to life as a whole; and when it comes to the actual building of the State, the Pakistan State of the Musalmans may be less Islamic than the Hindustan State of the Hindoos! That this may be possible can be averred from a very curious fact that whereas feudalism which is not only absolutely un-Islamic but even inhuman, is being sought to be abolished by the Hindoo Congress everywhere, the Musalman Landlords & Nawabs of the Muslim League are, shockingly enough, striving, with equal tenacity and determination, to maintain and perpetuate the same.[25]

What we have here is not a radically secular stand against communalism but an early example of a secular and Marxist interpretation of Islam that allows for (or even demands) a form of ethnic patriotism and nationalism that divides the Muslim universal community into various nations. Joyo does not seek a legitimization for his ethnic nationalism outside Islam but justifies it with Islam.

This implies that nationalism inevitably comes with various forms of reform, both social and Islamic, since those who claim to be Muslims are in fact not leading a Muslim life. Sometimes their conduct is even less Islamic than the life of non-Muslims. Joyo continues to argue that this is the case in Sindh. The second part of his treatise describes the sorry state of Sindhi society at the time of writing. In the present situation, Sindh is far removed from its own true self. Its truest sons of the soil—the peasants or *haris*—are ignorant, often violent and oppressed by their landlords and spiritual leaders (*pirs*) whom they worship as semi-gods. The landlords—the *zamindars* and *jagirdars*—are 'absentee, indifferent, unenlightened and in some cases oppressive and tyrannical'; they are 'the signposts symbolising and pointing to all that is evil'; they are 'the disturbers of peace, the traducers of Islam—the *mufsids* in Quranic phraseology'.[26] The middle classes (i.e., traders, merchants and clerks) are equally untrustworthy since they are either obsessed with money or the offspring of non-Muslim migrants from Gujarat and Bombay. Even the 'microscopic middle-class Intelligentsia' is easily misled by false ideologies like communalism.[27] Yet he claims there is hope. Despite stereotypical prejudices of them as 'weak and cowardly' (fostered by the fact that Sindhis have always considered it beyond their dignity and patriotic pride to join the British-colonial army [unlike Punjabis]), Sindhis are in fact brave and strong.[28] This is clear from the fact that everywhere in India the Sindhi is known for his fanaticism and violence: 'Sindhee students... wherever they go for taking education...leave a reputation there of their fighting qualities'.[29] Even 'Sindh's women-folk...are thought to be dangerous'.[30] All this force and potential, as rough and unpolished as it is, simply has to be refined by way of a proper education, class-consciousness, and nationalist awareness. The Sindhi people have to be given a proper cause to fight for. In his concluding remarks, Joyo appeals to the youth of Sindh and its student community to stand up and rescue their people. He extols them to devote themselves to education and reform and (with history and progress on their side) the youth of Sindh 'in collaboration with and at the head of our oppressed millions,' will 'march forward'.[31]

Joyo—with his references to history, culture, and geography—freely builds upon Khuhro's primordialist understanding of the Sindhi nation. However, he also introduces, in an admittedly rather undeveloped form, three interrelated themes that would become of pivotal importance for Sindhi nationalism after Independence. First, in opposition to communalism and the Two Nations Theory, he defends Sindh's sovereignty with the help of his own interpretation of Islam—an unorthodox and modern Islam that stresses the importance of individual conduct and social justice. Second, there is a close relation between nationalism and social reform. In Joyo's work, independence for Sindh is hardly an end in itself; it means nothing if it does not go hand in hand with the abolition of 'feudalism'. The stigmatization of the 'feudal landlord' and the love for the *hari* were later taken up, if sometimes only discursively, by many social workers and politicians in Sindh (including, most famously, the Pakistan People's Party of Zulfikar Ali Bhutto). Third, nationalism in Joyo's analysis is related to religious reform. Although the nation is a natural fact, it can only be realized fully if the people are ready to return to the true message of Islam. Although Joyo remains pretty implicit about this message, the notion of religious reform in relation to Sindhi nationalism will become the main theme in the work of his teacher, G.M. Syed.

THE REFORMATION OF SUFISM

More than anybody else, Ghulam Mustafa Syed (1904–1995) has shaped Sindhi nationalism after Independence. He was a remarkable man in many ways: a politician and one of the leading Sindhi members of the Muslim League in the 1930s and first half of the 1940s; a communal activist who was arrested for his involvement in Muslim-Hindu riots that took place in Upper Sindh in 1939; an original and largely autodidact and eclectic intellectual who created his own worldview out of a wide range of intellectual tradition (e.g., nineteenth century Islamic reform, Darwinian evolution theory, theosophy, eighteenth century Sindhi poetry, Marxism, classical Sufism, and German idealism); the son of a landowning *syed* family from the village of Sann who considered himself a worldly and spiritual leader for the landless poor (not unlike Mahatma Gandhi and Khan Abdul Ghaffar Khan before him); the promoter of modern education for the local Sindhi population who founded a school in his home village of Sann and became Minister of Education in the provincial government of Sindh; a Sindhi separatist and founder of the Jeay Sindh Movement who spent twenty-two years under house arrest for his Sindhi nationalist ideas; and finally, a religious reformer who modernized Sufism, who dubbed Sufism a main Sindhi trait and called Sindh the cradle of Sufism.[32] When he died in 1995, G.M. Syed was one of Pakistan's most controversial public figures. Many students, sympathizers, and former colleagues attended his funeral at which passages from the Quran, the Bhagavad Gita, the Bible, the Torah, and verses from Shah Abdul Latif were all read. In many homes in the interior of Sindh, I saw his portrait hanging on the wall (ironically often next to a picture of Zulfikar Ali Bhutto, his arch-enemy). His portrait was also placed in a photo gallery for Sindhi heroes at the Sindh Museum in Hyderabad. Nonetheless, although he personally reinterpreted the Sindhi national character in terms of a theosophic reading of Sufism, his political career had not been very successful. An independent Sindh no longer seemed a viable option and his Jeay Sindh Movement had ceased to be a political force to reckon with.

Perhaps the most significant crisis in his life took place around 1958. Put under house arrest soon after the military takeover by General Muhammad Ayub Khan, he was forced to leave party politics. He began to devote himself to studying the history of Sindh and reading about Sufism, which resulted in the publication of a highly controversial book called *Religion and Reality* in 1967. In this book G.M. Syed develops an evolutionary theory of religion and mysticism based on the notion of an outer domain of religious practice (e.g., rituals, dogmas, religious institutions, clergy and saints) and an inner realm of mysticism, in which the individual is taken up in the 'oneness of being' (i.e., *wahdat ul-wajud*). All religions share this mystical core but differ in terms of ritual and organization. In the spiritual evolution of mankind, there is a gradual movement from the outer domain to the inner domain, starting from Hinduism and onward to Buddhism, Christianity, Islam, and 'Science' and finally to true mysticism or Sufism (i.e., *tasawwuf*). He argues that the latter can never be the basis for nationalism, because mysticism is universal and the essence of any religious tradition. However, religious nationalism is based on the superficial outer domain of religious practice and organization and therefore creates false communities. For him, Pakistan is an artificial construct. The attachment to one's homeland is a natural feeling and a genuine, albeit lesser, form of the mystical love for the 'oneness of being'. The Sindhi people are therefore a natural community, sharing a homeland, a language and—above all—a tradition of mysticism.

Although controversial and highly unorthodox, G.M. Syed's redefinition of Sufism does share some characteristics with other modern examples of Islamic reform. G.M. Syed's Sufism is somewhat iconoclastic in the sense that it presupposes a totally spiritual, universal and timeless essence that is concealed by culture and tradition, both of which are bound to space and time and leads one away from the 'oneness of being' into the outer domain of superficial ritual. Like most Islamic reform in the nineteenth and twentieth century, G.M. Syed's Sufism does not recognize the authority of religious specialists. Whereas other reformists attacked the ignorance of the village mullah or the traditional mindset of the *ulama*, G.M. Syed is primarily critical of the holy man (*pir*) who acts as a middleman between his followers and the 'oneness of being'. True mysticism, G.M. Syed argues, has no intermediary. He criticizes the spiritual patron-client relations and factionalism of the *pir-muridi* brotherhoods as much as he condemns feudalism by arguing for more individualism and democratization in both. Finally, the universalism of reformed Islam sits uneasily with the nationalist agenda. In terms of reformist interpretations of Islam as a universal religion, Islamic nationalism is somewhat of a contradiction in terms. Whereas Muhammad Iqbal revived the notion of the *millat* to justify the existence of nations within the Muslim brotherhood, Maulana Mawdudi remained critical of Pakistan because he opined that the *umma* cannot be split into various communities. G.M. Syed deals with the same problem but how does he reconcile the universalism of Sufism (i.e., *wahdat ul-wajud*) with a Sindhi nationalist agenda?

To an extent he had already given the answer in a 1952 book entitled *Paigham-i-Latif* (or *The Message of Latif*) that addresses the poetry of Shah Abdul Latif. In this book we find the notion of Sindh as the land of mysticism *par excellence*. The Sindhi nation is not just a natural community based on homeland and language, just as any other nation. Sindh is also, implicitly, the best of nations (or in any case the most advanced) as it has always been hospitable to any wandering searcher for reality and has always remained indifferent to the waves of superficial religion that have held other nations in its grip. The many shrines of saints buried in the Sindhi soil testify to this and of all these saints Shah Abdul Latif was the greatest. Perhaps this mixture of universalism and nationalism is best expressed in *The Message of Latif's* foreword, written for the English translation by publisher Khadim Hussain Soomro:

> [I]n the view of G.M. Syed nationalism is a step toward ultimate destination of humanism. Shah Latif and Sain G.M. Syed…will be remembered as distinguished sons of the soil of Sindh. Their philosophical and logical approach will guide the world on the path of realism which is co-existence, cooperation, non-violence, peace, goodwill and tolerance.[33]

In other words, being a true son of the soil in no way contradicts a universalist ideology for all mankind.

What then is G.M. Syed's 'philosophical and logical' reading of Latif's poetry? The book starts with chapters on Shah Abdul Latif's life and times. Shah Latif, who lived in the eighteenth century, is described as a descendent of the Prophet through the lineage of Imam Hussain. He became a wandering ascetic and poet who took his inspiration from the Quran, the *Masnawi* of Jalaluddin Rumi, and the Sindhi verses of his great-grandfather Shah Karim. He was one of the first poets to compose his verses in the vernacular Sindhi and most of his verses are on themes he took from popular stories (i.e., the famous love story about Sassi and Punnu, or one about Marwi, a village girl who is married to the prince Umar but, despite the luxury she finds in her new home, dies of homesickness and longing for the simple life in her home village). Shah Abdul Latif won the admiration of the king, Ghulam Shah Kalhora, and settled in Bhitshah, a little village north of Hyderabad where his home became a centre for poetry and music.

After the introductory historical chapters, G.M. Syed continues by saying that nations have their particular poet who awaken the people and lead them into a new era of national awareness. The eighteenth century, the dawn of modern times, was precisely the right time for Shah Abdul Latif to spread his message to the Sindhi people. In many ways, G.M. Syed writes, Latif articulated in his poetry what was already present in the Sindhi people, even though the people themselves were not aware of it.

He was the mirror in which the Sindhi nation could recognize itself. What, then, did they see? There is a profound sense of patriotism expressed in the fate of Marwi, who prefers her modest village to the luxury of the court. There is a passion for freedom, a refusal to surrender to tyranny and a spirit of self-sacrifice—the latter found in Sassi's barefooted quest for Punnu, which she continues onto death despite the heat of the desert. There is also tolerance and, on the negative side, an inferiority complex and idleness of the common people, the opportunism of its leaders, and the tendency to fight each other.[34] Shah Abdul Latif, then, was also a reformer who encouraged the people to fight these evil tendencies. Besides, he was a seer whose concept of Sindh was a broad one that comprised not only present-day Sindh but parts of southern Punjab, Balochistan, and the former princely states of Jaisalmar and Jodhpur and Gujarat.[35]

In the next chapter on Shah Abdul Latif's concept of nationalism, G.M. Syed argues that the poet was a true nationalist in a period of time when there was much confusion about nationalism:

> [T]here existed three different ideas about nationalism in Sindh during the period of Shah Latif. They were the following: 1. Separate nationality of Sindh, and the idea of its self-determination and progress, 2. A united nationality of India, and the idea of its independence and progress, 3. A separate nationality of Muslims, and the idea of their domination and progress.[36]

G.M. Syed says that Shah Abdul Latif clearly did not advocate the last option:

> Due to his belief in Pantheistic philosophy he was convinced of the fundamental unity of all the religions. Due to the lack of united action…an artificial and customary division has developed between the people.[37]

He maintains that there was much hypocrisy and ignorance among the Muslims and especially among the mullahs and others who despised the mystics and helped kill them (just as they did to Makhdoom Bilawal [who was crushed in an oil press], to Sarmad [whom they hanged on the cross], to Shah Inayat [who was beheaded], and to other famous Sindhi poets and saints):

> All those people [i.e., mullahs] were responsible for these tragic events, who claimed to disseminate the Islamic Law, and whose entire history was replete with the deeds of darkness.[38]

The Sindhi people, in other words, have little but tragedy and oppression to expect from those who speak in the name of Islam. However, the option of a united India would also not be Shah Abdul Latif's choice. In years of travelling, he had met many different people with 'different faiths, social standards, languages, races and cultures'. To unite all these people was nothing but 'an artificial plan'.[39] For Shah Abdul Latif the only true concept of nationalism was a separate Sindhi nationality. He emphasized how Sindhis—be they Muslim or Hindu—shared a history and spirituality that was not only immune from both the violence of Muslim nationalism and the artificiality of a united India but also formed an alternative and remedy for these erroneous concepts of nationalism. This shared Sindhi spirituality was a mixture of the following ingredients:

> Due to the unbiased influence of Buddhism since the ancient times, the teaching of Guru Nanak, the preaching of Hindu saints and pious men and the non-sectarian and tolerant teaching of Muslim mystics, the Hindus living in Sindh were free from religious fundamentalism and narrow-mindedness as compared to the Hindus living in other provinces and were closer to the Muslims in their way of life.
>
> The Muslims were influenced by the mystics, the fundamental principle of whose teachings was love. Moreover on the one hand having no contact with the fanatic and narrow-minded Hindus, being the majority, and on the other hand having ruled for a long period of time they were unbiased and were firm advocates of religious tolerance.[40]

In short, both Sindhi Hindus and Muslims were influenced by mysticism and religious tolerance. This was the Sindhi essence that both Hindus and Muslims shared.

Having defined Sindh—or rather Shah Abdul Latif's view of Sindh—as a land of mysticism and tolerance, a fortunate blend of peace-loving trends that had left a mark on the subcontinent, a region untouched by narrow-mindedness and sectarianism (that had also shaped India in the name of religion and caste), G.M. Syed goes on to portray Shah Abdul Latif as the prophet of mysticism. To do this convincingly, G.M. Syed has to redefine mysticism. This is a common trait in any form of religious nationalism: when religion is turned into the distinctive feature of the nation, religion itself is also transformed. Thus, the second part of the book reads like an early sketch of *Religion and Reality,* published fifteen years later. G.M. Syed interprets Shah Abdul Latif's poetry in a way that (1) underlines reformed Sufism as a purely mystical tradition, and (2) has nothing to do with the hierarchical and institutionalized Sufism of the Sufi brotherhoods (i.e., with *pir-muridi* practices, the belief in *barakat*, or the annual pilgrimages to the shrines of *pirs* [*urs*]). This definition of Sufism radically dismisses the organizational institutions, rituals, and popular belief associated with Sufism for centuries. Consistent with his distinction between an inner and outer domain, G.M. Syed condenses Sufism (as well as Shah Abdul Latif's poetry) to an essence of mysticism, love, and *wahdat ul-wajud*. Sufism becomes thought and feeling. Its practice is Sindhi patriotism. True Sufi followers of Shah Abdul Latif, G.M. Syed concludes, fight for Sindh's independence.

G.M. Syed's reading of Shah Abdul Latif's poetry is obviously an anachronism. The three forms of nationalism he distinguishes were indeed manifest in the early 1950s (when G.M. Syed wrote) but hardly in the eighteenth century when Shah Abdul Latif composed his verses on Sassi, Marwi, and other popular heroines. Nationalism is ascribed to the eighteenth-century poet. In the last parts of his book, G.M. Syed attributes other twentieth-century ideologies to Shah Abdul Latif: a liking for democracy and socialism and an aversion toward dictatorship and capitalism.[41] Such an attribution is hardly remarkable. Many saints and poets of pre-colonial Sindh have been recovered from history to take their place in the pantheon of the Sufi saints of Sindhi nationalism (especially in the 1960s and 1970s) when the Sindhi nationalist movement became a socio-political factor in Pakistan. For example, the previously mentioned Shah Inayat of Jhok—an eighteenth-century charismatic leader in the Indus Delta—was christened a *socialist Sufi* by the Sindhi student leader Jam Saqi. The growing strength of the Sindhi nationalist movement went hand in hand with an avalanche of books, studies, and newspaper articles on a range of poets and charismatic leaders, all dubbed Sufis and Sindhi nationalists *avant la lettre*. Of all these poets and saints, Shah Abdul Latif became the most famous. His *shah jo risalo*, or collection of verses, became the national book of poems. His shrine in Bhit Shah became the cultural centre of Sindh, popular not only with Sindhi musicians (as it has been for many years) but, increasingly, with young students from Karachi, Hyderabad, and other towns for whom a visit to Bhit Shah became an important ritual of patriotism. It is important to realize that the discursive foundation for this had already been built in the early 1950s with G.M. Syed's study of Shah Abdul Latif's work. After Muhammad Ayub Khuhro's definition of Sindh in terms of culture and geography—to which was added Ibrahim Joyo's emphasis on the *hari* and his religiously informed critique of 'feudalism'—G.M. Syed added a third crucial element: the formulation of a distinct Sindhi religiosity in terms of a reformed Sufism of which Shah Abdul Latif was made, posthumously, the messenger.

CONCLUSIONS

Aware of the mobilizing potential of a reformed Sufism when combined with Third World socialism, Zulfikar Ali Bhutto tried to turn Shah Abdul Latif into the national poet of Pakistan rather than of Sindh. In 1974, he inaugurated a government sponsored Bhit Shah Cultural Complex, saying that 'Latif is not the poet of Sindh alone'.[42] This was also the time that the Sindh provincial government sponsored the international academic seminar on Sindhi history organized by Hamida Khuhro. Reformed political Sufism had been seized out of the hands of the Sindhi nationalist movement and its main intellectual leader (i.e., G.M. Syed) by the ruling Pakistan People's Party. The election campaign that had brought Bhutto to power had been full of the rhetoric of socialism, mysticism, and Sindh's unique history as the oppressed land of religious tolerance. He had gone to many Sufi shrines in rural Sindh to talk not of the concept of *wahdat ul-wajud* and preach the independence of Sindh, but to promise worldly goods to the rural poor and to pay his respect to the pirs venerated highly by the *haris*. Whereas G.M. Syed called for an independent Sindhudesh during the early 1970s, Bhutto promised his supporters to improve their life conditions within Pakistan. Bhutto won and G.M. Syed was put under house arrest, but in the first half of the 1970s—with the help of state funds and support—the notion of Sindh as a spiritual land with a profound mystical tradition, distinct from the religiosity of other ethnic groups in Pakistan, gained official status and academic validity.

Elsewhere, I have argued that the appropriation of Sindhi mysticism and culture by the Pakistan People's Party was part of a redefinition of Pakistani nationalism in which ethnic identity was no longer radically denied.[43] From independence onwards, Islam and ethnicity were seen as mutually exclusive. Islam was to be the inclusive force that would bring the new nation of Pakistan together while ethnicity was the dividing force that threatened to keep the various linguistic and regional groups apart. In this view, ethnicity was un-, or at least, a-Islamic. Particularly *muhajirs* who had migrated from India to Pakistan after Independence were known for a form of Pakistani nationalism that was hostile to ethnic loyalties. But not only *muhajirs* exhibited their hostilities. The infamous One Unit Scheme introduced by Ayub Khan (which abolished the provinces in former West Pakistan and brought them under one administrative unit) reduced regional influences to a minimum. However, this attempt to build a new nation by suppressing ethnic particularism proved counterproductive. Everywhere in Pakistan regional movements gained momentum, most forcefully in East Pakistan (now Bangladesh) and Sindh. While Bengali separatists won freedom for Bangladesh, Sindhi enthusiasts rose to power after the elections of 1970. Rather than fight them, Zulfikar Ali Bhutto successfully incorporated them by actively allowing for the expression of ethnic solidarity within the framework of Pakistani nationalism. To be a Muslim and a Pakistani was no longer enough: a Pakistani citizen was also supposed to have an ethnic identity. The way many Pakistanis have told me that they were Muslim first, Pakistani second, and Sindhis, *muhajirs*, or Punjabis third testified to the success of this three-fold national identity. Islam and ethnicity were no longer seen as mutually exclusive in the 1970s. On the contrary, ethnic TV shows and radio programmes made ethnicity *salonfähig*. In many ways, the 1970s were the high tide of Sindhi nationalism and Sufi revival.

What is clear from my genealogy of Sindhi nationalism is that the mixture of Islam and ethnicity was not merely an official state discourse from the 1970s. Much earlier the 'founders' of Sindhi culture themselves, despite their critical stand toward Muslim nationalism and other Muslim reformers like Muhammad Iqbal and Maulana Mawdudi, merged Sindhi culture with a distinct form of religiosity called Sufism or mysticism. This trend increased over time. Muhammad Ayub Khuhro never mentioned mysticism. For him, Sindh's unique position within India was a matter of culture, history, language, and geography. I think this is because Khuhro's struggle—Sindh's independence from the Bombay Presidency—was hardly cast in religious terms. In Sindh from the 1940s onwards, religion became so dominant (if not omnipresent) in debates about nationalism that it was a matter impossible to ignore. Moreover, after Independence, Muslim nationalism came with active and state-sponsored reform programmes to 'modernize' people's religious conduct. In defence against this double-edged sword of nation-building and religious reform, regional movements took to both ethnicity and religious syncretism in an attempt to preserve a space of influence. Asim Roy has written about this process for former East Pakistan in *The Islamic Syncretistic Tradition in Bengal*. In Sindh, this same process resulted in the formulation of a distinct form of Sufism that, while distinctively Sindhi, is also seen as the amalgam of the best of mystical traditions in India and the world of Islam.

I conclude with a final word about the ramifications of this socio-political process for that other large group living in Sindh since Independence, the *muhajirs*. The Sindhi revival in the 1970s under the rule of the Pakistan People's Party was not favourable for them. Although many left-wing *muhajirs* had joined the PPP and sympathized with

Bhutto's freely socialist and Sufi rhetoric, *muhajirs* were seen (partly also by themselves) as a people without ethnicity. Even in the 1990s, the concept of a *muhajir culture* was somewhat absurd to many *muhajirs*. The concept of culture belonged to ethnicity and regional languages, and originating from many different parts of India, *muhajirs* had neither. They had Islam and Urdu instead. *Muhajirs*, then, were never fully recognized as an ethnic group of their own by the Pakistan People's Party. Given that ethnic identity provided one with certain rights since the 1970s (e.g., as in for instance reservation programmes for admittance in educational institutions), it would not be surprising that *muhajirs* would also claim recognition as an ethnic group of their own. This was in fact one of the main demands of the Muhajir Qaumi Movement (MQM), established in the 1980s. Its position toward the Sindhis and Sindhi Sufism has always been somewhat ambiguous. Claiming that one had left home and hearth in India for Pakistan, not for Sindh, the MQM often repeated an earlier form of nationalism in which ethnicity and religious syncretism had no place. On the other hand, in times when the MQM sided with Sindhi organizations against parties that were seen as dominantly Punjabi, its leaders endorsed the distinct Sindhi religiosity by paying homage to Shah Abdul Latif and calling Sindh the land of religious tolerance. It even mimicked—largely in an absurdist manner—some Sindhi practices such as bestowing the spiritual power of saints on political leaders. The slogan *mast qalandar altaf hussain*, for instance, which linked the famous Qalandar saint Lal Shahbaz Qalandar of Sehwan Sharif with Altaf Hussain, the leader of the MQM, was popular in the early days of the party. Although the MQM was often fiercely anti-Sindhi in its actions, the party ideologically shared the Sindhi's distrust of 'fundamentalists' and fear of Punjabi domination. It even largely accepted the enduring relevance of ethnicity and, at times, subscribed to the notion of Sindh as the cradle of Sufism. Thus, while the Sindhi ethnic movement has not won independence for Sindh, it has gained recognition even by one of its main opponents.

NOTES

1. Hamida Khuhro, *Sind Through the Centuries* (Karachi: Oxford University Press, 1981), xiii.
2. G.M. Syed, *The Case of Sindh* (Karachi: Naeen Sindh Academy, 1995), 13.
3. Sarah F.D. Ansari, *Sufi Saints and State Power: The Pirs of Sind, 1843–1947* (Lahore: Vanguard, 1992).
4. E.H. Aitken, *Gazetteer of the Province of Sind* (Karachi: Indus, 1986), 472; H.T. Sorley,

The Gazetteer of West Pakistan: The Former Province of Sind—Including Khairpur State (Lahore: Government of West Pakistan, 1968), 154–162.

5. Khuhro, 173.
6. Muhammad Ayub Khuhro, 'A Story of the Sufferings of Sind: A Case for the Separation of Sind from the Bombay Presidency', in Hamida Khuhro, ed., *Documents on Separation of Sind From the Bombay Presidency* (Islamabad: Islamic University Press, 1982), 196.
7. Ibid., 205.
8. Ibid., 232.
9. Ibid., 234–5.
10. Muhammad Ibrahim Joyo, *Save Sind, Save the Continent—From Feudal Lords, Capitalists and Their Communalisms* (Karachi: Sind Renaissance Association, 1947), i.
11. Ibid., ii.
12. Ibid., i.
13. Ibid., iii–iv.
14. Ibid., iv.
15. Ibid., viii.
16. Ibid., v.
17. Ibid., 37.
18. Ibid., 39–40.
19. Ibid., 1.
20. Ibid., 1–2.
21. Ibid., 31.
22. Ibid., 71.
23. Ibid., 70–71.
24. Ibid., 45.
25. Ibid., 76–77.
26. Ibid., 105.
27. Ibid., 108 and 133–134.
28. Ibid., 118.
29. Ibid., 119.
30. Ibid., 120.
31. Ibid., 138–139.
32. Oskar Verkaaik, 'Reforming Mysticism: Sindhi Separatist Intellectuals in Pakistan', *International Review for Social History* 49 (2004): 65–86.
33. G.M. Syed, *Shah Latif and His Message* (Sehwan, Pakistan: Sain, 1996), ii.
34. Ibid., chapter 3.
35. Ibid., chapter 4.
36. Ibid., 103.
37. Ibid.
38. Ibid., 107.
39. Ibid., 108.
40. Ibid., 10–109.
41. Ibid., chapter 10.
42. Oskar Verkaaik, *Migrants and Militants: 'Fun' and Urban Violence in Pakistan* (Princeton: Princeton University Press, 2004), 37.
43. Ibid.

Contributors

Michel Boivin has a PhD in Oriental Languages, Civilisations and Societies from Université de la Sorbonne Nouvelle-Paris 3. He has a research position at the Centre for South Asian Studies, School of Advanced Studies in Social Sciences (EHESS), and the National Centre of Scientific Research (CNRS), Paris.

Matthew A. Cook has a PhD in anthropology from Columbia University. He is Assistant Professor of Postcolonial and South Asian Studies at North Carolina Central University. He is also a member of the North Carolina Consortium for South Asia Studies at Duke University.

Maya Khemlani David holds a PhD in Applied Linguistics from the University of Essex. She is Professor of Languages and Linguistics at the University of Malaya.

Paulo Lemos Horta has a PhD from the University of Toronto and is Assistant Professor of Literature at New York University, Abu Dhabi.

Farhana Ibrahim holds a PhD in anthropology from Cornell University. She is Assistant Professor of Sociology at the Indian Institute of Technology, Delhi.

Rita Kothari has a PhD from Gujarat University in English. She is Professor of Culture and Communication at the Mudra Institute of Communications in Ahmedabad, India.

Lata Parwani holds a MA in Indo-Muslim Culture from Harvard University. She is currently working toward a PhD in history at Tufts University.

Steven Ramey holds a PhD in Religious Studies from the University of North Carolina, Chapel Hill and is Assistant Professor of Religion at The University of Alabama.

Oskar Verkaaik holds a PhD from the University of Amsterdam. He is currently Assistant Professor at the University of Amsterdam's Research Centre for Religion and Society.

Vazira Fazila-Yacoobali Zamindar has a PhD in anthropology from Columbia University. She is Robert Gale Noyes Assistant Professor of the Humanities at Brown University.

Index

G

H

I

L

M

N